Computer Networking: An Innovative Approach

Computer Networking:
An Innovative Approach

Henry Martin

CLANRYE
INTERNATIONAL
www.clanryeinternational.com

Clanrye International,
750 Third Avenue, 9th Floor,
New York, NY 10017, USA

ISBN: 978-1-64726-095-8

Cataloging-in-Publication Data

Computer networking : an innovative approach / Henry Martin.
    p. cm.
Includes bibliographical references and index.
ISBN: 978-1-64726-095-8
1. Computer networks. 2. Electronic systems. 3. Cyberinfrastructure.
4. Network computers. I. Martin, Henry.
TK5105.5 .C66 2022
004.6--dc23

For information on all Clanrye International publications
visit our website at www.clanryeinternational.com

Table of Contents

Preface

The purpose of this book is to help students understand the fundamental concepts of this discipline. It is designed to motivate students to learn and prosper. I am grateful for the support of my colleagues. I would also like to acknowledge the encouragement of my family.

The digital communications network which facilitates the sharing of resources between nodes is termed as a telecommunication network. The process of sharing resources and data between two computers is called computer networking. The connections between them can be established using both cable media and wireless media. Some of the cable media which are used in computer networking are fiber-optic cables and twisted pair cables. A few of the other components of computer networks are generally classified on the basis of their bandwidth, network size, transmission medium and organizational intent. There are various applications and services which depend on computer networking such as World Wide Web, email, fax machines, shared use of printers, etc. This book provides comprehensive insights into the field of computer networking. It elucidates the concepts and innovative models around prospective developments with respect to this field. Coherent flow of topics, student-friendly language and extensive use of examples make this book an invaluable source of knowledge.

A foreword for all the chapters is provided below:

Chapter – What is Computer Networking?

Computer networks are the digital telecommunication networks that allow nodes to share resources. The practice of transporting and exchanging data between nodes over a shared medium is termed as computer networking. This is an introductory chapter which will introduce briefly all the significant aspects of computer networking including open and closed systems, circuit switching and network architecture.

Chapter – Types of Computer Networks

There are various types of networks such as LAN, WAN, MAN, PAN, VPN, CAN, BAN and NAN. The network which uses wireless data connections between network nodes is referred to as a wireless network. This chapter has been carefully written to provide an easy understanding of these types of networks.

Chapter – Topology of Computer Networks

The arrangement of the elements of a communication network is known as network topology. It can be classified as either physical topology or logical topology. The topics elaborated in this chapter will help in gaining a better perspective about network topology, its various types and the transmission modes in computer networks.

Chapter – Security of Computer Networks

Network security refers to the policies and practices that are used to prevent and monitor un-authorized access of a computer network. Some of its diverse types are access control, antivi-rus and antimalware software, application security, behavioral analytics, data loss prevention, email security, firewalls, mobile device security, etc. This chapter closely examines these key types of network security to provide an extensive understanding of the subject.

Chapter – Applications of Computer Networks

Computer networks are used in numerous fields and systems such as ethernet, world wide web, intranet, internet, extranet, deep web and cloud computing. The diverse applications of networks in these areas have been thoroughly discussed in this chapter.

Henry Martin

1
What is Computer Networking?

Computer networks are the digital telecommunication networks that allow nodes to share resources. The practice of transporting and exchanging data between nodes over a shared medium is termed as computer networking. This is an introductory chapter which will introduce briefly all the significant aspects of computer networking including open and closed systems, circuit switching and network architecture.

Network

A network, in computing, is a group of two or more devices that can communicate. In practice, a network is comprised of a number of different computer systems connected by physical and wireless connections. The scale can range from a single PC sharing out basic peripherals to massive data centers located around the World, to the Internet itself. Regardless of scope, all networks allow computers and individuals to share information and resources.

Computer networks serve a number of purposes, some of which include:

- Communications such as email, instant messaging, chat rooms, etc.
- Shared hardware such as printers and input devices.
- Shared data and information through the use of shared storage devices.
- Shared software, which is achieved by running applications on remote computers.

Besides physically connecting computer and communication devices, a network system serves the important function of establishing a cohesive architecture that allows a variety of equipment types to transfer information in a near-seamless fashion. Two popular architectures are ISO Open Systems Interconnection (OSI) and IBM's Systems Network Architecture (SNA).

The first computer networks were dedicated special-purpose systems such as SABRE (an airline reservation system) and AUTODIN I (a defense command-and-control system), both designed and implemented in the late 1950s and early 1960s. By the early 1960s computer manufacturers had begun to use semiconductor technology in commercial products, and both conventional batch-processing and time-sharing systems were in place in many large, technologically advanced companies. Time-sharing systems allowed a computer's resources to be shared in rapid succession with multiple users, cycling through the queue of users so quickly that the computer appeared dedicated to each user's tasks despite the existence of many others accessing the system "simultaneously." This led to the notion of sharing computer resources (called host computers or simply hosts) over an entire network. Host-to-host interactions were envisioned, along with access to specialized resources (such as supercomputers and mass storage systems) and interactive access by remote users to the computational powers of time-sharing systems located elsewhere. These ideas were first realized in ARPANET, which established the first host-to-host network connection on Oct. 29, 1969. It was created by the Advanced Research Projects Agency (ARPA) of the U.S. Department of Defense. ARPANET was one of the first general-purpose computer networks. It connected time-sharing computers at government-supported research sites, principally universities in the United States, and it soon became a critical piece of infrastructure for the computer science research community in the United States. Tools and applications—such as the simple mail transfer protocol (SMTP, commonly referred to as e-mail), for sending short messages, and the file transfer protocol (FTP), for longer transmissions—quickly emerged. In order to achieve cost-effective interactive communications between computers, which typically communicate in short bursts of data, ARPANET employed the new technology of packet switching. Packet switching takes large messages (or chunks of computer data) and breaks them into smaller, manageable pieces (known as packets) that can travel independently over any available circuit to the target destination, where the pieces are reassembled. Thus, unlike traditional voice communications, packet switching does not require a single dedicated circuit between each pair of users.

Open and Closed Systems

An open network can have many definitions depending on different requirements. An open network can refer to a network that must conform to open industry standards. Whether the device is used to interact within a network or externally, an architecture that is open every step of the way is needed. An open network can represent a network with an open ecosystem that defines the deployment scope of the solution set. An open network can mean an open source network that enables innovation in the marketplace while ensuring that the resulting product is constantly secured by the community that is contributing to it. An open network can indicate a network that provides access to the infrastructure in a programmable way through APIs (Application Programming Interfaces). However, those APIs are often closed out or only work with their solution. In summary, an open network allows a variety of entities to provide service on a reasonably equal basis versus each other and the network operator.

Likewise, a closed network also has different meanings. A closed network can refer to a private telephone network that has no external (public switched telephone network) connectivity. A closed network can imply a network that uses proprietary technology which is not directly interoperable with other standards-based networks. A closed network can signify a WLAN that does not send its name (SSID) in beacon frames. Stations must know the SSID (Service Set Identifier) in order to connect to access points in that network. A closed network can represent a private network that can only be used by authorized devices. Outsider use is prohibited and enforced through cryptographic means. In short, a closed network is one that sets aside a great deal of the network capacity for a limited set of providers, usually but not always limited to the network provider.

An open system, in the context of computing, is a computer system that combines portability and interoperability, and makes use of open software standards. It typically refers to a computer system that is interoperable between different vendors and standards, allowing for modularity so that hardware and software need not be attached to a single vendor or platform.

Before the popularity of the Windows OS and the PC, open systems used to refer to computer systems with Unix-like operating systems that accepted any modules or programs from any third party that used the same standard, as opposed to that era's closed systems such as IBM computers.

Circuit Switching and Packet Switching

Circuit switching and packet switching are the two switching methods that are used to connect the multiple communicating devices with one another. Circuit Switching was particularly designed for voice communication and it was less suitable for data transmission. So, a better solution evolved for data transmission called Packet switching. The main difference between circuit switching and packet switching is that Circuit Switching is connection oriented whereas, Packet Switching is connectionless. Let us learn some more differences between Circuit Switching and Packet Switching with the help of comparison chart shown below.

Circuit Switching vs Packet Switching

1. Comparison Chart.
2. Definition.
3. Key Differences.

Comparison Chart

Basis for Comparison	Circuit Switching	Packet Switching
Orientation	Connection oriented.	Connectionless.
Purpose	Initially designed for Voice communication.	Initially designed for Data Transmission.
Flexibility	Inflexible, because once a path is set all parts of a transmission follows the same path.	Flexible, because a route is created for each packet to travel to the destination.
Order	Message is received in the order, sent from the source.	Packets of a message are received out of order and assembled at the destination.
Technology/Approach	Circuit switching can be achieved using two technologies, either Space Division Switching or Time-Division Switching.	Packet Switching has two approaches Datagram Approach and Virtual Circuit Approach.
Layers	Circuit Switching is implemented at Physical Layer.	Packet Switching is implemented at Network Layer.

Circuit Switching

Circuit Switching establishes a physical path between the sender and receiver of the message before a message is delivered. When a connection is established between a sender and a receiver, the entire message travels through the established path from sender to the receiver. Once the message is delivered to the receiver, the source informs the network about the completion of transmission and all the switches released. Then the link and other connecting devices are used to set up another connection.

Circuit switching is always implemented at the Physical Layer. Circuit switching can be explained with an example of a telephone conversation. In a telephone conversation, once a connection is established, between a caller and the receiver, it remains connected, till the whole conversation is finished and both the caller and receiver hang up their phone. The Circuit switching is not appropriate for data transmission because data is transmitted in spurts (stream) and the line remains idle for most of the times and hence, the bandwidth is wasted. Circuit Switching can be implemented using two technologies either Space Division Switching or Time Division Switching.

Packet Switching

Packet Switching is connectionless as it doesn't establish any physical connection before the transmission starts. In packet switching before the message is transmitted, it is divided into some manageable parts called packets. These packets are routed one by one from source to destination. In packet switching, each packet may follow a different route to reach the destination. Packets arrived at the destination are out of order but, they are assembled in order before the destination forward it to the upper layer.

Packet Switching is always implemented at the Network Layer. Packet switching has two approaches Datagram Approach and Virtual Circuit Approach. In Datagram Approach each packet is independent of other though they belong to the same message and may also choose a different path to reach the destination. In Virtual Circuit Approach, the relationship between the packets that belong to the same message is preserved as the packet are not independent of each other, and all the packets that belong to a particular message follow the same route to travel to the destination.

Key Differences between Circuit Switching and Packet Switching

1. Circuit Switching is connection oriented that means a path is established between source and destination before the transmission occurs. On the other hand, Packet Switching is Connectionless that means a dynamic route is decided for each packet while transmission.

2. Circuit Switching was originally designed for voice communication whereas, Packet Switching was originally designed for data communication.

3. Circuit Switching is inflexible as once a path is established for transmission, it doesn't change while the duration of the session. On the other hand, Packet Switching is flexible as each packet may travel through a different route to reach its destination.

4. In packet switching, as each packet travels a different path hence, the packet are received out of order at the receiver side and later arranged in order. On the other hand, in circuit switching the entire message is received as it is as sent from a sender to receiver.

5. Space Division Switching or Time-Division Switching can be used to implement Circuit Switching whereas, Packet Switching can be implemented using two approaches Datagram Approach and Virtual Circuit Approach.

6. Circuit Switching is always implemented at physical layer whereas, Packet Switching is implemented on the network layer.

Integrated Service Digital Network (ISDN), shown in Figure below, is an example of a circuit-switched network.

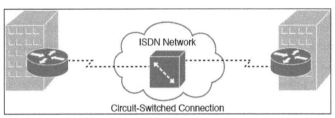

Circuit Switching ISDN Topology.

Circuit switching requires a dedicated physical connection between the sending and receiving devices. For example, parties involved in a phone call have a dedicated link between them for the duration of the conversation. When either party disconnects, the circuit is broken, and the data path is lost. This is an accurate representation of how circuit switching works with network and data transmissions. The sending system establishes a physical connection, and the data is transmitted between the two. When the transmission is complete, the channel is closed.

A Frame Relay network, shown in figure below, is an example of a packet-switched network.

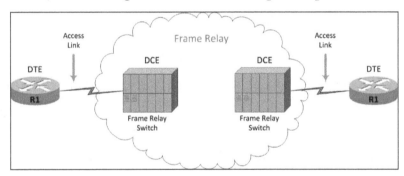

In packet switching, messages are broken into smaller pieces called packets. Each packet is assigned source and destination addresses. Packets are required to have this information because they do not always use the same path or route to get to their intended destination. Packets can take an alternative route if a particular route is unavailable for some reason.

Network Architecture

Network architecture is the design of a computer network. It is a framework for the specification of a network's physical components and their functional organization and configuration, its operational principles and procedures, as well as communication protocols used.

In telecommunication, the specification of a network architecture may also include a detailed description of products and services delivered via a communications network, as well as detailed rate and billing structures under which services are compensated.

The network architecture of the Internet is predominantly expressed by its use of the Internet Protocol Suite, rather than a specific model for interconnecting networks or nodes in the network, or the usage of specific types of hardware links.

OSI Model

The Open Systems Interconnection model (OSI model) is a conceptual model that characterizes and standardizes the communication functions of a telecommunication or computing system without regard to its underlying internal structure and technology. Its goal is the interoperability of diverse communication systems with standard communication protocols. The model partitions a communication system into abstraction layers. The original version of the model is defined by seven layers.

A layer serves the layer above it and is served by the layer below it. For example, a layer that provides error-free communications across a network provides the path needed by applications above it, while it calls the next lower layer to send and receive packets that constitute the contents of that path. Two instances at the same layer are visualized as connected by a horizontal connection in that layer.

The model is a product of the Open Systems Interconnection project at the International Organization for Standardization (ISO).

1. Physical layer: EIA/TIA-232, EIA/TIA-449, ITU-T V-Series, I.430, I.431, PDH, SONET/SDH, PON, OTN, DSL, IEEE 802.3, IEEE 802.11, IEEE 802.15, IEEE 802.16, IEEE 1394, ITU-T G.hn PHY, USB, Bluetooth, RS-232, RS-449

2. Data link layer: ATM, ARP, IS-IS, SDLC, HDLC, CSLIP, SLIP, GFP, PLIP, IEEE 802.2, LLC, MAC, L2TP, IEEE 802.3, Frame Relay, ITU-T G.hn DLL, PPP, X.25 LAPB, Q.922 LAPF

3. Network layer: IP, IPv4, IPv6, ICMP, IPsec, IGMP, IPX, AppleTalk, X.25 PLP

4. Transport layer: TCP, UDP, SCTP, DCCP, SPX

5. Session layer: Named pipe, NetBIOS, SAP, PPTP, RTP, SOCKS, SPDY

6. Presentation layer: MIME, XDR, ASN.1

7. Application layer: NNTP, SIP, SSI, DNS, FTP, Gopher, HTTP, NFS, NTP, SMPP, SMTP, SNMP, Telnet, DHCP, Netconf, *more*

Layer 1: Physical Layer

The physical layer is responsible for the transmission and reception of unstructured raw data between a device and a physical transmission medium. It converts the digital bits into electrical, radio, or optical signals. Layer specifications define characteristics such as voltage levels, the timing of voltage changes, physical data rates, maximum transmission distances, modulation scheme, channel access method and physical connectors. This includes the layout of pins, voltages, line impedance, cable specifications, signal timing and frequency for wireless devices. Bit rate control is done at the physical layer and may define transmission mode as simplex, half duplex, and full duplex. The components of a physical layer can be described in terms of a network topology. Bluetooth, Ethernet, and USB all have specifications for a physical layer.

Layer 2: Data Link Layer

The data link layer provides node-to-node data transfer—a link between two directly connected nodes. It detects and possibly corrects errors that may occur in the physical layer. It defines the protocol to establish and terminate a connection between two physically connected devices. It also defines the protocol for flow control between them.

IEEE 802 divides the data link layer into two sublayers:

- Medium access control (MAC) layer – responsible for controlling how devices in a network gain access to a medium and permission to transmit data.

- Logical link control (LLC) layer – responsible for identifying and encapsulating network layer protocols, and controls error checking and frame synchronization.

The MAC and LLC layers of IEEE 802 networks such as 802.3 Ethernet, 802.11 Wi-Fi, and 802.15.4 ZigBee operate at the data link layer.

The Point-to-Point Protocol (PPP) is a data link layer protocol that can operate over several different physical layers, such as synchronous and asynchronous serial lines.

The ITU-T G.hn standard, which provides high-speed local area networking over existing wires (power lines, phone lines and coaxial cables), includes a complete data link layer that provides both error correction and flow control by means of a selective-repeat sliding-window protocol.

Layer 3: Network Layer

The network layer provides the functional and procedural means of transferring variable length data sequences (called packets) from one node to another connected in "different networks". A network is a medium to which many nodes can be connected, on which every node has an *address* and which permits nodes connected to it to transfer messages to other nodes connected to it by merely providing the content of a message and the address of the destination node and letting the network find the way to deliver the message to the destination node, possibly routing it through intermediate nodes. If the message is too large to be transmitted from one node to another on the data link layer between those nodes, the network may implement message delivery by splitting the message into several fragments at one node, sending the fragments independently, and reassembling the fragments at another node. It may, but does not need to, report delivery errors.

Message delivery at the network layer is not necessarily guaranteed to be reliable; a network layer protocol may provide reliable message delivery, but it need not do so.

A number of layer-management protocols, a function defined in the *management annex*, ISO 7498/4, belong to the network layer. These include routing protocols, multicast group management, network-layer information and error, and network-layer address assignment. It is the function of the payload that makes these belong to the network layer, not the protocol that carries them.

Layer 4: Transport Layer

The transport layer provides the functional and procedural means of transferring variable-length data sequences from a source to a destination host, while maintaining the quality of service functions.

The transport layer controls the reliability of a given link through flow control, segmentation/desegmentation, and error control. Some protocols are state- and connection-oriented. This means that the transport layer can keep track of the segments and re-transmit those that fail delivery. The transport layer also provides the acknowledgement of the successful data transmission and sends the next data if no errors occurred. The transport layer creates segments out of the message received from the application layer. Segmentation is the process of dividing a long message into smaller messages.

OSI defines five classes of connection-mode transport protocols ranging from class 0 (which is also known as TP0 and provides the fewest features) to class 4 (TP4, designed for less reliable networks, similar to the Internet). Class 0 contains no error recovery, and was designed for use on network layers that provide error-free connections. Class 4 is closest to TCP, although TCP contains functions, such as the graceful close, which OSI assigns to the session layer. Also, all OSI TP connection-mode protocol classes provide expedited data and preservation of record boundaries.

An easy way to visualize the transport layer is to compare it with a post office, which deals with the dispatch and classification of mail and parcels sent. A post office inspects only the outer envelope of mail to determine its delivery. Higher layers may have the equivalent of double envelopes, such as cryptographic presentation services that can be read by the addressee only. Roughly speaking, tunneling protocols operate at the transport layer, such as carrying non-IP protocols such as IBM's SNA or Novell's IPX over an IP network, or end-to-end encryption with IPsec. While Generic Routing Encapsulation (GRE) might seem to be a network-layer protocol, if the encapsulation of the payload takes place only at the endpoint, GRE becomes closer to a transport protocol that uses IP headers but contains complete Layer 2 frames or Layer 3 packets to deliver to the endpoint. L2TP carries PPP frames inside transport segments.

Although not developed under the OSI Reference Model and not strictly conforming to the OSI definition of the transport layer, the Transmission Control Protocol (TCP) and the User Datagram Protocol (UDP) of the Internet Protocol Suite are commonly categorized as layer-4 protocols within OSI.

Layer 5: Session Layer

The session layer controls the dialogues (connections) between computers. It establishes, manages and terminates the connections between the local and remote application. It provides for full-duplex, half-duplex, or simplex operation, and establishes procedures for checkpointing, suspending, restarting, and terminating a session. In the OSI model, this layer is responsible for gracefully closing a session, which is handled in the Transmission Control Protocol at the transport layer in the Internet Protocol Suite. This layer is also responsible for session checkpointing and recovery, which is not usually used in the Internet Protocol Suite. The session layer is commonly implemented explicitly in application environments that use remote procedure calls.

Layer 6: Presentation Layer

The presentation layer establishes context between application-layer entities, in which the application-layer entities may use different syntax and semantics if the presentation service provides a mapping between them. If a mapping is available, presentation protocol data units are encapsulated into session protocol data units and passed down the protocol stack.

This layer provides independence from data representation by translating between application and network formats. The presentation layer transforms data into the form that the application accepts. This layer formats data to be sent across a network. It is sometimes called the syntax layer. The presentation layer can include compression functions. The Presentation Layer negotiates the Transfer Syntax.

The original presentation structure used the Basic Encoding Rules of Abstract Syntax Notation One (ASN.1), with capabilities such as converting an EBCDIC-coded text file to an ASCII-coded file, or serialization of objects and other data structures from and to XML. ASN.1 effectively makes an application protocol invariant with respect to syntax.

Layer 7: Application Layer

The application layer is the OSI layer closest to the end user, which means both the OSI application layer and the user interact directly with the software application. This layer interacts with software applications that implement a communicating component. Such application programs fall outside the scope of the OSI model. Application-layer functions typically include identifying communication partners, determining resource availability, and synchronizing communication. When identifying communication partners, the application layer determines the identity and availability of communication partners for an application with data to transmit. The most important distinction in the application layer is the distinction between the application-entity and the application. For example, a reservation website might have two application-entities: one using HTTP to communicate with its users, and one for a remote database protocol to record reservations. Neither of these protocols have anything to do with reservations. That logic is in the application itself. The application layer per se has no means to determine the availability of resources in the network.

Cross-layer Functions

Cross-layer functions are services that are not tied to a given layer, but may affect more than one layer. Some orthogonal aspects, such as management and security, involve all of the layers. These services are aimed at improving the CIA triad — confidentiality, integrity, and availability — of the transmitted data. Cross-layer functions are the norm, in practice, because the availability of a communication service is determined by the interaction between network design and network management protocols. Appropriate choices for both of these are needed to protect against denial of service.

Specific examples of cross-layer functions include the following:

- Security service (telecommunication) as defined by ITU-T X.800 recommendation.

- Management functions, i.e. functions that permit to configure, instantiate, monitor, terminate the communications of two or more entities: there is a specific application-layer protocol, common management information protocol (CMIP) and its corresponding service, common management information service (CMIS), they need to interact with every layer in order to deal with their instances.

- Multiprotocol Label Switching (MPLS), ATM, and X.25 are protocols. OSI divides the Network Layer into three roles: a) Subnetwork Access, b) Subnetwork Dependent Convergence and c) Subnetwork Independent Convergence. It was designed to provide a unified data-carrying service for both circuit-based clients and packet-switching clients which provide a datagram-based service model. It can be used to carry many different kinds of traffic, including IP packets, as well as native ATM, SONET, and Ethernet frames.

- Cross MAC and PHY Scheduling is essential in wireless networks because of the time varying nature of wireless channels. By scheduling packet transmission only in favorable channel conditions, which requires the MAC layer to obtain channel state information from the PHY layer, network throughput can be significantly improved and energy waste can be avoided.

TCP/IP Model

the TCP/IP model, it was designed and developed by Department of Defense (DoD) in 1960s and is based on standard protocols. It stands for Transmission Control Protocol/Internet Protocol. The TCP/IP model is a concise version of the OSI model. It contains four layers, unlike seven layers in the OSI model. The layers are:

- Process/Application Layer,

- Host-to-Host/Transport Layer,

- Internet Layer,

- Network Access/Link Layer.

The first layer is the Process layer on the behalf of the sender and Network Access layer on the behalf of the receiver.

1. Network Access Layer:

This layer corresponds to the combination of Data Link Layer and Physical Layer of the OSI model. It looks out for hardware addressing and the protocols present in this layer allows for the physical transmission of data.

We just talked about ARP being a protocol of Internet layer, but there is a conflict about declaring it as a protocol of Internet Layer or Network access layer. It is described as residing in layer 3, being encapsulated by layer 2 protocols.

2. Internet Layer:

This layer parallels the functions of OSI's Network layer. It defines the protocols which are responsible for logical transmission of data over the entire network. The main protocols residing at this layer are:

IP – stands for Internet Protocol and it is responsible for delivering packets from the source host to the destination host by looking at the IP addresses in the packet headers. IP has 2 versions: IPv4 and IPv6. IPv4 is the one that most of the websites are using currently. But IPv6 is growing as the number of IPv4 addresses are limited in number when compared to the number of users.

ICMP – stands for Internet Control Message Protocol. It is encapsulated within IP datagrams and is responsible for providing hosts with information about network problems.

ARP – stands for Address Resolution Protocol. Its job is to find the hardware address of a host from a known IP address. ARP has several types: Reverse ARP, Proxy ARP, Gratuitous ARP and Inverse ARP.

3. Host-to-Host Layer:

This layer is analogous to the transport layer of the OSI model. It is responsible for end-to-end communication and error-free delivery of data. It shields the upper-layer applications from the complexities of data. The two main protocols present in this layer are:

- Transmission Control Protocol (TCP) – It is known to provide reliable and error-free communication between end systems. It performs sequencing and segmentation of data. It also has acknowledgment feature and controls the flow of the data through flow control mechanism. It is a very effective protocol but has a lot of overhead due to such features. Increased overhead leads to increased cost.

- User Datagram Protocol (UDP) – On the other hand does not provide any such features. It is the go-to protocol if your application does not require reliable transport as it is very cost-effective. Unlike TCP, which is connection-oriented protocol, UDP is connectionless.

4. Process Layer:

This layer performs the functions of top three layers of the OSI model: Application, Presentation and Session Layer. It is responsible for node-to-node communication and controls user-interface specifications. Some of the protocols present in this layer are: HTTP, HTTPS, FTP, TFTP, Telnet, SSH, SMTP, SNMP, NTP, DNS, DHCP, NFS, X Window, LPD. Other protocols are:

- HTTP and HTTPS – HTTP stands for Hypertext transfer protocol. It is used by the World Wide Web to manage communications between web browsers and servers. HTTPS stands for HTTP-Secure. It is a combination of HTTP with SSL (Secure Socket Layer). It is efficient in cases where the browser need to fill out forms, sign in, authenticate and carry out bank transactions.

- SSH – SSH stands for Secure Shell. It is a terminal emulations software similar to Telnet. The reason SSH is more preferred is because of its ability to maintain the encrypted connection. It sets up a secure session over a TCP/IP connection.

- NTP – NTP stands for Network Time Protocol. It is used to synchronize the clocks on our computer to one standard time source. It is very useful in situations like bank transactions.

Peer-To-Peer Network

- Peer-To-Peer network is a network in which all the computers are linked together with equal privilege and responsibilities for processing the data.

- Peer-To-Peer network is useful for small environments, usually up to 10 computers.

- Peer-To-Peer network has no dedicated server.

- Special permissions are assigned to each computer for sharing the resources, but this can lead to a problem if the computer with the resource is down.

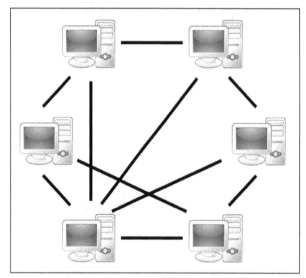

Computer Network Architecture.

Advantages of Peer-To-Peer Network:

- It is less costly as it does not contain any dedicated server.

- If one computer stops working but, other computers will not stop working.

- It is easy to set up and maintain as each computer manages itself.

Disadvantages of Peer-To-Peer Network:

- In the case of Peer-To-Peer network, it does not contain the centralized system. Therefore, it cannot back up the data as the data is different in different locations.

- It has a security issue as the device is managed itself.

Architecture

A peer-to-peer network is designed around the notion of equal *peer* nodes simultaneously functioning as both "clients" and "servers" to the other nodes on the network. This model of network arrangement differs from the client–server model where communication is usually to and from a central server. A typical example of a file transfer that uses the client-server model is the File Transfer Protocol (FTP) service in which the client and server programs are distinct: the clients initiate the transfer, and the servers satisfy these requests.

Routing and Resource Discovery

Peer-to-peer networks generally implement some form of virtual overlay network on top of the physical network topology, where the nodes in the overlay form a subset of the nodes in the physical network. Data is still exchanged directly over the underlying TCP/IP network, but at the application layer peers are able to communicate with each other directly, via the logical overlay links (each of which corresponds to a path through the underlying physical network). Overlays are used for indexing and peer discovery, and make the P2P system independent from the physical network topology. Based on how the nodes are linked to each other within the overlay network, and how resources are indexed and located, we can classify networks as *unstructured* or *structured* (or as a hybrid between the two).

Unstructured Networks

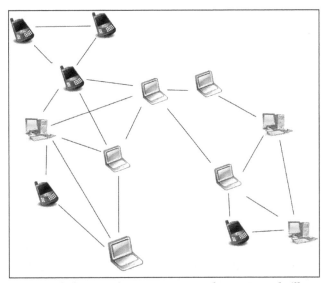

Overlay network diagram for an unstructured P2P network, illustrating
the ad hoc nature of the connections between nodes.

Unstructured peer-to-peer networks do not impose a particular structure on the overlay network by design, but rather are formed by nodes that randomly form connections to each other. (Gnutella, Gossip, and Kazaa are examples of unstructured P2P protocols). Because there is no structure globally imposed upon them, unstructured networks are easy to build and allow for localized optimizations to different regions of the overlay. Also, because the role of all peers in the network is the same, unstructured networks are highly robust in the face of high rates of "churn"—that is, when large numbers of peers are frequently joining and leaving the network.

However, the primary limitations of unstructured networks also arise from this lack of structure. In particular, when a peer wants to find a desired piece of data in the network, the search query must be flooded through the network to find as many peers as possible that share the data. Flooding causes a very high amount of signaling traffic in the network, uses more CPU/memory (by requiring every peer to process all search queries), and does not ensure that search queries will always be resolved. Furthermore, since there is no correlation between a peer and the content managed by it, there is no guarantee that flooding will find a peer that has the desired data. Popular content is likely to be available at several peers and any peer searching for it is likely to find the same thing. But if a peer is looking for rare data shared by only a few other peers, then it is highly unlikely that search will be successful.

Structured Networks

In structured peer-to-peer networks the overlay is organized into a specific topology, and the protocol ensures that any node can efficiently search the network for a file/resource, even if the resource is extremely rare.

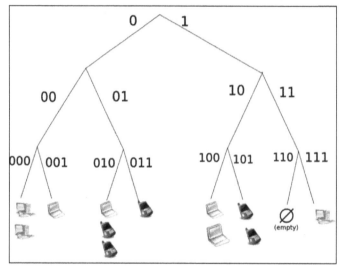

Overlay network diagram for a structured P2P network, using a distributed
hash table (DHT) to identify and locate nodes/resources.

The most common type of structured P2P networks implement a distributed hash table (DHT), in which a variant of consistent hashing is used to assign ownership of each file to a particular peer. This enables peers to search for resources on the network using a hash table: that is, (key, value) pairs are stored in the DHT, and any participating node can efficiently retrieve the value associated with a given key.

However, in order to route traffic efficiently through the network, nodes in a structured overlay must maintain lists of neighbors that satisfy specific criteria. This makes them less robust in networks with a high rate of *churn* (i.e. with large numbers of nodes frequently joining and leaving the network). More recent evaluation of P2P resource discovery solutions under real workloads have pointed out several issues in DHT-based solutions such as high cost of advertising/discovering resources and static and dynamic load imbalance.

Notable distributed networks that use DHTs include Tixati, an alternative to BitTorrent's distributed tracker, the Kad network, the Storm botnet, YaCy, and the Coral Content Distribution Network. Some prominent research projects include the Chord project, Kademlia, PAST storage utility, P-Grid, a self-organized and emerging overlay network, and CoopNet content distribution system. DHT-based networks have also been widely utilized for accomplishing efficient resource discovery for grid computing systems, as it aids in resource management and scheduling of applications.

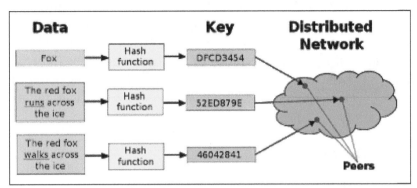

Distributed hash tables.

Hybrid Models

Hybrid models are a combination of peer-to-peer and client-server models. A common hybrid model is to have a central server that helps peers find each other. Spotify was an example of a hybrid model. There are a variety of hybrid models, all of which make trade-offs between the centralized functionality provided by a structured server/client network and the node equality afforded by the pure peer-to-peer unstructured networks. Currently, hybrid models have better performance than either pure unstructured networks or pure structured networks because certain functions, such as searching, do require a centralized functionality but benefit from the decentralized aggregation of nodes provided by unstructured networks.

Coopnet Content Distribution System

CoopNet (Cooperative Networking) was a proposed system for off-loading serving to peers who have recently downloaded content, proposed by computer scientists Venkata N. Padmanabhan and Kunwadee Sripanidkulchai, working at Microsoft Research and Carnegie Mellon University. Basically when a server experiences an increase in load it redirects incoming peers to other peers who have agreed to mirror the content, thus off-loading balance from the server. All of the information is retained at the server. This system makes use of the fact that the bottle-neck is most likely in the outgoing bandwidth than the CPU, hence its server-centric design. It assigns peers to other peers who are 'close in IP' to its neighbors in an attempt to use locality. If multiple peers are found with the same file it designates that the node choose the fastest of its neighbors. Streaming media is transmitted by having clients cache the previous stream, and then transmit it piece-wise to new nodes.

Security and Trust

Peer-to-peer systems pose unique challenges from a computer security perspective.

Like any other form of software, P2P applications can contain vulnerabilities. What makes this particularly dangerous for P2P software, however, is that peer-to-peer applications act as servers as well as clients, meaning that they can be more vulnerable to remote exploits.

Routing Attacks

Also, since each node plays a role in routing traffic through the network, malicious users can perform a variety of "routing attacks", or denial of service attacks. Examples of common routing attacks include "incorrect lookup routing" whereby malicious nodes deliberately forward requests incorrectly or return false results, "incorrect routing updates" where malicious nodes corrupt the routing tables of neighboring nodes by sending them false information, and "incorrect routing network partition" where when new nodes are joining they bootstrap via a malicious node, which places the new node in a partition of the network that is populated by other malicious nodes.

Corrupted Data and Malware

The prevalence of malware varies between different peer-to-peer protocols. Studies analyzing the spread of malware on P2P networks found, for example, that 63% of the answered download requests on the gnutella network contained some form of malware, whereas only 3% of the content on OpenFT contained malware. In both cases, the top three most common types of malware accounted for the large majority of cases (99% in gnutella, and 65% in OpenFT). Another study analyzing traffic on the Kazaa network found that 15% of the 500,000 file sample taken were infected by one or more of the 365 different computer viruses that were tested for.

Corrupted data can also be distributed on P2P networks by modifying files that are already being shared on the network. For example, on the FastTrack network, the RIAA managed to introduce faked chunks into downloads and downloaded files (mostly MP3 files). Files infected with the RIAA virus were unusable afterwards and contained malicious code. The RIAA is also known to have uploaded fake music and movies to P2P networks in order to deter illegal file sharing. Consequently, the P2P networks of today have seen an enormous increase of their security and file verification mechanisms. Modern hashing, chunk verification and different encryption methods have made most networks resistant to almost any type of attack, even when major parts of the respective network have been replaced by faked or nonfunctional hosts.

Resilient and Scalable Computer Networks

The decentralized nature of P2P networks increases robustness because it removes the single point of failure that can be inherent in a client-server based system. As nodes arrive and demand on the system increases, the total capacity of the system also increases, and the likelihood of failure decreases. If one peer on the network fails to function properly, the whole network is not compromised or damaged. In contrast, in a typical client–server architecture, clients share only their demands with the system, but not their resources. In this case, as more clients join the system, fewer resources are available to serve each client, and if the central server fails, the entire network is taken down.

Distributed Storage and Search

Search results for the query "software libre", using YaCy a free distributed search engine that runs on a peer-to-peer network instead making requests to centralized index servers (like Google, Yahoo, and other corporate search engines).

There are both advantages and disadvantages in P2P networks related to the topic of data back-up, recovery, and availability. In a centralized network, the system administrators are the only forces controlling the availability of files being shared. If the administrators decide to no longer distribute a file, they simply have to remove it from their servers, and it will no longer be available to users. Along with leaving the users powerless in deciding what is distributed throughout the community, this makes the entire system vulnerable to threats and requests from the government and other large forces. For example, YouTube has been pressured by the RIAA, MPAA, and entertainment industry to filter out copyrighted content. Although server-client networks are able to monitor and manage content availability, they can have more stability in the availability of the content they choose to host. A client should not have trouble accessing obscure content that is being shared on a stable centralized network. P2P networks, however, are more unreliable in sharing unpopular files because sharing files in a P2P network requires that at least one node in the network has the requested data, and that node must be able to connect to the node requesting the data. This requirement is occasionally hard to meet because users may delete or stop sharing data at any point.

In this sense, the community of users in a P2P network is completely responsible for deciding what content is available. Unpopular files will eventually disappear and become unavailable as more people stop sharing them. Popular files, however, will be highly and easily distributed. Popular files on a P2P network actually have more stability and availability than files on central networks. In a centralized network, a simple loss of connection between the server and clients is enough to cause a failure, but in P2P networks, the connections between every node must be lost in order to cause a data sharing failure. In a centralized system, the administrators are responsible for all data recovery and backups, while in P2P systems, each node requires its own backup system. Because of the lack of central authority in P2P networks, forces such as the recording industry, RIAA, MPAA, and the government are unable to delete or stop the sharing of content on P2P systems.

Applications

Content Delivery

In P2P networks, clients both provide and use resources. This means that unlike client-server systems, the content-serving capacity of peer-to-peer networks can actually *increase* as more users begin to access the content (especially with protocols such as Bittorrent that require users to share, refer a performance measurement study). This property is one of the major advantages of using P2P networks because it makes the setup and running costs very small for the original content distributor.

File-sharing Networks

Many file peer-to-peer file sharing networks, such as Gnutella, G2, and the eDonkey network popularized peer-to-peer technologies.

- Peer-to-peer content delivery networks.

- Peer-to-peer content services, e.g. caches for improved performance such as Correli Caches.

- Software publication and distribution (Linux distribution, several games); via file sharing networks.

Copyright Infringements

Peer-to-peer networking involves data transfer from one user to another without using an intermediate server. Companies developing P2P applications have been involved in numerous legal cases, primarily in the United States, over conflicts with copyright law. Two major cases are Grokster vs RIAA and MGM Studios, Inc. v. Grokster, Ltd. In the last case, the Court unanimously held that defendant peer-to-peer file sharing companies Grokster and Streamcast could be sued for inducing copyright infringement.

Multimedia

- The P2PTV and PDTP protocols.

- Some proprietary multimedia applications use a peer-to-peer network along with streaming servers to stream audio and video to their clients.

- Peercasting for multicasting streams.

- Pennsylvania State University, MIT and Simon Fraser University are carrying on a project called LionShare designed for facilitating file sharing among educational institutions globally.

- Osiris is a program that allows its users to create anonymous and autonomous web portals distributed via P2P network.

Energy Trading

Companies such as Power Ledger and Bovlabs employ peer-to-peer energy trading platforms.

Other P2P Applications

- Bitcoin and alternatives such as Ether, Nxt and Peercoin are peer-to-peer-based digital cryptocurrencies.

- Dalesa, a peer-to-peer web cache for LANs (based on IP multicasting).

- FAROO, a peer-to-peer web search engine

- Filecoin is an open source, public, cryptocurrency and digital payment system intended to be a blockchain-based cooperative digital storage and data retrieval method.

- I2P, an overlay network used to browse the Internet anonymously.

- Infinit is an unlimited and encrypted peer to peer file sharing application for digital artists written in C++.

- The InterPlanetary File System (IPFS) is a protocol and network designed to create a content-addressable, peer-to-peer method of storing and sharing hypermedia distribution protocol. Nodes in the IPFS network form a distributed file system.

- JXTA, a peer-to-peer protocol designed for the Java platform.

- Netsukuku, a Wireless community network designed to be independent from the Internet.

- Open Garden, connection sharing application that shares Internet access with other devices using Wi-Fi or Bluetooth.

- Research like the Chord project, the PAST storage utility, the P-Grid, and the CoopNet content distribution system.

- Tradepal and M-commerce applications that power real-time marketplaces.

- The U.S. Department of Defense is conducting research on P2P networks as part of its modern network warfare strategy. In May 2003, Anthony Tether, then director of DARPA, testified that the United States military uses P2P networks.

- WebTorrent is a P2P streaming torrent client in JavaScript for use in web browsers, as well as in the WebTorrent Desktop stand alone version that bridges WebTorrent and BitTorrent serverless networks.

- Tor (anonymity network)

- Microsoft in Windows 10 uses a proprietary peer to peer technology called "'Delivery Optimization" to deploy operating system updates using end-users PCs either on the local network or other PCs. According to Microsoft's Channel 9 it led to a 3%-50% reduction in Internet bandwidth usage.

- Artisoft's LANtastic was built as a peer-to-peer operating system. Machines can be servers and workstations at the same time.

Social Implications

Incentivizing Resource Sharing and Cooperation

Cooperation among a community of participants is key to the continued success of P2P systems aimed at casual human users; these reach their full potential only when large numbers of nodes contribute resources. But in current practice, P2P networks often contain large numbers of users who utilize resources shared by other nodes, but who do not share anything themselves (often referred to as the "freeloader problem"). Freeloading can have a profound impact on the network and in some cases can cause the community to collapse. In these types of networks "users have natural disincentives to cooperate because cooperation consumes their own resources and may degrade their own performance." Studying the social attributes of P2P networks is challenging due to large populations of turnover, asymmetry of interest and zero-cost identity. A variety of incentive mechanisms have been implemented to encourage or even force nodes to contribute resources.

Some researchers have explored the benefits of enabling virtual communities to self-organize and introduce incentives for resource sharing and cooperation, arguing that the social aspect missing from today's P2P systems should be seen both as a goal and a means for self-organized virtual communities to be built and fostered. Ongoing research efforts for designing effective incentive mechanisms in P2P systems, based on principles from game theory, are beginning to take on a more psychological and information-processing direction.

Privacy and Anonymity

Some peer-to-peer networks (e.g. Freenet) place a heavy emphasis on privacy and anonymity—that is, ensuring that the contents of communications are hidden from eavesdroppers, and that the identities/locations of the participants are concealed. Public key cryptography can be used to provide encryption, data validation, authorization, and authentication for data/messages. Onion routing and other mix network protocols (e.g. Tarzan) can be used to provide anonymity.

Here are a few examples of common use cases for P2P networks:

- When you connect the Windows computers in your home to a Homegroup, you create a peer-to-peer network between them. The Homegroup is a small group of computers that are connected between themselves to share storage and printers. This is one of the most common uses for peer-to-peer technology. Some people might say that Homegroups can't be peer-to-peer because the computers in the network are connected to a router. However, keep in mind that the router has nothing in common with managing what the computers from the Homegroup share among themselves. The router does not work as a server but merely as an interface or gate between the local network and the internet. If you want, you can find more information about the way Microsoft chose to implement the P2P technology.

- When you create an ad-hoc network between two computers, you create a peer-to-peer network between them.

- Sharing large files over the internet is often done using a P2P network architecture. For example, some online gaming platforms use P2P for downloading games between users. Blizzard Entertainment distributes Diablo III, StarCraft II and World of Warcraft using P2P. Another large publisher, Wargaming, does the same with their World of Tanks, World of Warships and World of Warplanes games. Others, like Steam or GOG, choose not to use P2P and prefer maintaining dedicated download servers around the world.

- Windows 10 updates are delivered both from Microsoft's servers and through P2P.

- Many Linux operating systems are distributed via BitTorrent downloads that use P2P transfers. Such examples are Ubuntu, Linux Mint, and Manjaro.

Client/Server Network

Client/Server network is a network model designed for the end users called clients, to access the resources such as songs, video, etc. from a central computer known as Server. The central controller is known as a server while all other computers in the network are called clients.

A server performs all the major operations such as security and network management. A server is responsible for managing all the resources such as files, directories, printer, etc.

All the clients communicate with each other through a server. For example, if client1 wants to send some data to client 2, then it first sends the request to the server for the permission. The server sends the response to the client 1 to initiate its communication with the client 2.

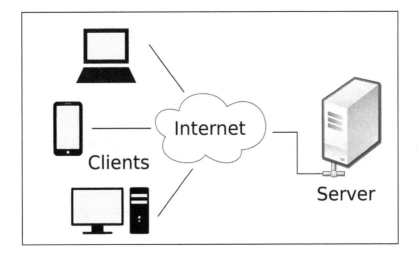

Advantages of Client/Server Network

- A Client/Server network contains the centralized system. Therefore we can back up the data easily.

- A Client/Server network has a dedicated server that improves the overall performance of the whole system.

- Security is better in Client/Server network as a single server administers the shared resources.

- It also increases the speed of the sharing resources.

Disadvantages of Client/Server Network

- Client/Server network is expensive as it requires the server with large memory.

- A server has a Network Operating System (NOS) to provide the resources to the clients, but the cost of NOS is very high.

- It requires a dedicated network administrator to manage all the resources.

Client and Server Role

The *client-server* characteristic describes the relationship of cooperating programs in an application. The server component provides a function or service to one or many clients, which initiate requests for such services. Servers are classified by the services they provide. For example, a web server serves web pages and a file server serves computer files. A shared resource may be any of the server computer's software and electronic components, from programs and data to processors and storage devices. The sharing of resources of a server constitutes a *service*.

Whether a computer is a client, a server, or both, is determined by the nature of the application that requires the service functions. For example, a single computer can run web server and file server software at the same time to serve different data to clients making different kinds of requests. Client software can also communicate with server software within the same computer.

Communication between servers, such as to synchronize data, is sometimes called *inter-server* or *server-to-server* communication.

Client and Server Communication

In general, a service is an abstraction of computer resources and a client does not have to be concerned with how the server performs while fulfilling the request and delivering the response. The client only has to understand the response based on the well-known application protocol, i.e. the content and the formatting of the data for the requested service.

Clients and servers exchange messages in a request–response messaging pattern. The client sends a request, and the server returns a response. This exchange of messages is an example of inter-process communication. To communicate, the computers must have a common language, and they must follow rules so that both the client and the server know what to expect. The language and rules of communication are defined in a communications protocol. All client-server protocols operate in the application layer. The application layer protocol defines the basic patterns of the dialogue. To formalize the data exchange even further, the server may implement an application programming interface (API). The API is an abstraction layer for accessing a service. By restricting communication to a specific content format, it facilitates parsing. By abstracting access, it facilitates cross-platform data exchange.

A server may receive requests from many distinct clients in a short period of time. A computer can only perform a limited number of tasks at any moment, and relies on a scheduling system to prioritize incoming requests from clients to accommodate them. To prevent abuse and maximize availability, server software may limit the availability to clients. Denial of service attacks are designed to exploit a server's obligation to process requests by overloading it with excessive request rates.

Centralized Computing

The client–server model does not dictate that server-hosts must have more resources than client-hosts. Rather, it enables any general-purpose computer to extend its capabilities by using the shared resources of other hosts. Centralized computing, however, specifically allocates a large amount of resources to a small number of computers. The more computation is offloaded from client-hosts to the central computers, the simpler the client-hosts can be. It relies heavily on network resources (servers and infrastructure) for computation and storage. A diskless node loads even its operating system from the network, and a computer terminal has no operating system at all; it is only an input/output interface to the server. In contrast, a fat client, such as a personal computer, has many resources, and does not rely on a server for essential functions.

As microcomputers decreased in price and increased in power from the 1980s to the late 1990s, many organizations transitioned computation from centralized servers, such as mainframes and minicomputers, to fat clients. This afforded greater, more individualized dominion over computer resources, but complicated information technology management. During the 2000s, web applications matured enough to rival application software developed for a specific microarchitecture. This maturation, more affordable mass storage, and the advent of service-oriented architecture were among the factors that gave rise to the cloud computing trend of the 2010s.

Comparison with Peer-to-Peer Architecture

In addition to the client–server model, distributed computing applications often use the peer-to-peer (P2P) application architecture.

In the client–server model, the server is often designed to operate as a centralized system that serves many clients. The computing power, memory and storage requirements of a server must be scaled appropriately to the expected work-load (*i.e.*, the number of clients connecting simultaneously). Load-balancing and failover systems are often employed to scale the server implementation.

In a peer-to-peer network, two or more computers (*peers*) pool their resources and communicate in a decentralized system. Peers are coequal, or equipotent nodes in a non-hierarchical network. Unlike clients in a client–server or client–queue–client network, peers communicate with each other directly. In peer-to-peer networking, an algorithm in the peer-to-peer communications protocol balances load, and even peers with modest resources can help to share the load. If a node becomes unavailable, its shared resources remain available as long as other peers offer it. Ideally, a peer does not need to achieve high availability because other, redundant peers make up for any resource downtime; as the availability and load capacity of peers change, the protocol reroutes requests.

Both client-server and master-slave are regarded as sub-categories of distributed peer-to-peer systems.

Benefits of Client Server Networks

The main benefits of the client server network is allowing a shared database or site to be accessed or updated by multiple computers while maintaining only one control center for the action. This makes it possible for companies to distribute information, upload data, or reach the program without being tied down to one individual computer site. Because the information is stored online, a client server model creates more power and control over what is being saved.

Additionally, this model has an increased security, often with encryption, ensuring that the data is only available to qualified individuals. A client server model also makes it easier to back up important information than if it was stored across multiple devices. A network administrator can simply configure a backup for the server, and if the original data were to be destroyed, he or she would only need to restore the single backup.

Disadvantages of Client Server Networks

Under a client server model, the main disadvantage is running the risk of a system overload due to not having enough resources to serve all the clients. If too many different clients attempt to reach the shared network at the same time, there may be a failure or a slowing down of the connection. Furthermore, if the network is down, this disables access to the information from any site or client anywhere. This can be detrimental to major businesses who are unable to reach their pertinent data.

References

- Network, 5537, definition: techopedia.com, Retrieved 12 July, 2019

- Computer-network, technology: britannica.com, Retrieved 11 January 2019

- Internet, technology: britannica.com, Retrieved 1 August, 2019

- Open-network-vs-closed-network-choose: fiber-optical-networking.com, Retrieved 5, March, 2019

- Open-system, 21204, definition: techopedia.com, Retrieved 8 June, 2019

- Difference-between-circuit-switching-and-packet-switching: techdifferences.com, Retrieved 5 February, 2019

- Barkai, david (2001). Peer-to-peer computing : technologies for sharing and collaborating on the net. Hillsboro, or: intel press. Isbn 978-0970284679. Oclc 49354877

- Computer-network-tcpip-model: geeksforgeeks.org, Retrieved 16 January, 2019

- "the osi model's seven layers defined and functions explained". Microsoft support. Retrieved 28 december 2014

- Computer-network-architecture: javatpoint.com, Retrieved 15 July, 2019

- Ahson, syed a.; ilyas, mohammad, eds. (2008). Sip handbook: services, technologies, and security of session initiation protocol. Taylor & francis. P. 204. Isbn 9781420066043

- Computer-network-architecture: javatpoint.com, Retrieved 27 May, 2019

- What-is-a-client-server-network: techwalla.com, Retrieved 23 February, 2019

2
Types of Computer Networks

There are various types of networks such as LAN, WAN, MAN, PAN, VPN, CAN, BAN and NAN. The network which uses wireless data connections between network nodes is referred to as a wireless network. This chapter has been carefully written to provide an easy understanding of these types of networks.

LAN

A Local Area Network (LAN) is a network that is confined to a relatively small area. It is generally limited to a geographic area such as a writing lab, school, or building.

Computers connected to a network are broadly categorized as servers or workstations. Servers are generally not used by humans directly, but rather run continuously to provide "services" to the other computers (and their human users) on the network. Services provided can include printing and faxing, software hosting, file storage and sharing, messaging, data storage and retrieval, complete access control (security) for the network's resources, and many others.

Workstations are called such because they typically do have a human user which interacts with the network through them. Workstations were traditionally considered a desktop, consisting of a computer, keyboard, display, and mouse, or a laptop, with with integrated keyboard, display, and touchpad. With the advent of the tablet computer, and the touch screen devices such as iPad and iPhone, our definition of workstation is quickly evolving to include those devices, because of their ability to interact with the network and utilize network services.

Servers tend to be more powerful than workstations, although configurations are guided by needs. For example, a group of servers might be located in a secure area, away from humans, and only accessed through the network. In such cases, it would be common for the servers to operate without a dedicated display or keyboard. However, the size and speed of the server's processor(s), hard drive, and main memory might add dramatically to the cost of the system. On the other hand, a workstation might not need as much storage or working memory, but might require an expensive display to accommodate the needs of its user. Every computer on a network should be appropriately configured for its use.

On a single LAN, computers and servers may be connected by cables or wirelessly. Wireless access to a wired network is made possible by wireless access points (WAPs). These WAP devices provide a bridge between computers and networks. A typical WAP might have the theoretical capacity to connect hundreds or even thousands of wireless users to a network, although practical capacity might be far less.

Nearly always servers will be connected by cables to the network, because the cable connections remain the fastest. Workstations which are stationary (desktops) are also usually connected by a cable to the network, although the cost of wireless adapters has dropped to the point that, when installing workstations in an existing facility with inadequate wiring, it can be easier and less expensive to use wireless for a desktop.

Home Area Network

A home network or home area network (HAN) is a type of computer network that facilitates communication among devices within the close vicinity of a home. Devices capable of participating in this network, for example, smart devices such as network printers and handheld mobile computers, often gain enhanced emergent capabilities through their ability to interact. These additional capabilities can be used to increase the quality of life inside the home in a variety of ways, such as automation of repetitive tasks, increased personal productivity, enhanced home security, and easier access to entertainment.

Infrastructure Devices

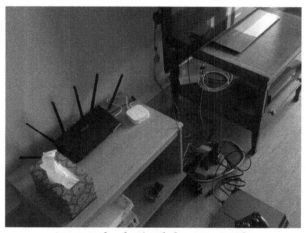

An example of a simple home network.

A home network usually relies on one or more of the following equipment to establish physical layer, data link layer, and network layer connectivity among internal devices, also known as the LAN, and external devices outside the LAN networks or the WAN. The following are examples of typical LAN devices:

- A modem exposes an Ethernet interface to a service provider's native telecommunications infrastructure. In homes these usually come in the form of a DSL modem or cable modem.

- A router manages network layer connectivity between a WAN and the HAN. It performs the key function of network address translation enabling multiple devices to share the home's single WAN address. Most home networks feature a particular class of small, passively cooled, table-top device with an integrated wireless access point and 4 port Ethernet switch. These devices aim to make the installation, configuration, and management of a home network as automated, user friendly, and "plug-and-play" as possible.

- A network switch is used to allow devices on the home network to talk to one another via Ethernet. While the needs of most home networks are satisfied with the built-in wireless and switching capabilities of their router, some situations require the addition of a separate switch with advanced capabilities. For example:

  ○ A typical home router has 4 to 6 Ethernet LAN ports, so a router's switching capacity could be exceeded.

  ○ A network device might require a non-standard port feature such as power over Ethernet (PoE).

- A wireless access point is required for connecting wireless devices to a network. Most home networks rely on a wireless router, which has a built in wireless access point, to fill this role.

- A home automation controller enables low-power wireless communications with simple, non-data-intensive devices such as smart light bulbs (Philips Hue) and smart locks (August Home).

- A network bridge connects two networks, often in order to grant a wired-only device, e.g. Xbox, access to a wireless network medium.

Triple Play

A service provider's triple play solution features a rented modem/wireless router combination device, such as an Arris SURFboard SBG6580, that only requires the setting of a password to complete the installation and configuration. In most situations, there is no longer a need to acquire additional infrastructure devices or even for the user to possess advanced technical knowledge to successfully distribute internet access throughout the home.

Physical Connectivity and Protocols

Home networking standards	
Common name	IEEE standard
HomePlug HD-PLC	1901
Wi-Fi	802.11a
	802.11b
	802.11g
	802.11n
	802.11ac
Common name	ITU-T recommendation
HomePNA 2.0	G.9951–3
HomePNA 3.1/HomeGrid	G.9954
G.hn/HomeGrid	G.9960 (PHY)

G.hn/HomeGrid	G.9961 (DLL/MAC)
G.hn/HomeGrid	G.9962 (Management Plane)
G.hn-mimo	G.9963
G.hn/HomeGrid	G.9964 (PSD Management)
G.hnta	G.9970
G.cx	G.9972

Home networks can use either wired or wireless technologies to connect endpoints. Wireless is the predominant option in homes due to the ease of installation, lack of unsightly cables, and network performance characteristics sufficient for residential activities.

Wireless

Wireless LAN

One of the most common ways of creating a home network is by using wireless radio signal technology; the 802.11 network as certified by the IEEE. Most wireless-capable residential devices operate at a frequency of 2.4 GHz under 802.11b and 802.11g or 5 GHz under 802.11a. Some home networking devices operate in both radio-band signals and fall within the 802.11n or 802.11ac standards. Wi-Fi is a marketing and compliance certification for IEEE 802.11 technologies. The Wi-Fi Alliance has tested compliant products, and certifies them for interoperability.

Wireless PAN

Low power, close range communication based on IEEE 802.15 standards has a strong presence in homes. Bluetooth continues to be the technology of choice for most wireless accessories such as keyboards, mice, headsets, and game controllers. These connections are often established in a transient, ad-hoc manner and are not thought of as permanent residents of a home network.

Low-rate Wireless Pan

A "low-rate" version of the original WPAN protocol was used as the basis of ZigBee. Despite originally being conceived as a standard for low power machine-to-machine communication in industrial environments. The technology has been found to be well suited for integration into embedded "Smart Home" offerings that are expected to run on battery for extended periods of time. ZigBee utilizes mesh networking to overcome the distance limitations associated with traditional WPAN in order to establish a single network of addressable devices spread across the entire building. Z-Wave is an additional standard also built on 802.15.4, that was developed specifically with the needs of home automation device makers in mind.

Twisted Pair Cables

Most wired network infrastructures found in homes utilize Category 5 or Category 6 twisted pair cabling with RJ45 compatible terminations. This medium provides physical connectivity between the Ethernet interfaces present on a large number of residential IP-aware devices. Depending on the grade of cable and quality of installation, speeds of up to 10 Mbit/s, 100 Mbit/s, 1 Gbit/s, or 10Gbit/s are supported.

Fiber Optics

Newer upscale neighborhoods can feature fiber optic cables running directly into the homes. This enables service providers to offer internet services with much higher bandwidth and lower latency characteristics associated with end-to-end optical signaling.

Telephone Wires

- VDSL and VDSL2.

- HomePNA support up to 160 Mbit/s.

Coaxial Cables

The following standards allow devices to communicate over coaxial cables, which are frequently installed to support multiple television sets throughout homes.

- DOCSIS.

- The Multimedia over Coax Alliance (MoCA) standard can achieve up to 270 Mbit/s.

- CWave.

- HomePNA support up to 320 Mbit/s.

Power Lines

The ITU-T G.hn and IEEE Powerline standard, which provide high-speed (up to 1 Gbit/s) local area networking over existing home wiring, are examples of home networking technology designed specifically for IPTV delivery. Recently, the IEEE passed proposal P1901 which grounded a standard within the market for wireline products produced and sold by companies that are part of the HomePlug Alliance. The IEEE is continuously working to push for P1901 to be completely recognized worldwide as the sole standard for all future products that are produced for Home Networking.

- HomePlug and HomePNA are associated standards.

- Universal Powerline Association.

Endpoint Devices and Services

Traditionally, data-centric equipment such as computers and media players have been the primary tenants of a home network. However, due to the lowering cost of computing and the ubiquity of smartphone usage, many traditionally non-networked home equipment categories now include new variants capable of control or remote monitoring through an app on a smartphone. Newer startups and established home equipment manufacturers alike have begun to offer these products as part of a "Smart" or "Intelligent" or "Connected Home" portfolio. The control and monitoring interfaces for these products can be accessed through proprietary smartphone applications specific to that product line.

General Purpose

- Personal computers such as desktops, laptops, netbooks, and tablets.

- A network attached storage (NAS) device can be easily accessed via the CIFS or NFS protocols for general storage or for backup purposes.

- A print server can be used to share any directly connected printers with other computers on the network.

- IP phones or smartphones (when connected via Wi-Fi) utilizing VoIP technologies.

Entertainment

- Smart speakers.

- Television: Some new TVs and DVRs include integrated WiFi connectivity which allows the user to access services such as Netflix and YouTube.

- Home audio: Digital audio players, and stereo systems with network connectivity can allow a user to easily access their music library, often using Bonjour to discover and interface with an instance of iTunes running on a remote PC.

- Gaming: Video game consoles rely on connectivity to the home network to enable a significant portion of their overall features, such as the multiplayer in games, social network integration, ability to purchase or demo new games, and receive software updates. Recent consoles have begun more aggressively pursuing the role of the sole entertainment and media hub of the home.

- DLNA is a common protocol used for interoperability between networked media-centric devices in the home.

Some older entertainment devices may not feature the appropriate network interfaces required for home network connectivity. In some situations, USB dongles and PCI Network Interface Cards are available as accessories that enable this functionality.

Lighting

- Connected light bulbs such as Lifx, Philips Hue, Samsung Smart Bulb, GE Link.

- ZigBee Light Link is the open standards protocol used by current major "Connected" light bulb vendors.

Home Security and Access Control

- Garage door and gate openers: Liftmaster MyQ, GoGogate.

Environmental Monitoring and Conditioning

- HVAC: Nest Learning Thermostat.

- Smoke/CO detectors: Nest Protect.

Cloud Services

The convenience, availability, and reliability of externally managed cloud computing resources continues to become an appealing choice for many home-dwellers without interest or experience in IT. For these individuals, the subscription fees and privacy risks associated with such services are often perceived as lower cost than having to configure and maintain similar facilities within a home network. In such situations, local services along with the devices maintaining them are replaced by those in an external data center and made accessible to the home-dweller's computing devices via a WAN connection.

Network Management

Embedded Devices

Small standalone embedded home network devices typically require remote configuration from a PC on the same network. For example, broadband modems are often configured through a web browser running on a PC in the same network. These devices usually use a minimal Linux distribution with a lightweight HTTP server running in the background to allow the user to conveniently modify system variables from a GUI rendered in their browser. These pages use HTML forms extensively and make attempts to offer styled, visually appealing views that are also descriptive and easy to use.

Apple Ecosystem Devices

Apple devices aim to make networking as hidden and automatic as possible, utilizing a zero-configuration networking protocol called Bonjour embedded within their otherwise proprietary line of software and hardware products.

Microsoft Ecosystem Devices

Microsoft offers simple access control features built into their Windows operating system. Homegroup is a feature that allows shared disk access, shared printer access and shared scanner access among all computers and users (typically family members) in a home, in a similar fashion as in a small office workgroup, e.g., by means of distributed peer-to-peer networking (without a central server). Additionally, a home server may be added for increased functionality. The *Windows HomeGroup* feature was introduced with Microsoft Windows 7 in order to simplify file sharing in residences. All users (typically all family members), except guest accounts, may access any shared library on any computer that is connected to the home group. Passwords are not required from the family members during logon. Instead, secure file sharing is possible by means of a temporary password that is used when adding a computer to the HomeGroup.

Common Issues and Concerns

Wireless Signal Loss

The wireless signal strength of the standard residential wireless router may not be powerful enough to cover the entire house or may not be able to get through to all floors of multiple floor residences. In such situations, the installation of one or more wireless repeaters may be necessary.

Leaky Wi-Fi

WiFi often extends beyond the boundaries of a home and can create coverage where it is least wanted, offering a channel through which non-residents could compromise a system and retrieve personal data. To prevent this it is usually sufficient to enforce the use of authentication, encryption, or VPN that requires a password for network connectivity.

However new Wi-Fi standards working at 60 GHz, such as 802.11ad, enable confidence that the LAN will not trespass physical barriers, as at such frequencies a simple wall would attenuate the signal considerably.

Electrical Grid Noise

For home networks relying on powerline communication technology, how to deal with electrical noise injected into the system from standard household appliances remains the largest challenge. Whenever any appliance is turned on or turned off it creates noise that could possibly disrupt data transfer through the wiring. IEEE products that are certified to be HomePlug 1.0 compliant have been engineered to no longer interfere with, or receive interference from other devices plugged into the same home's electrical grid.

Administration

The administration of proliferating devices and software in home networks, and the growing amount of private data, is fast becoming an issue by itself. Keeping overview, applying without delay SW updates and security patches, keeping juniors internet use within safe boundaries, structuring of storage and access levels for private files and other data, data backups, detection and cleaning of any infections, operating virtual private networks for easy access to resources in the home network when away, etc. Such things are all issues that require attention and planned careful work in order to provide a secure, resilient, and stable home network easy to use for all members of the household and their guests.

Storage Area Network

A storage area network (SAN) or storage network is a Computer network which provides access to consolidated, block-level data storage. SANs are primarily used to enhance accessibility of storage devices, such as disk arrays and tape libraries, to servers so that the devices appear to the operating system as locally-attached devices. A SAN typically is a dedicated network of storage devices not accessible through the local area network (LAN) by other devices, thereby preventing interference of LAN traffic in data transfer.

The cost and complexity of SANs dropped in the early 2000s to levels allowing wider adoption across both enterprise and small to medium-sized business environments. A SAN does not provide file abstraction, only block-level operations. However, file systems built on top of SANs do provide file-level access, and are known as shared-disk file systems.

Storage Architectures

Storage area networks (SANs) are sometimes referred to as *network behind the servers* and historically developed out of the centralised data storage model, but with its own data network.

A SAN is, at its simplest, a dedicated network for data storage. In addition to storing data, SANs allow for the automatic backup of data, and the monitoring of the storage as well as the backup process. A SAN is a combination of hardware and software. It grew out of data-centric mainframe architectures, where clients in a network can connect to several servers that store different types of data. To scale storage capacities as the volumes of data grew, direct-attached storage (DAS) was developed, where disk arrays or just a bunch of disks (JBODs) were attached to servers. In this architecture storage devices can be added to increase storage capacity. However, the server through which the storage devices are accessed is a single point of failure, and a large part of the LAN network bandwidth is used for accessing, storing and backing up data. To solve the single point of failure issue, a *direct-attached shared storage* architecture was implemented, where several servers could access the same storage device.

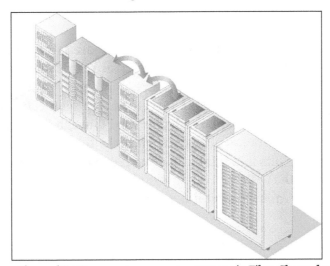

The Fibre Channel SAN connects servers to storage via Fibre Channel switches.

DAS was the first network storage system and is still widely implemented where data storage requirements are not very high. Out of it developed the network-attached storage (NAS) architecture, where one or more dedicated file server or storage devices are made available in a LAN. Therefore, the transfer of data, particularly for backup, still takes place over the existing LAN. If more than a terabyte of data was stored at any one time, LAN bandwidth became a bottleneck. Therefore, SANs were developed, where a dedicated storage network was attached to the LAN, and terabytes of data are transferred over a dedicated high speed and bandwidth network. Within the storage network, storage devices are interconnected. Transfer of data between storage devices, such as for backup, happens behind the servers and is meant to be transparent. While in a NAS architecture data is transferred using the TCP and IP protocols over Ethernet, distinct protocols were developed for SANs, such as Fibre Channel, iSCSI, Infiniband. Therefore, SANs often have their own network and storage devices, which have to be bought, installed, and configured. This makes SANs inherently more expensive than NAS architectures.

Components

SANs have their own networking devices, such as SAN switches. To access the SAN so-called SAN servers are used, which in turn connect to SAN interfaces. Within the SAN a range of data storage devices may be interconnected, such as SAN capable disk arrays, JBODS and tape libraries.

Dual port 8 Gb FC host bus adapter card.

Host Layer

Servers that allow access to the SAN and its storage devices are said to form the *host layer* of the SAN. Such servers have host bus adapters (HBAs), which are cards that attach to slots on the server main board (usually PCI slots) and run with a corresponding firmware and driver. Through the host bus adapters the operating system of the server can communicate with the storage devices in the SAN. A cable connects to the host bus adapter card through the gigabit interface converter (GBIC). These interface converters are also attached to switches and storage devices within the SAN, and they convert digital bits into light impulses that can then be transmitted over the Fiber Channel cables. Conversely, the GBIC converts incoming light impulses back into digital bits. The predecessor of the GBIC was called gigabit link module (GLM). This is applicable for Fiber Channel deployments only.

Fabric Layer

Qlogic SAN-switch with optical Fibre Channel connectors installed.

The fabric layer consists of SAN networking devices that include SAN switches, routers, protocol bridges, gateway devices, and cables. SAN network devices move data within the SAN, or between an *initiator*, such as an HBA port of a server, and a *target*, such as the port of a storage device. SAN networks are usually built with redundancy, so SAN switches are connected with redundant links. SAN switches connect the servers with the storage devices and are typically non-blocking, thus transmitting data across all attached wires at the same time. When SANs were first built, hubs were the only devices that were Fibre Channel capable, but Fibre Channel switches were developed and hubs are now rarely found in SANs. Switches have the advantage over hubs that they allow all attached devices to communicate simultaneously, as a switch provides a dedicated link to connect all its ports with one another. SAN switches are for redundancy purposes set up in a meshed topology. A single SAN switch can have as few as 8 ports, up to 32 ports with modular extensions. So called director class switches can have as many as 128 ports. When SANs were first built Fibre Channel had to be implemented over copper cables, these days multimode optical fibre cables are used in SANs. In switched SANs the Fibre Channel switched fabric protocol FC-SW-6 is used, where every device in the SAN has a hardcoded World Wide Name (WWN) address in the host bus adapter (HBA). If a device is connected to the SAN its WWN is registered in the SAN switch name server. In place of a WWN, or worldwide port name (WWPN), SAN Fibre Channel storage device vendors may also hardcode a worldwide node name (WWNN). The ports of storage devices often have an WWN starting with 5, while the bus adapters of servers start with 10 or 21.

Storage Layer

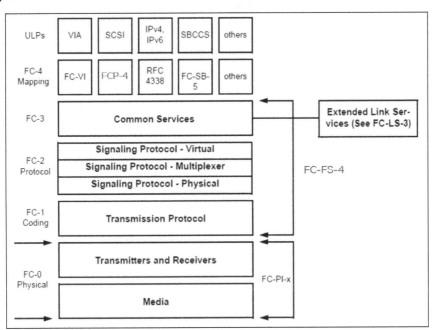

Fibre Channel is a layered technology that starts at the physical layer and progresses through the protocols to the upper level protocols like SCSI and SBCCS.

On top of the Fibre Channel-Switched Protocol is often the serialized Small Computer Systems Interface (SCSI) protocol, implemented in servers and SAN storage devices. It allows software applications to communicate, or encode data, for storage devices. The internet Small Computer Systems Interface (iSCSI) over Ethernet and the Infiniband protocols may also be found implemented in SANs, but are often bridged into the Fibre Channel SAN. However, Infiniband and iSCSI storage devices, in particular, disk arrays, are available.

The various storage devices in a SAN are said to form the *storage layer*. It can include a variety of hard disk and magnetic tape devices that store data. In SANs disk arrays are joined through a RAID, which makes a lot of hard disks look and perform like one big storage device. Every storage device, or even partition on that storage device, has a logical unit number (LUN) assigned to it. This is a unique number within the SAN and every node in the SAN, be it a server or another storage device, can access the storage through the LUN. The LUNs allow for the storage capacity of a SAN to be segmented and for the implementation of access controls. A particular server, or a group of servers, may, for example, be only given access to a particular part of the SAN storage layer, in the form of LUNs. When a storage device receives a request to read or write data, it will check its access list to establish whether the node, identified by its LUN, is allowed to access the storage area, also identified by a LUN. LUN masking is a technique whereby the host bus adapter and the SAN software of a server restrict the LUNs for which commands are accepted. In doing so LUNs that should in any case not be accessed by the server are masked. Another method to restrict server access to particular SAN storage devices is fabric-based access control, or zoning, which has to be implemented on the SAN networking devices and the servers. Thereby server access is restricted to storage devices that are in a particular SAN zone.

Network Protocols

Most storage networks use the SCSI protocol for communication between servers and disk drive devices. A mapping layer to other protocols is used to form a network:

- ATA over Ethernet (AoE), mapping of ATA over Ethernet.

- Fibre Channel Protocol (FCP), the most prominent one, is a mapping of SCSI over Fibre Channel.

- Fibre Channel over Ethernet (FCoE).

- ESCON over Fibre Channel (FICON), used by mainframe computers.

- HyperSCSI, mapping of SCSI over Ethernet.

- iFCP or SANoIP mapping of FCP over IP.

- iSCSI, mapping of SCSI over TCP/IP.

- iSCSI Extensions for RDMA (iSER), mapping of iSCSI over InfiniBand.

- SCSI RDMA Protocol (SRP), another SCSI implementation for RDMA transports.

Storage networks may also be built using SAS and SATA technologies. SAS evolved from SCSI direct-attached storage. SATA evolved from IDE direct-attached storage. SAS and SATA devices can be networked using SAS Expanders.

Table: Examples of stacked protocols using SCSI.

Applications						
SCSI Layer						
FCP	FCP	FCP	FCP	iSCSI	iSER	SRP
		FCIP	iFCP			
		TCP			RDMA Transport	
	FCoE	IP			IP or InfiniBand Network	
FC	Ethernet				Ethernet or InfiniBand Link	

Software

A SAN is primarily defined as a special purpose network, the Storage Networking Industry Association (SNIA) defines a SAN as "a network whose primary purpose is the transfer of data between computer systems and storage elements". But a SAN does not just consist of a communication infrastructure, it also has a software *management layer*. This software organizes the servers, storage devices, and the network so that data can be transferred and stored. Because a SAN is not a direct attached storage (DAS), the storage devices in the SAN are not owned and managed by a server. Potentially the data storage capacity that can be accessed by a single server through a SAN is infinite, and this storage capacity may also be accessible by other servers. Moreover, SAN software must ensure that data is directly moved between storage devices within the SAN, with minimal server intervention.

SAN management software is installed on one or more servers and management clients on the storage devices. Two approaches have developed to SAN management software: in-band management means that management data between server and storage devices is transmitted on the same network as the storage data. While out-of-band management means that management data is transmitted over dedicated links. SAN management software will collect management data from all storage devices in the storage layer, including info on read and write failure, storage capacity bottlenecks and failure of storage devices. SAN management software may integrate with the Simple Network Management Protocol (SNMP).

In 1999, an open standard was introduced for managing storage devices and provide interoperability, the Common Information Model (CIM). The web-based version of CIM is called Web-Based Enterprise Management (WBEM) and defines SAN storage device objects and process transactions. Use of these protocols involves a CIM object manager (CIMOM), to manage objects and interactions, and allows for the central management of SAN storage devices. Basic device management for SANs can also be achieved through the Storage Management Interface Specification (SMI-S), were CIM objects and processes are registered in a directory. Software applications and subsystems can then draw on this directory. Management software applications are also available to configure SAN storage devices, allowing, for example, the configuration of zones and logical unit numbers (LUNs).

Ultimately SAN networking and storage devices are available from many vendors. Every SAN vendor has its own management and configuration software. Common management in SANs that include devices from different vendors is only possible if vendors make the application programming interface (API) for their devices available to other vendors. In such cases, upper-level SAN management software can manage the SAN devices from other vendors.

File Systems Support

In a SAN data is transferred, stored and accessed on a block level. As such a SAN does not provide data file abstraction, only block-level storage and operations. But file systems have been developed to work with SAN software to provide file-level access. These are known as SAN file systems, or shared disk file system. Server operating systems maintain their own file systems on their own dedicated, non-shared LUNs, as though they were local to themselves. If multiple systems were simply to attempt to share a LUN, these would interfere with each other and quickly corrupt the data. Any planned sharing of data on different computers within a LUN requires software, such as SAN file systems or clustered computing.

In Media and Entertainment

Video editing systems require very high data transfer rates and very low latency. SANs in media and entertainment are often referred to as serverless due to the nature of the configuration which places the video workflow (ingest, editing, playout) desktop clients directly on the SAN rather than attaching to servers. Control of data flow is managed by a distributed file system such as StorNext by Quantum. Per-node bandwidth usage control, sometimes referred to as quality of service (QoS), is especially important in video editing as it ensures fair and prioritized bandwidth usage across the network.

Quality of Service

SAN Storage QoS enables the desired storage performance to be calculated and maintained for network customers accessing the device. Some factors that affect SAN QoS are:

- Bandwidth – The rate of data throughput available on the system.

- Latency – The time delay for a read/write operation to execute.

- Queue depth – The number of outstanding operations waiting to execute to the underlying disks (traditional or solid-state drives).

QoS can be impacted in a SAN storage system by an unexpected increase in data traffic (usage spike) from one network user that can cause performance to decrease for other users on the same network. This can be known as the "noisy neighbor effect." When QoS services are enabled in a SAN storage system, the "noisy neighbor effect" can be prevented and network storage performance can be accurately predicted.

Using SAN storage QoS is in contrast to using disk over-provisioning in a SAN environment. Over-provisioning can be used to provide additional capacity to compensate for peak network traffic loads. However, where network loads are not predictable, over-provisioning can eventually cause all bandwidth to be fully consumed and latency to increase significantly resulting in SAN performance degradation.

Storage Virtualization

Storage virtualization is the process of abstracting logical storage from physical storage. The physical storage resources are aggregated into storage pools, from which the logical storage is created. It presents to the user a logical space for data storage and transparently handles the process of mapping it to the physical location, a concept called location transparency. This is implemented in modern disk arrays, often using vendor proprietary technology. However, the goal of storage virtualization is to group multiple disk arrays from different vendors, scattered over a network, into a single storage device. The single storage device can then be managed uniformly.

Wireless LAN

A wireless LAN (WLAN) is a wireless computer network that links two or more devices using wireless communication to form a local area network (LAN) within a limited area such as a home, school, computer laboratory, campus, office building etc. This gives users the ability to move around within the area and yet still be connected to the network. Through a gateway, a WLAN can also provide a connection to the wider Internet.

Most modern WLANs are based on IEEE 802.11 standards and are marketed under the Wi-Fi brand name. Wireless LANs have become popular for use in the home, due to their ease of installation and use. They are also popular in commercial properties that offer wireless access to their employees and customers.

Architecture

Stations

All components that can connect into a wireless medium in a network are referred to as stations (STA). All stations are equipped with wireless network interface controllers (WNICs). Wireless stations fall into two categories: wireless access points, and clients. Access points (APs), normally wireless routers, are base stations for the wireless network. They transmit and receive radio frequencies for wireless enabled devices to communicate with. Wireless clients can be mobile devices such as laptops, personal digital assistants, IP phones and other smartphones, or non-portable devices such as desktop computers, printers, and workstations that are equipped with a wireless network interface.

Basic Service Set

The basic service set (BSS) is a set of all stations that can communicate with each other at PHY layer. Every BSS has an identification (ID) called the BSSID, which is the MAC address of the access point servicing the BSS.

There are two types of BSS: Independent BSS (also referred to as IBSS), and infrastructure BSS. An independent BSS (IBSS) is an ad hoc network that contains no access points, which means they cannot connect to any other basic service set.

Independent Basic Service Set

An IBSS is a set of STAs configured in ad hoc (peer-to-peer)mode.

Extended Service Set

An extended service set (ESS) is a set of connected BSSs. Access points in an ESS are connected by a distribution system. Each ESS has an ID called the SSID which is a 32-byte (maximum) character string.

Distribution System

A distribution system (DS) connects access points in an extended service set. The concept of a DS can be used to increase network coverage through roaming between cells.

DS can be wired or wireless. Current wireless distribution systems are mostly based on WDS or MESH protocols, though other systems are in use.

Types of Wireless LANs

The IEEE 802.11 has two basic modes of operation: infrastructure and *ad hoc* mode. In *ad hoc* mode, mobile units transmit directly peer-to-peer. In infrastructure mode, mobile units communicate through an access point that serves as a bridge to other networks (such as Internet or LAN).

Since wireless communication uses a more open medium for communication in comparison to wired LANs, the 802.11 designers also included encryption mechanisms: Wired Equivalent Privacy (WEP, now insecure), Wi-Fi Protected Access (WPA, WPA2, WPA3), to secure wireless computer networks. Many access points will also offer Wi-Fi Protected Setup, a quick (but now insecure) method of joining a new device to an encrypted network.

Infrastructure

Most Wi-Fi networks are deployed in infrastructure mode.

In infrastructure mode, a base station acts as a wireless access point hub, and nodes communicate through the hub. The hub usually, but not always, has a wired or fiber network connection, and may have permanent wireless connections to other nodes.

Wireless access points are usually fixed, and provide service to their client nodes within range.

Wireless clients, such as laptops, smartphones etc. connect to the access point to join the network.

Sometimes a network will have a multiple access points, with the same 'SSID' and security arrangement. In that case connecting to any access point on that network joins the client to the network. In that case, the client software will try to choose the access point to try to give the best service, such as the access point with the strongest signal.

Peer-to-Peer

Peer-to-Peer or ad hoc wireless LAN.

An ad hoc network is a network where stations communicate only peer to peer (P2P). There is no base and no one gives permission to talk. This is accomplished using the Independent Basic Service Set (IBSS). A WiFi Direct network is another type of network where stations communicate peer to peer.

In a Wi-Fi P2P group, the group owner operates as an access point and all other devices are clients. There are two main methods to establish a group owner in the Wi-Fi Direct group. In one approach, the user sets up a P2P group owner manually. This method is also known as Autonomous Group Owner (autonomous GO). In the second method, also called negotiation-based group creation, two devices compete based on the group owner intent value. The device with higher intent value becomes a group owner and the second device becomes a client. Group owner intent value can depend on whether the wireless device performs a cross-connection between an infrastructure WLAN service and a P2P group, remaining power in the wireless device, whether the wireless device is already a group owner in another group and a received signal strength of the first wireless device.

A peer-to-peer network allows wireless devices to directly communicate with each other. Wireless devices within range of each other can discover and communicate directly without involving central access points. This method is typically used by two computers so that they can connect to each other to form a network. This can basically occur in devices within a closed range.

If a signal strength meter is used in this situation, it may not read the strength accurately and can be misleading, because it registers the strength of the strongest signal, which may be the closest computer.

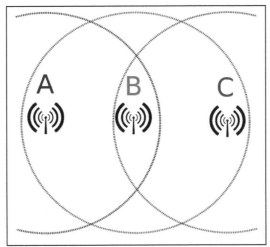

Hidden node problem: Devices A and C are both communicating with B, but are unaware of each other.

IEEE 802.11 defines the physical layer (PHY) and MAC (Media Access Control) layers based on CSMA/CA (Carrier Sense Multiple Access with Collision Avoidance). This is in contrast to Ethernet which uses CSMA-CD (Carrier Sense Multiple Access with Collision Detection). The 802.11 specification includes provisions designed to minimize collisions, because two mobile units may both be in range of a common access point, but out of range of each other.

Bridge

A bridge can be used to connect networks, typically of different types. A wireless Ethernet bridge allows the connection of devices on a wired Ethernet network to a wireless network. The bridge acts as the connection point to the Wireless LAN.

Wireless Distribution System

A wireless distribution system (WDS) enables the wireless interconnection of access points in an IEEE 802.11 network. It allows a wireless network to be expanded using multiple access points without the need for a wired backbone to link them, as is traditionally required. The notable advantage of a WDS over other solutions is that it preserves the MAC addresses of client packets across links between access points.

An access point can be either a main, relay or remote base station. A main base station is typically connected to the wired Ethernet. A relay base station relays data between remote base stations, wireless clients or other relay stations to either a main or another relay base station. A remote base station accepts connections from wireless clients and passes them to relay or main stations. Connections between clients are made using MAC addresses rather than by specifying IP assignments.

All base stations in a WDS must be configured to use the same radio channel, and share WEP keys or WPA keys if they are used. They can be configured to different service set identifiers. WDS also requires that every base station be configured to forward to others in the system.

WDS capability may also be referred to as repeater mode because it appears to bridge and accept wireless clients at the same time (unlike traditional bridging). Throughput in this method is halved for all clients connected wirelessly. When it is difficult to connect all of the access points in a network by wires, it is also possible to put up access points as repeaters.

Roaming

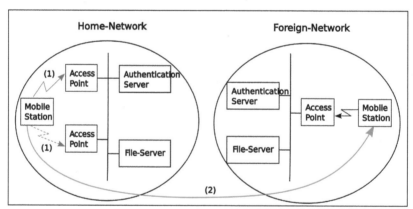

Roaming among Wireless Local Area Networks.

There are two definitions for wireless LAN roaming:

1. Internal roaming: The Mobile Station (MS) moves from one access point (AP) to another AP within a home network if the signal strength is too weak. An authentication server (RADIUS) performs the re-authentication of MS via 802.1x (e.g. with PEAP). The billing of QoS is in the home network. A Mobile Station roaming from one access point to another often interrupts the flow of data among the Mobile Station and an application connected to the network. The Mobile Station, for instance, periodically monitors the presence of alternative access points (ones that will provide a better connection). At some point, based on proprietary mechanisms, the Mobile Station decides to re-associate with an access point having a stronger wireless signal. The Mobile Station, however, may lose a connection with an access point before associating with another access point. In order to provide reliable connections with applications, the Mobile Station must generally include software that provides session persistence.

2. External roaming: The MS (client) moves into a WLAN of another Wireless Internet Service Provider (WISP) and takes their services (Hotspot). The user can use a foreign network independently from their home network, provided that the foreign network allows visiting users on their network. There must be special authentication and billing systems for mobile services in a foreign network.

Applications

Wireless LANs have a great deal of applications. Modern implementations of WLANs range from small in-home networks to large, campus-sized ones to completely mobile networks on airplanes and trains.

Users can access the Internet from WLAN hotspots in restaurants, hotels, and now with portable devices that connect to 3G or 4G networks. Oftentimes these types of public access points require no registration or password to join the network. Others can be accessed once registration has occurred and a fee is paid.

Existing Wireless LAN infrastructures can also be used to work as indoor positioning systems with no modification to the existing hardware.

WAN

The textbook definition of a WAN is a computer network spanning regions, countries, or even the world. However, in terms of the application of computer networking protocols and concepts, it may be best to view WANs as computer networking technologies used to transmit data over long distances, and between different LANs, MANs and other localised computer networking architectures. This distinction stems from the fact that common LAN technologies operating at lower layers of the OSI model (such as the forms of Ethernet or Wi-Fi) are often designed for physically proximal networks, and thus cannot transmit data over tens, hundreds, or even thousands of miles or kilometres.

WANs do not just necessarily connect physically disparate LANs. A CAN, for example, may have a localized backbone of a WAN technology, which connects different LANs within a campus. This could be to facilitate higher bandwidth applications or provide better functionality for users in the CAN.

WANs are used to connect LANs and other types of networks together so that users and computers in one location can communicate with users and computers in other locations. Many WANs are built for one particular organization and are private. Others, built by Internet service providers, provide connections from an organization's LAN to the Internet. WANs are often built using leased lines. At each end of the leased line, a router connects the LAN on one side with a second router within the LAN on the other. Leased lines can be very expensive. Instead of using leased lines, WANs can also be built using less costly circuit switching or packet switching methods. Network protocols including TCP/IP deliver transport and addressing functions. Protocols including Packet over SONET/SDH, Multiprotocol Label Switching (MPLS), Asynchronous Transfer Mode (ATM) and Frame Relay are often used by service providers to deliver the links that are used in WANs. X.25 was an important early WAN protocol, and is often considered to be the "grandfather" of Frame Relay as many of the underlying protocols and functions of X.25 are still in use today (with upgrades) by Frame Relay.

Academic research into wide area networks can be broken down into three areas: mathematical models, network emulation, and network simulation.

Performance improvements are sometimes delivered via wide area file services or WAN optimization.

Connection Technology

Many technologies are available for wide area network links. Examples include circuit-switched telephone lines, radio wave transmission, and optical fiber. New developments in technologies have successively increased transmission rates. In ca. 1960, a 110 bit/s (bits per second) line was normal on the edge of the WAN, while core links of 56 kbit/s to 64 kbit/s were considered fast. As of 2014, households are connected to the Internet with Dial-Up, ADSL, Cable, Wimax, 4G or fiber. The speeds that people can currently use range from 28.8 kbit/s through a 28K modem over a telephone connection to speeds as high as 100 Gbit/s over an Ethernet 100GBaseY connection.

The following communication and networking technologies have been used to implement WANs.

- Asynchronous Transfer Mode,
- Cable modem,
- Dial-up internet,
- Digital subscriber line,
- Fiber-optic communication,
- Frame Relay,
- ISDN,
- Leased line,
- SD-WAN,
- Synchronous optical networking,
- X.25.

400 Gigabit Ethernet

AT&T conducted trials in 2017 for business use of 400 gigabit Ethernet. Researchers Robert Maher, Alex Alvarado, Domaniç Lavery, and Polina Bayvel of University College London were able to increase networking speeds to 1.125 terabits per second. Christos Santis, graduate student Scott

Steger, Amnon Yariv, Martin and Eileen Summerfield developed a new laser that quadruples transfer speeds with fiber optics. If these two technologies were combined, then a transfer speed of up to 4.5 terabits per second could potentially be achieved.

MAN

A metropolitan area network (MAN) is a computer network that interconnects users with computer resources in a geographic region of the size of a metropolitan area. The term MAN is applied to the interconnection of local area networks (LANs) in a city into a single larger network which may then also offer efficient connection to a wide area network. The term is also used to describe the interconnection of several local area networks in a metropolitan area through the use of point-to-point connections between them.

Internet Exchanges (IXs), also known as Exchange Points (XPs), have historically been important for the connection of metropolitan area networks (MANs) to the national or global Internet. The Boston Metropolitan Exchange Point (Boston MXP) enabled metro Ethernet providers, such as the HarvardNet to exchange data with national carriers, such as the Sprint Corporation and AT&T. Exchange points also serve as low-latency link between campus area networks, thus the Massachusetts Institute of Technology and the Boston University could exchange data, voice and video using the Boston MXP. Further examples of metropolitan Internet Exchanges in the USA that were operational by 2002 include the Anchorage Metropolitan Access Point (AMAP), the Seattle Internet Exchange (SIX), the Dallas-Fort Worth Metropolitan Access Point (DFMAP) and the Denver Internet Exchange (IX-Denver). Verizon put into operation three regional metropolitan exchanges to interconnect MANs and give them access to the Internet. The MAE-West serves the MANs of San Jose, Los Angeles and California. The MAE-East interconnects the MANs of New York City, Washington, D.C., and Miami. While the MAE-Central interconnects the MANs of Dallas, Texas, and Illinois.

In larger cities several local providers may have built a dark fibre MAN backbone. In London the metro Ethernet rings of several providers make up the London MAN infrastructure. Like other MANs, the London MAN primarily serves the needs of its urban customers, who typically need a high number of connections with low bandwidth, a fast transit to other MAN providers, as well as high bandwidth access to national and international long-haul providers. Within the MAN of larger cities, metropolitan exchange points now play a vital role. The London Internet Exchange (LINX) had by 2005 built up several exchange points across the Greater London region.

Cities that host one of the international Internet Exchanges have become a preferred location for companies and data centres. The Amsterdam Internet Exchange (AMS-IX) is the world second largest Internet Exchange and has attracted companies to Amsterdam that are dependent on high speed internet access. The Amsterdam metropolitan area network has benefited too from high speed Internet access. Similarly Frankfurt has become a magnet for data centres of international companies because it hosts the non-profit DE-CIX, the largest Internet Exchange in the world. DE-CIX has gone on to establish carrier neutral metropolitan Internet Exchanges in New

York, Madrid, Dubai, Marseille, Dallas, Hamburg, Munich, Duesseldorf, Berlin, Istanbul, Palermo, Lisbon, Mumbai, Delhi, Kolkata, Chennai, and Moscow. The business model of the metro DE-CIX is to reduce the transit cost for local carriers by keeping data in the metropolitan area or region, while at the same time allowing long-haul low-latency peering globally with other major MANs.

PAN

A personal area network (PAN) is a computer network for interconnecting devices centered on an individual person's workspace. A PAN provides data transmission among devices such as computers, smartphones, tablets and personal digital assistants. PANs can be used for communication among the personal devices themselves, or for connecting to a higher level network and the Internet where one master device takes up the role as gateway. A PAN may be wireless or carried over wired interfaces such as USB.

A wireless personal area network (WPAN) is a PAN carried over a low-powered, short-distance wireless network technology such as IrDA, Wireless USB, Bluetooth or ZigBee. The reach of a WPAN varies from a few centimeters to a few meters.

Wireless Personal Area Network

A wireless personal area network (WPAN) is a personal area network in which the connections are wireless. IEEE 802.15 has produced standards for several types of PANs operating in the ISM band including Bluetooth. The Infrared Data Association has produced standards for WPANs which operate using infrared communications.

Bluetooth

Bluetooth uses short-range radio waves. Uses in a WPAN include, for example, Bluetooth devices such as keyboards, pointing devices, audio head sets, printers may connect to personal digital assistants (PDAs), cell phones, or computers. A Bluetooth WPAN is also called a *piconet*, and is composed of up to 8 active devices in a master-slave relationship (a very large number of additional devices can be connected in "parked" mode). The first Bluetooth device in the piconet is the master, and all other devices are slaves that communicate with the master. A piconet typically has a range of 10 metres (33 ft), although ranges of up to 100 metres (330 ft) can be reached under ideal circumstances. Long-range Bluetooth routers with augmented antenna arrays connect Bluetooth devices up to 1,000 feet.

With Bluetooth mesh networking the range and number of devices is extended by using mesh networking techniques to relay information from one to another. Such a network doesn't have a master device and may or may not be treated as a WPAN.

IrDA

Infrared Data Association (IrDA) uses infrared light, which has a frequency below the human eye's sensitivity. Infrared is used in other wireless communications applications, for instance, in remote controls. Typical WPAN devices that use IrDA include printers, keyboards, and other serial communication interfaces.

VPN

VPN stands for Virtual Private Network (VPN), that allows a user to connect to a private network over the Internet securely and privately. VPN creates an encrypted connection that is called VPN tunnel, and all Internet traffic and communication is passed through this secure tunnel.

Virtual Private Network (VPN) is basically of 2 types:

- Remote Access VPN: Remote Access VPN permits a user to connect to a private network and access all its services and resources remotely. The connection between the user and the private network occurs through the Internet and the connection is secure and private. Remote Access VPN is useful for home users and business users both.

  An employee of a company, while he/she is out of station, uses a VPN to connect to his/her company's private network and remotely access files and resources on the private network. Private users or home users of VPN, primarily use VPN services to bypass regional restrictions on the Internet and access blocked websites. Users aware of Internet security also use VPN services to enhance their Internet security and privacy.

- Site to Site VPN: A Site-to-Site VPN is also called as Router-to-Router VPN and is commonly used in the large companies. Companies or organizations, with branch offices in different locations, use Site-to-site VPN to connect the network of one office location to the network at another office location.

  - Intranet based VPN: When several offices of the same company are connected using Site-to-Site VPN type, it is called as Intranet based VPN.

  - Extranet based VPN: When companies use Site-to-site VPN type to connect to the office of another company, it is called as Extranet based VPN.

Basically, Site-to-site VPN create a imaginary bridge between the networks at geographically distant offices and connect them through the Internet and sustain a secure and private communication between the networks. In Site-to-site VPN one router acts as a VPN Client and another router as a VPN Server as it is based on Router-to-Router communication. When the authentication is validated between the two routers only then the communication starts.

Types of Virtual Private Network Protocols

- Internet Protocol Security (IPSec): Internet Protocol Security, known as IPSec, is used to secure Internet communication across an IP network. IPSec secures Internet Protocol communication by verifying the session and encrypts each data packet during the connection.

IPSec runs in 2 modes:

- Transport mode,
- Tunneling mode.

The work of transport mode is to encrypt the message in the data packet and the tunneling mode encrypts the whole data packet. IPSec can also be used with other security protocols to improve the security system.

- Layer 2 Tunneling Protocol (L2TP): L2TP or Layer 2 Tunneling Protocol is a tunneling protocol that is often combined with another VPN security protocol like IPSec to establish a highly secure VPN connection. L2TP generates a tunnel between two L2TP connection points and IPSec protocol encrypts the data and maintains secure communication between the tunnel.

- Point–to–Point Tunneling Protocol (PPTP): PPTP or Point-to-Point Tunneling Protocol generates a tunnel and confines the data packet. Point-to-Point Protocol (PPP) is used to encrypt the data between the connection. PPTP is one of the most widely used VPN protocol and has been in use since the early release of Windows. PPTP is also used on Mac and Linux apart from Windows.

- SSL and TLS: SSL (Secure Sockets Layer) and TLS (Transport Layer Security) generate a VPN connection where the web browser acts as the client and user access is prohibited to specific applications instead of entire network. Online shopping websites commonly uses SSL and TLS protocol. It is easy to switch to SSL by web browsers and with almost no action required from the user as web browsers come integrated with SSL and TLS. SSL connections have "https" in the initial of the URL instead of "http".

- OpenVPN: OpenVPN is an open source VPN that is commonly used for creating Point-to-Point and Site-to-Site connections. It uses a traditional security protocol based on SSL and TLS protocol.

- Secure Shell (SSH): Secure Shell or SSH generates the VPN tunnel through which the data transfer occurs and also ensures that the tunnel is encrypted. SSH connections are generated by a SSH client and data is transferred from a local port on to the remote server through the encrypted tunnel.

CAN

A campus network, campus area network, corporate area network or CAN is a computer network made up of an interconnection of local area networks (LANs) within a limited geographical area. The networking equipments (switches, routers) and transmission media (optical fiber, copper plant, Cat5 cabling etc.) are almost entirely owned by the campus tenant/owner: an enterprise, university, government etc. A campus area network is larger than a local area network but smaller than a metropolitan area network (MAN) or wide area network (WAN).

University Campuses

College or university campus area networks often interconnect a variety of buildings, including administrative buildings, academic buildings, university libraries, campus or student centers, residence halls, gymnasiums, and other outlying structures, like conference centers, technology centers, and training institutes.

Early examples include the Stanford University Network at Stanford University, Project Athena at MIT, and the Andrew Project at Carnegie Mellon University.

Corporate Campuses

Much like a university campus network, a corporate campus network serves to connect buildings. Examples of such are the networks at Googleplex and Microsoft's campus. Campus networks are normally interconnected with high speed Ethernet links operating over optical fiber such as gigabit Ethernet and 10 Gigabit Ethernet.

Area Range

The range of CAN is 1 km to 5 km. If two buildings have the same domain and they are connected with a network, then it will be considered as CAN only. Though the CAN is mainly used for corporate campuses so the data link will be high speed.

BAN

A body area network (BAN), also referred to as a *wireless body area network* (WBAN) or a *body sensor network* (BSN) or a *medical body area network* (MBAN), is a wireless network of wearable computing devices. BAN devices may be embedded inside the body, implants, may be surface-mounted on the body in a fixed position wearable technology or may be accompanied devices which humans can carry in different positions, in clothes pockets, by hand or in various bags. Whilst there is a trend towards the miniaturization of devices, in particular, networks consisting of several miniaturized body sensor units (BSUs) together with a single body central unit (BCU). Larger decimeter (tab and pad) sized smart devices, accompanied devices, still play an important role in terms of acting as a data hub, data gateway and providing a user interface to view and manage BAN applications, in-situ. The development of WBAN technology started around 1995 around the idea of using wireless personal area network (WPAN) technologies to implement communications on, near, and around the human body. About six years later, the term "BAN" came to refer to systems where communication is entirely within, on, and in the immediate proximity of a human body. A WBAN system can use WPAN wireless technologies as gateways to reach longer ranges. Through gateway devices, it is possible to connect the wearable devices on the human body to the internet. This way, medical professionals can access patient data online using the internet independent of the patient location.

The rapid growth in physiological sensors, low-power integrated circuits, and wireless communication has enabled a new generation of wireless sensor networks, now used for purposes such as: monitoring traffic, crops, infrastructure, and health. The body area network field is an interdisciplinary area which could allow inexpensive and continuous health monitoring with real-time updates of medical records through the Internet. A number of intelligent physiological sensors can be integrated into a wearable wireless body area network, which can be used for computer-assisted rehabilitation or early detection of medical conditions. This area relies on the feasibility of implanting very small biosensors inside the human body that are comfortable and that don't impair normal activities. The implanted sensors in the human body will collect various physiological changes in order to monitor the patient's health status no matter their location. The information will be transmitted wirelessly to an external processing unit. This device will instantly transmit all information in real time to the doctors throughout the world. If an emergency is detected, the physicians will immediately inform the patient through the computer system by sending appropriate messages or alarms. Currently the level of information provided and energy resources capable of powering the sensors are limiting. While the technology is still in its primitive stage it is being widely researched and once adopted, is expected to be a breakthrough invention in healthcare, leading to concepts like telemedicine and mHealth becoming real.

Applications

Initial applications of BANs are expected to appear primarily in the healthcare domain, especially for continuous monitoring and logging vital parameters of patients suffering from chronic diseases such as diabetes, asthma and heart attacks.

- A BAN network in place on a patient can alert the hospital, even before they have a heart attack, through measuring changes in their vital signs.

- A BAN network on a diabetic patient could auto inject insulin through a pump, as soon as their insulin level declines.

Other applications of this technology include sports, military, or security. Extending the technology to new areas could also assist communication by seamless exchanges of information between individuals, or between individual and machines.

Standards

The latest international standard for BANs is the IEEE 802.15.6 standard.

Components

A typical BAN or BSN requires vital sign monitoring sensors, motion detectors (through accelerometers) to help identify the location of the monitored individual and some form of communication, to transmit vital sign and motion readings to medical practitioners or care givers. A typical body area network kit will consist of sensors, a processor, a transceiver and a battery. Physiological sensors, such as ECG and SpO2 sensors, have been developed. Other sensors such as a blood pressure sensor, EEG sensor and a PDA for BSN interface are under development.

Wireless Communication

The FCC has approved the allocation of 40 MHz of spectrum bandwidth for medical BAN low-power, wide-area radio links at the 2360–2400 MHz band. This will allow off-loading MBAN communication from the already saturated standard Wi-Fi spectrum to a standard band.

The 2360–2390 MHz frequency range is available on a secondary basis. The FCC will expand the existing Medical Device Radiocommunication (MedRadio) Service in Part 95 of its rules. MBAN devices using the band will operate under a 'license-by-rule' basis which eliminates the need to apply for individual transmitter licenses. Usage of the 2360–2390 MHz frequencies are restricted to indoor operation at health-care facilities and are subject to registration and site approval by coordinators to protect aeronautical telemetry primary usage. Operation in the 2390–2400 MHz band is not subject to registration or coordination and may be used in all areas including residential.

Challenges

Problems with the use of this technology could include:

- Data Quality: Data generated and collected through BANs can play a key role in the patient care process. It is essential that the quality of this data is of a high standard to ensure that the decisions made are based on the best information possible.

- Data Management: As BANs generate large volumes of data, the need to manage and maintain these datasets is of utmost importance.

- Sensor Validation: Pervasive sensing devices are subject to inherent communication and hardware constraints including unreliable wired/wireless network links, interference and limited power reserves. This may result in erroneous datasets being transmitted back to the end user. It is of the utmost importance especially within a healthcare domain that all sensor readings are validated. This helps to reduce false alarm generation and to identify possible weaknesses within the hardware and software design.

- Data Consistency: Data residing on multiple mobile devices and wireless patient notes need to be collected and analysed in a seamless fashion. Within body area networks, vital patient datasets may be fragmented over a number of nodes and across a number of networked PCs or Laptops. If a medical practitioner's mobile device does not contain all known information then the quality of patient care may degrade.

- Security: Considerable effort would be required to make WBAN transmission secure and accurate. It would have to be made sure that the patient "secure" data is only derived from each patient's dedicated WBAN system and is not mixed up with other patient's data. Further, the data generated from WBAN should have secure and limited access. Although security is a high priority in most networks, little study has been done in this area for WBANs. As WBANs are resource-constrained in terms of power, memory, communication rate and computational capability, security solutions proposed for other networks may not be applicable to WBANs. Confidentiality, authentication, integrity, and freshness of data together with availability and secure management are the security requirements in WBAN. The IEEE 802.15.6 standard, which is latest standard for WBAN, tried to provide security in WBAN. However, it has several security problems.

- Interoperability: WBAN systems would have to ensure seamless data transfer across standards such as Bluetooth, ZigBee etc. to promote information exchange, plug and play device interaction. Further, the systems would have to be scalable, ensure efficient migration across networks and offer uninterrupted connectivity.

- System devices: The sensors used in WBAN would have to be low on complexity, small in form factor, light in weight, power efficient, easy to use and reconfigurable. Further, the storage devices need to facilitate remote storage and viewing of patient data as well as access to external processing and analysis tools via the Internet.

- Invasion of privacy: People might consider the WBAN technology as a potential threat to freedom, if the applications go beyond "secure" medical usage. Social acceptance would be key to this technology finding a wider application.

- Interference: The wireless link used for body sensors should reduce the interference and increase the coexistence of sensor node devices with other network devices available in the environment. This is especially important for large scale implementation of WBAN systems.

- Cost: Today's consumers expect low cost health monitoring solutions which provide high functionality. WBAN implementations will need to be cost optimized to be appealing alternatives to health conscious consumers.

- Constant Monitoring: Users may require different levels of monitoring, for example those at risk of cardiac ischemia may want their WBANs to function constantly, while others at risk of falls may only need WBANs to monitor them while they are walking or moving. The level of monitoring influences the amount of energy required and the life cycle of the BAN before the energy source is depleted.

- Constrained deployment: The WBAN needs to be wearable, lightweight and non intrusive. It should not alter or encumber the user's daily activities. The technology should ultimately be transparent to the user i.e., it should perform its monitoring tasks without the user realising it.

- Consistent performance: The performance of the WBAN should be consistent. Sensor measurements should be accurate and calibrated, even when the WBAN is switched off and switched on again. The wireless links should be robust and work under various user environments.

NAN

A near-me area network (NAN) is a communication network that focuses on wireless communication among devices in close proximity.

Unlike local area networks (LANs), where the devices are in the same network segment and share the same broadcast domain, the devices in a NAN can belong to different proprietary network infrastructures (for example, different mobile carriers). If two devices are geographically close, the communication path between them might, in fact, traverse a long distance, going from a LAN, through the Internet, and to another LAN.

NAN applications focus on two-way communications among devices within a certain proximity to each other, but don't generally concern themselves with the devices' exact locations.

Examples of Applications

Some services are meaningful only to a group of people in close proximity, which has generated the need for NANs. The following scenarios show some example NAN applications:

- Ben is going to the ABC supermarket to buy three bottles of red wine. The supermarket offers a 30 percent discount on the purchase of six bottles, so he sends a message to other customers to see if they would like to buy the other three bottles of wine.

- Susan bought a movie ticket 15 minutes ago, but she now feels dizzy and can't watch the film. She sends out messages to people around the cinema to see if anyone will purchase her ticket at 50 percent off.

- In a theme park, guests would like to know each ride's queue status to reduce their waiting time. So, they take a photo of the queue they're in and share it with other guests through a NAN application.

- Ann works at Causeway Bay and would like to find someone to have lunch with. She checks her friend list to see who is closest to her at this moment and invites that friend to join her.

- Carol just lost her son in the street, so she sends out his picture, which is stored in her mobile device, to passers-by to see if they can find him.

Types of Wireless Networks

Wireless Links

- Terrestrial microwave – Terrestrial microwave communication uses Earth-based transmitters and receivers resembling satellite dishes. Terrestrial microwaves are in the low gigahertz range, which limits all communications to line-of-sight. Relay stations are spaced approximately 48 km (30 mi) apart.

- Communications satellites – Satellites communicate via microwave radio waves, which are not deflected by the Earth's atmosphere. The satellites are stationed in space, typically in geosynchronous orbit 35,400 km (22,000 mi) above the equator. These Earth-orbiting systems are capable of receiving and relaying voice, data, and TV signals.

- Cellular and PCS systems use several radio communications technologies. The systems divide the region covered into multiple geographic areas. Each area has a low-power transmitter or radio relay antenna device to relay calls from one area to the next area.

- Radio and spread spectrum technologies – Wireless local area networks use a high-frequency radio technology similar to digital cellular and a low-frequency radio technology. Wireless LANs use spread spectrum technology to enable communication between multiple devices in a limited area. IEEE 802.11 defines a common flavor of open-standards wireless radio-wave technology known as.

- Free-space optical communication uses visible or invisible light for communications. In most cases, line-of-sight propagation is used, which limits the physical positioning of communicating devices.

Types of Wireless Networks

Wireless PAN

Wireless personal area networks (WPANs) connect devices within a relatively small area, that is generally within a person's reach. For example, both Bluetooth radio and invisible infrared light provides a WPAN for interconnecting a headset to a laptop. ZigBee also supports WPAN applications. Wi-Fi PANs are becoming commonplace (2010) as equipment designers start to integrate Wi-Fi into a variety of consumer electronic devices. Intel "My WiFi" and Windows 7 "virtual Wi-Fi" capabilities have made Wi-Fi PANs simpler and easier to set up and configure.

Wireless LAN

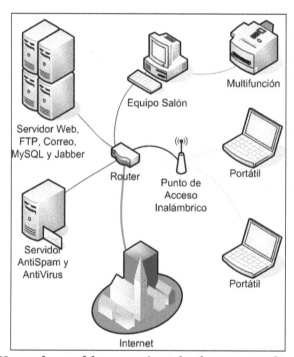

Wireless LANs are often used for connecting to local resources and to the Internet.

A wireless local area network (WLAN) links two or more devices over a short distance using a wireless distribution method, usually providing a connection through an access point for internet access. The use of spread-spectrum or OFDM technologies may allow users to move around within a local coverage area, and still remain connected to the network.

Products using the IEEE 802.11 WLAN standards are marketed under the Wi-Fi brand name. Fixed wireless technology implements point-to-point links between computers or networks at two distant locations, often using dedicated microwave or modulated laser light beams over line of sight paths. It is often used in cities to connect networks in two or more buildings without installing a wired link. To connect to Wi-Fi, sometimes are used devices like a router or connecting HotSpot using mobile smartphones.

Wireless Ad Hoc Network

A wireless ad hoc network, also known as a wireless mesh network or mobile ad hoc network (MANET), is a wireless network made up of radio nodes organized in a mesh topology. Each node forwards messages on behalf of the other nodes and each node performs routing. Ad hoc networks can "self-heal", automatically re-routing around a node that has lost power. Various network layer protocols are needed to realize ad hoc mobile networks, such as Distance Sequenced Distance Vector routing, Associativity-Based Routing, Ad hoc on-demand Distance Vector routing, and Dynamic source routing.

Wireless MAN

Wireless metropolitan area networks are a type of wireless network that connects several wireless LANs. WiMAX is a type of Wireless MAN and is described by the IEEE 802.16 standard.

Wireless WAN

Wireless wide area networks are wireless networks that typically cover large areas, such as between neighbouring towns and cities, or city and suburb. These networks can be used to connect branch offices of business or as a public Internet access system. The wireless connections between access points are usually point to point microwave links using parabolic dishes on the 2.4 GHz and 5.8 Ghz band, rather than omnidirectional antennas used with smaller networks. A typical system contains base station gateways, access points and wireless bridging relays. Other configurations are mesh systems where each access point acts as a relay also. When combined with renewable energy systems such as photovoltaic solar panels or wind systems they can be stand alone systems.

Cellular Network

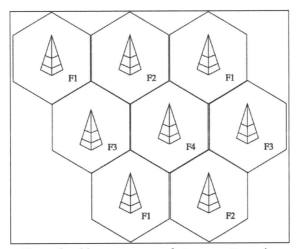

Example of frequency reuse factor or pattern 1/4.

A cellular network or mobile network is a radio network distributed over land areas called cells, each served by at least one fixed-location transceiver, known as a cell site or base station. In a cellular network, each cell characteristically uses a different set of radio frequencies from all their immediate neighbouring cells to avoid any interference.

When joined together these cells provide radio coverage over a wide geographic area. This enables a large number of portable transceivers (e.g., mobile phones, pagers, etc.) to communicate with each other and with fixed transceivers and telephones anywhere in the network, via base stations, even if some of the transceivers are moving through more than one cell during transmission.

Although originally intended for cell phones, with the development of smartphones, cellular telephone networks routinely carry data in addition to telephone conversations:

- Global System for Mobile Communications (GSM): The GSM network is divided into three major systems: the switching system, the base station system, and the operation and support system. The cell phone connects to the base system station which then connects to the operation and support station; it then connects to the switching station where the call is transferred to where it needs to go. GSM is the most common standard and is used for a majority of cell phones.

- Personal Communications Service (PCS): PCS is a radio band that can be used by mobile phones in North America and South Asia. Sprint happened to be the first service to set up a PCS.

- D-AMPS: Digital Advanced Mobile Phone Service, an upgraded version of AMPS, is being phased out due to advancement in technology. The newer GSM networks are replacing the older system.

Global Area Network

A global area network (GAN) is a network used for supporting mobile across an arbitrary number of wireless LANs, satellite coverage areas, etc. The key challenge in mobile communications is handing off user communications from one local coverage area to the next. In IEEE Project 802, this involves a succession of terrestrial wireless LANs.

Space Network

Space networks are networks used for communication between spacecraft, usually in the vicinity of the Earth. The example of this is NASA's Space Network.

Uses

Some examples of usage include cellular phones which are part of everyday wireless networks, allowing easy personal communications. Another example, Intercontinental network systems, use radio satellites to communicate across the world. Emergency services such as the police utilize wireless networks to communicate effectively as well. Individuals and businesses use wireless networks to send and share data rapidly, whether it be in a small office building or across the world.

Properties

In a general sense, wireless networks offer a vast variety of uses by both business and home users.

"Now, the industry accepts a handful of different wireless technologies. Each wireless technology is defined by a standard that describes unique functions at both the Physical and the Data Link layers of the OSI model. These standards differ in their specified signaling methods, geographic ranges, and frequency usages, among other things. Such differences can make certain technologies better suited to home networks and others better suited to network larger organizations."

Performance

Each standard varies in geographical range, thus making one standard more ideal than the next depending on what it is one is trying to accomplish with a wireless network. The performance of wireless networks satisfies a variety of applications such as voice and video. The use of this technology also gives room for expansions, such as from 2G to 3G and, 4G and 5G technologies, which stand for the fourth and fifth generation of cell phone mobile communications standards. As wireless networking has become commonplace, sophistication increases through configuration of network hardware and software, and greater capacity to send and receive larger amounts of data, faster, is achieved. Now the wireless network has been running on LTE, which is a 4G mobile communication standard. Users of an LTE network should have data speeds that are 10x faster than a 3G network.

Space

Space is another characteristic of wireless networking. Wireless networks offer many advantages when it comes to difficult-to-wire areas trying to communicate such as across a street or river, a warehouse on the other side of the premises or buildings that are physically separated but operate as one. Wireless networks allow for users to designate a certain space which the network will be able to communicate with other devices through that network.

Space is also created in homes as a result of eliminating clutters of wiring. This technology allows for an alternative to installing physical network mediums such as TPs, coaxes, or fiber-optics, which can also be expensive.

Home

For homeowners, wireless technology is an effective option compared to Ethernet for sharing printers, scanners, and high-speed Internet connections. WLANs help save the cost of installation of cable mediums, save time from physical installation, and also creates mobility for devices connected to the network. Wireless networks are simple and require as few as one single wireless access point connected directly to the Internet via a router.

Wireless Network Elements

The telecommunications network at the physical layer also consists of many interconnected wireline network elements (NEs). These NEs can be stand-alone systems or products that are either supplied by a single manufacturer or are assembled by the service provider (user) or system integrator with parts from several different manufacturers.

Wireless NEs are the products and devices used by a wireless carrier to provide support for the backhaul network as well as a mobile switching center (MSC).

Reliable wireless service depends on the network elements at the physical layer to be protected against all operational environments and applications.

What are especially important are the NEs that are located on the cell tower to the base station (BS) cabinet. The attachment hardware and the positioning of the antenna and associated closures and cables are required to have adequate strength, robustness, corrosion resistance, and resistance against wind, storms, icing, and other weather conditions. Requirements for individual components, such as hardware, cables, connectors, and closures, shall take into consideration the structure to which they are attached.

Difficulties

Interference

Compared to wired systems, wireless networks are frequently subject to electromagnetic interference. This can be caused by other networks or other types of equipment that generate radio waves that are within, or close, to the radio bands used for communication. Interference can degrade the signal or cause the system to fail.

Absorption and Reflection

Some materials cause absorption of electromagnetic waves, preventing it from reaching the receiver, in other cases, particularly with metallic or conductive materials reflection occurs. This can cause dead zones where no reception is available. Aluminium foiled thermal isolation in modern homes can easily reduce indoor mobile signals by 10 dB frequently leading to complaints about the bad reception of long-distance rural cell signals.

Multipath Fading

In multipath fading two or more different routes taken by the signal, due to reflections, can cause the signal to cancel out at certain locations, and to be stronger in other places (upfade).

Hidden Node Problem

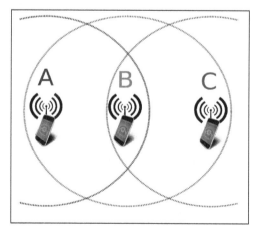

In a hidden node problem Station A can communicate with Station B. Station C can also communicate with Station B. However, Stations A and C cannot communicate with each other, but their signals can interfere at B.

The hidden node problem occurs in some types of network when a node is visible from a wireless access point (AP), but not from other nodes communicating with that AP. This leads to difficulties in media access control (collisions).

Exposed Terminal Node Problem

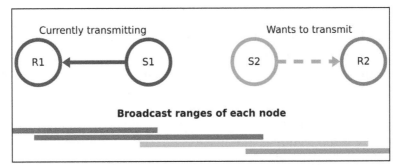

The exposed terminal problem is when a node on one network is unable to send because of co-channel interference from a node that is on a different network.

Shared Resource Problem

The wireless spectrum is a limited resource and shared by all nodes in the range of its transmitters. Bandwidth allocation becomes complex with multiple participating users. Often users are not aware that advertised numbers (e.g., for IEEE 802.11 equipment or LTE networks) are not their capacity, but shared with all other users and thus the individual user rate is far lower. With increasing demand, the capacity crunch is more and more likely to happen. User-in-the-loop (UIL) may be an alternative solution to ever upgrading to newer technologies for over-provisioning.

Capacity

Channel

Understanding of SISO, SIMO, MISO and MIMO. Using multiple antennas and transmitting in different frequency channels can reduce fading, and can greatly increase the system capacity.

Shannon's theorem can describe the maximum data rate of any single wireless link, which relates to the bandwidth in hertz and to the noise on the channel.

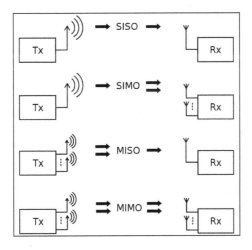

One can greatly increase channel capacity by using MIMO techniques, where multiple aerials or multiple frequencies can exploit multiple paths to the receiver to achieve much higher throughput – by a factor of the product of the frequency and aerial diversity at each end. Under Linux, the Central Regulatory Domain Agent (CRDA) controls the setting of channels.

Network

The total network bandwidth depends on how dispersive the medium is (more dispersive medium generally has better total bandwidth because it minimises interference), how many frequencies are available, how noisy those frequencies are, how many aerials are used and whether a directional antenna is in use, whether nodes employ power control and so on.

Cellular wireless networks generally have good capacity, due to their use of directional aerials, and their ability to reuse radio channels in non-adjacent cells. Additionally, cells can be made very small using low power transmitters this is used in cities to give network capacity that scales linearly with population density.

Safety

Wireless access points are also often close to humans, but the drop off in power over distance is fast, following the inverse-square law. The position of the United Kingdom's Health Protection Agency (HPA) is that "radio frequency (RF) exposures from WiFi are likely to be lower than those from mobile phones." It also saw "no reason why schools and others should not use WiFi equipment." In October 2007, the HPA launched a new "systematic" study into the effects of WiFi networks on behalf of the UK government, in order to calm fears that had appeared in the media in a recent period up to that time". Dr Michael Clark, of the HPA, says published research on mobile phones and masts does not add up to an indictment of WiFi.

References

- Barkai, David (2001). Peer-to-peer computing: technologies for sharing and collaborating on the net. Hillsboro, OR: Intel Press. ISBN 978-0970284679. OCLC 49354877

- "History of Wireless". Johns Hopkins Bloomberg School of Public Health. Archived from the original on 2007-02-10. Retrieved 2007-02-1

- Ahson, Syed A.; Ilyas, Mohammad, eds. (2008). SIP Handbook: Services, Technologies, and Security of Session Initiation Protocol. Taylor & Francis. P. 204. ISBN 9781420066043

- "Network (sunet — The Stanford University Network)". Stanford University Information Technology Services. July 16, 2010. Retrieved May 4, 2011

- Richard Barker & Paul Massiglia (2002). Storage Area Network Essentials: A Complete Guide to Understanding and Implementing sans. John Wiley & Sons. P. 198. ISBN 9780471267119

- "History of Wireless". Johns Hopkins Bloomberg School of Public Health. Archived from the original on 2007-02-10. Retrieved 2007-02-17

- Groth, David and Skandler, Toby (2005). Network+ Study Guide, Fourth Edition. Sybex, Inc. ISBN 0-7821-4406-3

- "GPS Mobile Phones: the Privacy and Regulatory Issues". Research and Markets. February 2008. Retrieved 27 June 2017

- Jeffrey S. Beasley & Piyasat Nilkaew (2012). Networking Essentials: Networking Essentials. Pearson Education. P. 10-4. ISBN 9780133381702

- Types-of-virtual-private-network-vpn-and-its-protocols: geeksforgeeks.org, Retrieved 23 February, 2019

- Gary B. Shelly & Jennifer Campbell (2011). Discovering the Internet: Complete. Cengage Learning. P. 345. ISBN 978-1-111-82072-5

3

Topology of Computer Networks

The arrangement of the elements of a communication network is known as network topology. It can be classified as either physical topology or logical topology. The topics elaborated in this chapter will help in gaining a better perspective about network topology, its various types and the transmission modes in computer networks.

Network Topology

A network topology describes the configuration of a communication network and the physical and logical arrangement of the nodes that form it.

The way in which the elements of a network are mapped or arranged is known as a network topology. It describes the physical and logical interconnection between the different nodes of a network and defines the way in which they communicate with each other. Network topologies are classified as physical, logical, and signal.

Centralization

The star topology reduces the probability of a network failure by connecting all of the peripheral nodes (computers, etc.) to a central node. When the physical star topology is applied to a logical bus network such as Ethernet, this central node (traditionally a hub) rebroadcasts all transmissions received from any peripheral node to all peripheral nodes on the network, sometimes including the originating node. All peripheral nodes may thus communicate with all others by transmitting to, and receiving from, the central node only. The failure of a transmission line linking any peripheral node to the central node will result in the isolation of that peripheral node from all others, but the remaining peripheral nodes will be unaffected. However, the disadvantage is that the failure of the central node will cause the failure of all of the peripheral nodes.

A tree topology (hierarchical topology) can be viewed as a collection of star networks arranged in a hierarchy. This tree has individual peripheral nodes (e.g. leaves) which are required to transmit to and receive from one other node only and are not required to act as repeaters or regenerators. Unlike the star network, the functionality of the central node may be distributed.

As in the conventional star network, individual nodes may thus still be isolated from the network by a single-point failure of a transmission path to the node. If a link connecting a leaf fails, that leaf is isolated; if a connection to a non-leaf node fails, an entire section of the network becomes isolated from the rest.

To alleviate the amount of network traffic that comes from broadcasting all signals to all nodes, more advanced central nodes were developed that are able to keep track of the identities of the nodes that are connected to the network. These network switches will "learn" the layout of the network by "listening" on each port during normal data transmission, examining the data packets and recording the address/identifier of each connected node and which port it is connected to in a lookup table held in memory. This lookup table then allows future transmissions to be forwarded to the intended destination only.

Decentralization

In a partially connected mesh topology, there are at least two nodes with two or more paths between them to provide redundant paths in case the link providing one of the paths fails. Decentralization is often used to compensate for the single-point-failure disadvantage that is present when using a single device as a central node (e.g., in star and tree networks). A special kind of mesh, limiting the number of hops between two nodes, is a hypercube. The number of arbitrary forks in mesh networks makes them more difficult to design and implement, but their decentralized nature makes them very useful. In 2012, the Institute of Electrical and Electronics Engineers (IEEE) published the Shortest Path Bridging protocol to ease configuration tasks and allows all paths to be active which increases bandwidth and redundancy between all devices.

This is similar in some ways to a grid network, where a linear or ring topology is used to connect systems in multiple directions. A multidimensional ring has a toroidal topology, for instance.

A fully connected network, complete topology, or full mesh topology is a network topology in which there is a direct link between all pairs of nodes. In a fully connected network with n nodes, there are n(n-1)/2 direct links. Networks designed with this topology are usually very expensive to set up, but provide a high degree of reliability due to the multiple paths for data that are provided by the large number of redundant links between nodes. This topology is mostly seen in military applications.

Physical Topology

A physical topology describes the placement of network nodes and the physical connections between them. This includes the arrangement and location of network nodes and the way in which they are connected.

Types

Bus Topology

Bus topology is a network type in which every computer and network device is connected to single cable. When it has exactly two endpoints, then it is called Linear Bus topology.

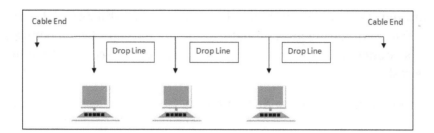

Features of Bus Topology

1. It transmits data only in one direction.

2. Every device is connected to a single cable.

Advantages of Bus Topology

1. It is cost effective.

2. Cable required is least compared to other network topology.

3. Used in small networks.

4. It is easy to understand.

5. Easy to expand joining two cables together.

Disadvantages of Bus Topology

1. Cables fails then whole network fails.

2. If network traffic is heavy or nodes are more the performance of the network decreases.

3. Cable has a limited length.

4. It is slower than the ring topology.

Ring Topology

It is called ring topology because it forms a ring as each computer is connected to another computer, with the last one connected to the first. Exactly two neighbours for each device.

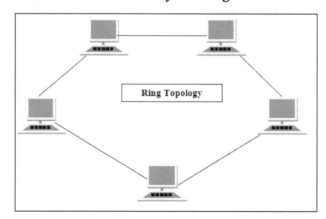

Features of Ring Topology

1. A number of repeaters are used for Ring topology with large number of nodes, because if someone wants to send some data to the last node in the ring topology with 100 nodes, then the data will have to pass through 99 nodes to reach the 100th node. Hence to prevent data loss repeaters are used in the network.

2. The transmission is unidirectional, but it can be made bidirectional by having 2 connections between each Network Node, it is called Dual Ring Topology.

3. In Dual Ring Topology, two ring networks are formed, and data flow is in opposite direction in them. Also, if one ring fails, the second ring can act as a backup, to keep the network up.

4. Data is transferred in a sequential manner that is bit by bit. Data transmitted, has to pass through each node of the network, till the destination node.

Advantages of Ring Topology

1. Transmitting network is not affected by high traffic or by adding more nodes, as only the nodes having tokens can transmit data.

2. Cheap to install and expand.

Disadvantages of Ring Topology

1. Troubleshooting is difficult in ring topology.

2. Adding or deleting the computers disturbs the network activity.

3. Failure of one computer disturbs the whole network.

Star Topology

In this type of topology all the computers are connected to a single hub through a cable. This hub is the central node and all others nodes are connected to the central node.

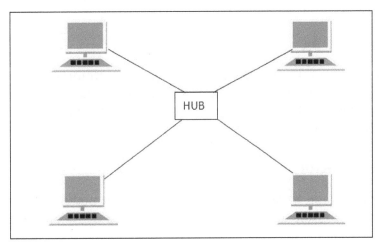

Features of Star Topology

1. Every node has its own dedicated connection to the hub.

2. Hub acts as a repeater for data flow.

3. Can be used with twisted pair, Optical Fibre or coaxial cable.

Advantages of Star Topology

1. Fast performance with few nodes and low network traffic.

2. Hub can be upgraded easily.

3. Easy to troubleshoot.

4. Easy to setup and modify.

5. Only that node is affected which has failed, rest of the nodes can work smoothly.

Disadvantages of Star Topology

1. Cost of installation is high.

2. Expensive to use.

3. If the hub fails then the whole network is stopped because all the nodes depend on the hub.

4. Performance is based on the hub that is it depends on its capacity

Mesh Topology

It is a point-to-point connection to other nodes or devices. All the network nodes are connected to each other. Mesh has n(n-1)/2 physical channels to link n devices.

There are two techniques to transmit data over the Mesh topology, they are:

1. Routing.

2. Flooding.

Mesh Topology: Routing

In routing, the nodes have a routing logic, as per the network requirements. Like routing logic to direct the data to reach the destination using the shortest distance. Or, routing logic which has information about the broken links, and it avoids those node etc. We can even have routing logic, to re-configure the failed nodes.

Mesh Topology: Flooding

In flooding, the same data is transmitted to all the network nodes, hence no routing logic is required. The network is robust, and the its very unlikely to lose the data. But it leads to unwanted load over the network.

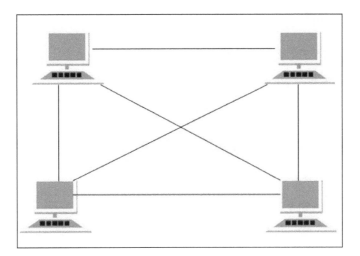

Types of Mesh Topology

1. Partial Mesh Topology: In this topology some of the systems are connected in the same fashion as mesh topology but some devices are only connected to two or three devices.

2. Full Mesh Topology: Each and every nodes or devices are connected to each other.

Features of Mesh Topology

1. Fully connected.

2. Robust.

3. Not flexible.

Advantages of Mesh Topology

1. Each connection can carry its own data load.

2. It is robust.

3. Fault is diagnosed easily.

4. Provides security and privacy.

Disadvantages of Mesh Topology

1. Installation and configuration is difficult.

2. Cabling cost is more.

3. Bulk wiring is required.

Tree Topology

It has a root node and all other nodes are connected to it forming a hierarchy. It is also called hierarchical topology. It should at least have three levels to the hierarchy.

Features of Tree Topology

1. Ideal if workstations are located in groups.

2. Used in Wide Area Network.

Advantages of Tree Topology

1. Extension of bus and star topologies.

2. Expansion of nodes is possible and easy.

3. Easily managed and maintained.

4. Error detection is easily done.

Disadvantages of Tree Topology

1. Heavily cabled.

2. Costly.

3. If more nodes are added maintenance is difficult.

4. Central hub fails, network fails.

Hybrid Topology

It is two different types of topologies which is a mixture of two or more topologies. For example if in an office in one department ring topology is used and in another star topology is used, connecting these topologies will result in Hybrid Topology (ring topology and star topology).

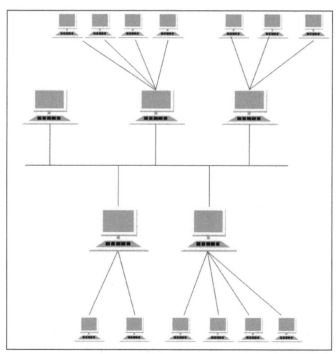

Features of Hybrid Topology

1. It is a combination of two or topologies.

2. Inherits the advantages and disadvantages of the topologies included.

Advantages of Hybrid Topology

1. Reliable as Error detecting and trouble shooting is easy.

2. Effective.

3. Scalable as size can be increased easily.

4. Flexible.

Disadvantages of Hybrid Topology

1. Complex in design.

2. Costly.

Point-to-Point

Point-to-point networks contains exactly two hosts such as computer, switches or routers, servers connected back to back using a single piece of cable. Often, the receiving end of one host is connected to sending end of the other and vice-versa.

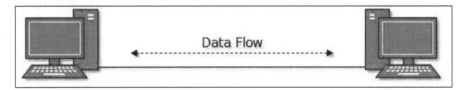

If the hosts are connected point-to-point logically, then may have multiple intermediate devices. But the end hosts are unaware of underlying network and see each other as if they are connected directly.

Daisy Chain

This topology connects all the hosts in a linear fashion. Similar to Ring topology, all hosts are connected to two hosts only, except the end hosts. Means, if the end hosts in daisy chain are connected then it represents Ring topology.

Each link in daisy chain topology represents single point of failure. Every link failure splits the network into two segments. Every intermediate host works as relay for its immediate hosts.

Dual Ring Topology

If ring topologies are configured to be bidirectional then they are referred to as dual ring topologies. Dual ring topologies provide each node with two connections, one in each direction. Thus, data can flow in a clockwise or counterclockwise direction.

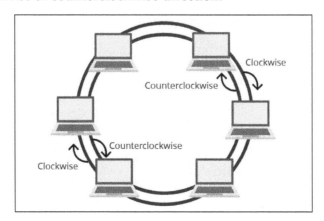

Logical Topology

Logical topology is the arrangement of devices on a computer network and how they communicate with one another. Logical topologies describe how signals act on the network.

In contrast, a physical topology defines how nodes in a network are physically linked and includes aspects such as geographic location of nodes and physical distances between nodes. The logical topology defines how nodes in a network communicate across its physical topology. The logical topology can be considered isomorphic to the physical topology, as vice versa.

Early twisted pair Ethernet with a single hub is a logical bus topology with a physical star topology. While token ring is a logical ring topology with a physical star topology.

Token Ring

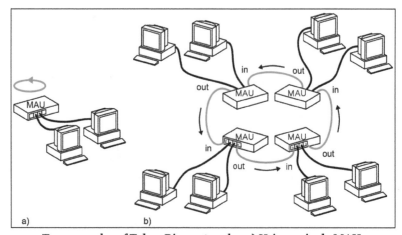

Two examples of Token Ring networks: a) Using a single MAU,
b) Using several MAUs connected to each other.

Token Ring local area network (LAN) technology is a communications protocol for local area networks. It uses a special three-byte frame called a "token" that travels around a logical "ring" of workstations or servers. This token passing is a channel access method providing fair access for all stations, and eliminating the collisions of contention-based access methods.

Introduced by IBM in 1984, it was then standardized with protocol IEEE 802.5 and was fairly successful, particularly in corporate environments, but gradually eclipsed by the later versions of Ethernet.

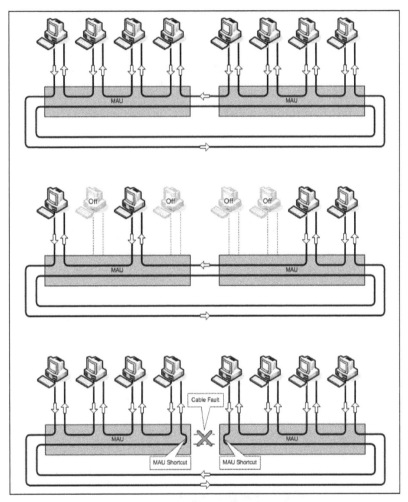

Token Ring network: operation of a MAU.

Operation

Stations on a Token Ring LAN are logically organized in a ring topology with data being transmitted sequentially from one ring station to the next with a control token circulating around the ring controlling access. Similar token passing mechanisms are used by ARCNET, token bus, 100VG-AnyLAN (802.12) and FDDI, and they have theoretical advantages over the CSMA/CD of early Ethernet.

A Token Ring network can be modeled as a polling system where a single server provides service to queues in a cyclic order.

Access Control

The data transmission process goes as follows:

- Empty information frames are continuously circulated on the ring.

- When a computer has a message to send, it seizes the token. The computer will then be able to send the frame.

- The frame is then examined by each successive workstation. The workstation that identifies itself to be the destination for the message copies it from the frame and changes the token back to 0.

- When the frame gets back to the originator, it sees that the token has been changed to 0 and that the message has been copied and received. It removes the message from the frame.

- The frame continues to circulate as an "empty" frame, ready to be taken by a workstation when it has a message to send.

Multistation Access Units and Controlled Access Units

Physically, a Token Ring network is wired as a star, with 'MAUs' in the center, 'arms' out to each station, and the loop going out-and-back through each.

A MAU could present in the form of a hub or a switch; since Token Ring had no collisions many MAUs were manufactured as hubs. Although Token Ring runs on LLC, it includes source routing to forward packets beyond the local network. The majority of MAUs are configured in a 'concentration' configuration by default, but later MAUs also supporting a feature to act as splitters and not concentrators exclusively such as on the IBM 8226.

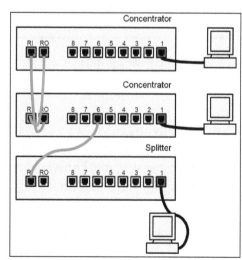

Later IBM would release Controlled Access Units that could support multiple MAU modules known as a Lobe Attachment Module. The CAUs supported features such as Dual-Ring Redundancy for alternate routing in the event of a dead port, modular concentration with LAMs, and multiple interfaces like most later MAUs. This offered a more reliable setup and remote management than with an unmanaged MAU hub.

Cabling and Interfaces

Cabling is generally IBM "Type-1", a heavy two-pair 150 Ohm shielded twisted pair cable. This was the basic cable for the "IBM Cabling System", a structured cabling system that IBM hoped would be widely adopted. Unique hermaphroditic connectors, commonly referred to as IBM Data Connectors in formal writing or colloquially as Boy George connectors were used. The connectors have the disadvantage of being quite bulky, requiring at least 3 x 3 cm panel space, and being relatively fragile. The advantages of the connectors being that they are genderless and have superior shielding over standard unshielded 8P8C. Connectors at the computer were usually DE-9 female.

In later implementations of Token Ring, Cat 4 cabling was also supported, so 8P8C ("RJ45") connectors were used on both of the MAUs, CAUs and NICs; with many of the network cards supporting both 8P8C and DE-9 for backwards compatibility.

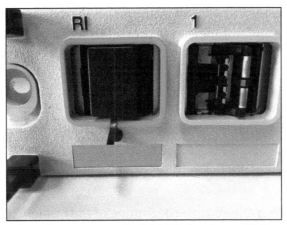

Data Connectors on the Multistation Access Unit.

8P8C 'Media Filters' that plug into a Connector
converting it for use with 8P8C connectors.

Frame Types

Token

When no station is sending a frame, a special token frame circles the loop. This special token frame is repeated from station to station until arriving at a station that needs to send data.

Tokens are 3 bytes in length and consist of a start delimiter, an access control byte, and an end delimiter.

Start Delimiter	Access Control	End Delimiter
8-bits	8-bits	8-bits

Abort Frame

Used to abort transmission by the sending station.

SD	ED
8 bits	8 bits

Data

Data frames carry information for upper-layer protocols, while command frames contain control information and have no data for upper-layer protocols. Data/command frames vary in size, depending on the size of the Information field.

SD	AC	FC	DA	SA	PDU from LLC (IEEE 802.2)	CRC	ED	FS
8 bits	8 bits	8 bits	48 bits	48 bits	up to 4500x8 bits	32 bits	8 bits	8 bits

Starting Delimiter

Consists of a special bit pattern denoting the beginning of the frame. The bits from most significant to least significant are J, K, 0, J, K, 0, 0, 0. J and K are code violations. Since Manchester encoding is self-clocking, and has a transition for every encoded bit 0 or 1, the J and K codings violate this, and will be detected by the hardware. Both the Starting Delimiter and Ending Delimiter fields are used to mark frame boundaries.

J	K	0	J	K	0	0	0
1 bit	1 bit	1 bit	1 bit	1 bit	1 bit	1 bit	1 bit

Access Control

This byte field consists of the following bits from most significant to least significant bit order: P, P, P, T, M, R, R, R. The P bits are priority bits, T is the token bit which when set specifies that this is a token frame, M is the monitor bit which is set by the Active Monitor (AM) station when it sees this frame, and R bits are reserved bits.

+	Bits 0–2	3	4	5–7
0	Priority	Token	Monitor	Reservation

Frame Control

A one-byte field that contains bits describing the data portion of the frame contents which indicates whether the frame contains data or control information. In control frames, this byte specifies the type of control information.

+	Bits 0–1	Bits 2–7
0	Frame type	Control Bits

Frame type – 01 indicates LLC frame IEEE 802.2 (data) and ignore control bits; 00 indicates MAC frame and control bits indicate the type of MAC control frame.

Destination Address

A six-byte field used to specify the destination(s) physical address.

Source Address

Contains physical address of sending station. It is a six-byte field that is either the local assigned address (LAA) or universally assigned address (UAA) of the sending station adapter.

Data

A variable length field of 0 or more bytes, the maximum allowable size depending on ring speed containing MAC management data or upper layer information. Maximum length of 4500 bytes.

Frame Check Sequence

A four-byte field used to store the calculation of a CRC for frame integrity verification by the receiver.

Ending Delimiter

The counterpart to the starting delimiter, this field marks the end of the frame and consists of the following bits from most significant to least significant: J, K, 1, J, K, 1, I, E. I is the intermediate frame bit and E is the error bit.

J	K	1	J	K	1	I	E
1	1 bit	1 bit	1 bit	1 bit	1 bit	1 bit	1 bit

Frame Status

A one-byte field used as a primitive acknowledgment scheme on whether the frame was recognized and copied by its intended receiver.

A	C	0	0	A	C	0	0
1 bit	1 bit	1 bit	1 bit	1 bit	1 bit	1 bit	1 bit

Where, A = 1, Address recognized C = 1, Frame copied.

Other Technical Details

Active and Standby Monitors

Every station in a Token Ring network is either an active monitor (AM) or standby monitor (SM) station. There can be only one active monitor on a ring at a time. The active monitor is chosen through an election or monitor contention process.

The monitor contention process is initiated when the following happens:

- A loss of signal on the ring is detected.

- An active monitor station is not detected by other stations on the ring.

- A particular timer on an end station expires such as the case when a station hasn't seen a token frame in the past 7 seconds.

When any of the above conditions take place and a station decides that a new monitor is needed, it will transmit a "claim token" frame, announcing that it wants to become the new monitor. If that token returns to the sender, it is OK for it to become the monitor. If some other station tries to become the monitor at the same time then the station with the highest MAC address will win the election process. Every other station becomes a standby monitor. All stations must be capable of becoming an active monitor station if necessary.

The active monitor performs a number of ring administration functions. The first function is to operate as the master clock for the ring in order to provide synchronization of the signal for stations on the wire. Another function of the AM is to insert a 24-bit delay into the ring, to ensure that there is always sufficient buffering in the ring for the token to circulate. A third function for the AM is to ensure that exactly one token circulates whenever there is no frame being transmitted, and to detect a broken ring. Lastly, the AM is responsible for removing circulating frames from the ring.

Token Ring Insertion Process

Token Ring stations must go through a 5-phase ring insertion process before being allowed to participate in the ring network. If any of these phases fail, the Token Ring station will not insert into the ring and the Token Ring driver may report an error.

- Phase 0 (Lobe Check) — A station first performs a lobe media check. A station is wrapped at the MSAU and is able to send 2000 test frames down its transmit pair which will loop back to its receive pair. The station checks to ensure it can receive these frames without error.

- Phase 1 (Physical Insertion) — A station then sends a 5-volt signal to the MSAU to open the relay.

- Phase 2 (Address Verification) — A station then transmits MAC frames with its own MAC address in the destination address field of a Token Ring frame. When the frame returns and if the Address Recognized (AR) and Frame Copied (FC) bits in the frame-status are set to 0 (indicating that no other station currently on the ring uses that address), the station must participate in the periodic (every 7 seconds) ring poll process. This is where stations identify themselves on the network as part of the MAC management functions.

- Phase 3 (Participation in ring poll) — A station learns the address of its Nearest Active Upstream Neighbour (NAUN) and makes its address known to its nearest downstream neighbour, leading to the creation of the ring map. Station waits until it receives an AMP or SMP frame with the AR and FC bits set to 0. When it does, the station flips both bits (AR and FC) to 1, if enough resources are available, and queues an SMP frame for transmission. If no such frames are received within 18 seconds, then the station reports a failure to open and de-inserts from the ring. If the station successfully participates in a ring poll, it proceeds into the final phase of insertion, request initialization.

- Phase 4 (Request Initialization) — Finally a station sends out a special request to a parameter server to obtain configuration information. This frame is sent to a special functional address, typically a Token Ring bridge, which may hold timer and ring number information the new station needs to know.

Optional Priority Scheme

In some applications there is an advantage to being able to designate one station having a higher priority. Token Ring specifies an optional scheme of this sort, as does the CAN Bus, (widely used in automotive applications) - but Ethernet does not.

In the Token Ring priority MAC, eight priority levels, 0–7, are used. When the station wishing to transmit receives a token or data frame with a priority less than or equal to the station's requested priority, it sets the priority bits to its desired priority. The station does not immediately transmit; the token circulates around the medium until it returns to the station. Upon sending and receiving its own data frame, the station downgrades the token priority back to the original priority.

Here are the following eight access priority and traffic types for devices that support 802.1Q and 802.1p:

Priority bits	Traffic type
x'000'	Normal data traffic
x'001'	Not used
x'010'	Not used
x'011'	Not used
x'100'	Normal data traffic (forwarded from other devices)
x'101'	Data sent with time sensitivity requirements
x'110'	Data with real time sensitivity (i.e. VoIP)
x'111'	Station management

Bridging Token Ring and Ethernet

Both Token Ring and Ethernet interfaces on the 2210-24 M.

Bridging solutions for Token Ring and Ethernet networks included the AT&T StarWAN 10:4 Bridge, the IBM 9208 LAN Bridge and the Microcom LAN Bridge. Alternative connection solutions incorporated a router that could be configured to dynamically filter traffic, protocols and interfaces, such as the IBM 2210-24M Multiprotocol Router which contained both Ethernet and Token Ring interfaces.

Ethernet over Twisted Pair

Ethernet over twisted pair technologies use twisted-pair cables for the physical layer of an Ethernet computer network. They are a subset of all Ethernet physical layers.

Early Ethernet had used various grades of coaxial cable, but in 1984, StarLAN showed the potential of simple unshielded twisted pair. This led to the development of 10BASE-T and its successors 100BASE-TX, 1000BASE-T and 10GBASE-T, supporting speeds of 10, 100 Mbit/s and 1 and 10 Gbit/s respectively.

All these standards use 8P8C connectors, while the cables range from Cat 3 to Cat 8.

Ethernet over twisted-pair cable.

8P8C plug.

The first two early designs of twisted pair networking were StarLAN, standardized by the IEEE Standards Association as IEEE 802.3e in 1986, at one megabit per second, and LattisNet, developed in January 1987, at 10 megabit per second. Both were developed before the 10BASE-T standard and used different signalling, so they were not directly compatible with it.

In 1988 AT&T released StarLAN 10, named for working at 10 Mbit/s. The StarLAN 10 signalling was used as the basis of 10BASE-T, with the addition of link beat to quickly indicate connection status.

Using twisted pair cabling, in a star topology, for Ethernet addressed several weaknesses of the previous standards:

- Twisted pair cables were already in use for telephone service and were already present in many office buildings, lowering overall cost.

- The centralized star topology already in use for telephone service and was a more common approach to cabling than the bus in earlier standards and easier to manage.

- Using point-to-point links was less prone to failure and greatly simplified troubleshooting compared to a shared bus.

- Exchanging cheap repeater hubs for more advanced switching hubs provided a viable upgrade path.

- Mixing different speeds in a single network became possible with the arrival of Fast Ethernet.

- Depending on cable grades, subsequent upgrading to Gigabit Ethernet or faster could be accomplished by replacing the network switches.

Although 10BASE-T is rarely used as a normal-operation signaling rate today, it is still in wide use with NICs in Wake-on-LAN power-down mode and for special, low-power, low-bandwidth applications. 10BASE-T is still supported on most twisted-pair Ethernet ports with up to Gigabit Ethernet speed.

The common names for the standards derive from aspects of the physical media. The leading number (10 in 10BASE-T) refers to the transmission speed in Mbit/s. BASE denotes that baseband transmission is used. The T designates twisted pair cable. Where there are several standards for the same transmission speed, they are distinguished by a letter or digit following the T, such as TX or T4, referring to the encoding method and number of lanes.

Shared Cable

10BASE-T and 100BASE-TX require only two pairs (pins 1–2, 3–6) to operate. Since common category 5 cable has four pairs, it is possible to use the spare pairs (pins 4–5, 7–8) in 10- and 100-Mbit/s configurations for other purposes. The spare pairs may be used for power over Ethernet (PoE), for two plain old telephone service (POTS) lines, or for a second 10BASE-T or 100BASE-TX connection. In practice, great care must be taken to separate these pairs as 10/100-Mbit/s Ethernet equipment electrically terminate the unused pins. Shared cable is not an option for Gigabit Ethernet as 1000BASE-T requires all four pairs to operate.

Single-pair

In addition to the more computer-oriented two and four-pair variants, the 100BASE-T1 and 1000BASE-T1 single-pair Ethernet PHYs are intended for automotive applications or as optional data channels in other interconnect applications. The single pair operates at full duplex and has a maximum reach of 15 m (100BASE-T1, 1000BASE-T1 link segment type A) or up to 40 m (1000BASE-T1 link segment type B) with up to four in-line connectors. Both PHYs require a balanced twisted pair with an impedance of 100 Ω. The cable must be capable of transmitting 600 MHz for 1000BASE-T1 and 66 MHz for 100BASE-T1.

Similar to PoE, Power over Data Lines (PoDL) can provide up to 50 W to a device.

Autonegotiation and Duplex

Ethernet over twisted pair standards up to Gigabit Ethernet define both full-duplex and half-duplex communication. However, half-duplex operation for gigabit speed isn't supported by any existing hardware. Higher speed standards, 2.5GBASE-T up to 40GBASE-T running at 2.5 to 40 Gbit/s, consequently define only full-duplex point-to-point links which are generally connected by network switches, and don't support the traditional shared-medium CSMA/CD operation.

Many different modes of operations (10BASE-T half duplex, 10BASE-T full duplex, 100BASE-TX half duplex, etc.) exist for Ethernet over twisted pair, and most network adapters are capable of different modes of operation. 1000BASE-T requires autonegotiation to be on in order to operate.

When two linked interfaces are set to different duplex modes, the effect of this duplex mismatch is a network that functions much more slowly than its nominal speed. Duplex mismatch may be inadvertently caused when an administrator configures an interface to a fixed mode (e.g. 100 Mbit/s full duplex) and fails to configure the remote interface, leaving it set to autonegotiate. Then, when the autonegotiation process fails, half duplex is assumed by the autonegotiating side of the link.

Transmission Modes in Computer Networks

Transmission mode refers to the mechanism of transferring of data between two devices connected over a network. It is also called Communication Mode. These modes direct the direction of flow of information. There are three types of transmission modes. They are:

1. Simplex Mode.

2. Half duplex Mode.

3. Full duplex Mode.

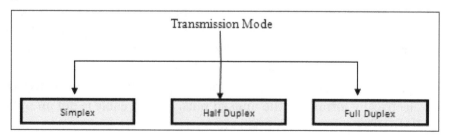

Simplex Mode

In this type of transmission mode, data can be sent only in one direction i.e. communication is uni-directional. We cannot send a message back to the sender. Unidirectional communication is done in Simplex Systems where we just need to send a command/signal, and do not expect any response back. Examples of simplex Mode are loudspeakers, television broadcasting, television and remote, keyboard and monitor etc.

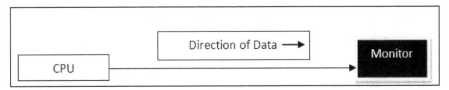

Half Duplex Mode

Half-duplex data transmission means that data can be transmitted in both directions on a signal carrier, but not at the same time.

For example, on a local area network using a technology that has half-duplex transmission, one workstation can send data on the line and then immediately receive data on the line from the same direction in which data was just transmitted. Hence half-duplex transmission implies a bidirectional line (one that can carry data in both directions) but data can be sent in only one direction at a time. Example of half duplex is a walkie- talkie in which message is sent one at a time but messages are sent in both the directions.

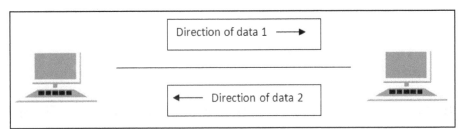

Full Duplex Mode

In full duplex system we can send data in both the directions as it is bidirectional at the same time in other words, data can be sent in both directions simultaneously.

Example of Full Duplex is a Telephone Network in which there is communication between two persons by a telephone line, using which both can talk and listen at the same time.

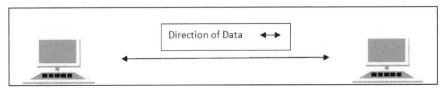

In full duplex system there can be two lines one for sending the data and the other for receiving data.

Transmission Mediums in Computer Networks

Data is represented by computers and other telecommunication devices using signals. Signals are transmitted in the form of electromagnetic energy from one device to another. Electromagnetic signals travel through vacuum, air or other transmission mediums to move from one point to another (from sender to receiver).

Electromagnetic energy (includes electrical and magnetic fields) consists of power, voice, visible light, radio waves, ultraviolet light, gamma rays etc.

Transmission medium is the means through which we send our data from one place to another. The first layer (physical layer) of Communication Networks OSI Seven layer model is dedicated to the transmission media, we will study the OSI Model later.

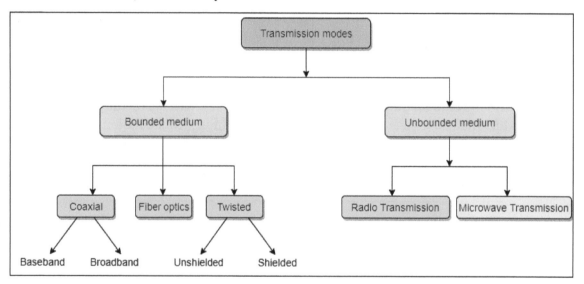

Factors to be Considered while Selecting a Transmission Medium

1. Transmission Rate.

2. Cost and Ease of Installation.

3. Resistance to Environmental Conditions.

4. Distances.

Bounded or Guided Transmission Media

Guided media, which are those that provide a conduit from one device to another, include Twisted-Pair Cable, Coaxial Cable, and Fibre-Optic Cable.

A signal travelling along any of these media is directed and contained by the physical limits of the medium. Twisted-pair and coaxial cable use metallic (copper) conductors that accept and transport signals in the form of electric current. Optical fibre is a cable that accepts and transports signals in the form of light.

Twisted Pair Cable

This cable is the most commonly used and is cheaper than others. It is lightweight, cheap, can be installed easily, and they support many different types of network. Some important points :

- Its frequency range is 0 to 3.5 kHz.

- Typical attenuation is 0.2 dB/Km at 1 kHz.

- Typical delay is 50 µs/km.

- Repeater spacing is 2 km.

A twisted pair consists of two conductors (normally copper), each with its own plastic insulation, twisted together. One of these wires is used to carry signals to the receiver, and the other is used only as ground reference. The receiver uses the difference between the two. In addition to the signal sent by the sender on one of the wires, interference (noise) and crosstalk may affect both wires and create unwanted signals. If the two wires are parallel, the effect of these unwanted signals is not the same in both wires because they are at different locations relative to the noise or crosstalk sources. This results in a difference at the receiver.

Twisted pair is of two types:

- Unshielded Twisted Pair (UTP).

- Shielded Twisted Pair (STP).

Unshielded Twisted Pair Cable

It is the most common type of telecommunication when compared with Shielded Twisted Pair Cable which consists of two conductors usually copper, each with its own colour plastic insulator. Identification is the reason behind coloured plastic insulation.

UTP cables consist of 2 or 4 pairs of twisted cable. Cable with 2 pair use RJ-11 connector and 4 pair cable use RJ-45 connector.

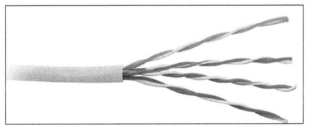

Unshielded Twisted Pair Cable.

Advantages of Unshielded Twisted Pair Cable

- Installation is easy,

- Flexible,

- Cheap,

- It has high speed capacity,

- 100 meter limit

- Higher grades of UTP are used in LAN technologies like Ethernet.

It consists of two insulating copper wires (1 mm thick). The wires are twisted together in a helical form to reduce electrical interference from similar pair.

Disadvantages of Unshielded Twisted Pair Cable

- Bandwidth is low when compared with Coaxial Cable.

- Provides less protection from interference.

Shielded Twisted Pair Cable

This cable has a metal foil or braided-mesh covering which encases each pair of insulated conductors. Electromagnetic noise penetration is prevented by metal casing. Shielding also eliminates crosstalk.

It has same attenuation as unshielded twisted pair. It is faster the unshielded and coaxial cable. It is more expensive than coaxial and unshielded twisted pair.

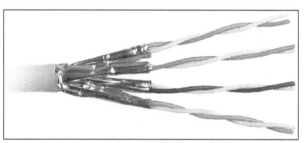

Shielded Twisted Pair Cable.

Advantages of Shielded Twisted Pair Cable

- Easy to install,

- Performance is adequate,

- Can be used for Analog or Digital transmission,

- Increases the signalling rate,

- Higher capacity than unshielded twisted pair,

- Eliminates crosstalk.

Disadvantages of Shielded Twisted Pair Cable

- Difficult to manufacture,

- Heavy.

Performance of Shielded Twisted Pair Cable

One way to measure the performance of twisted-pair cable is to compare attenuation versus frequency and distance. As shown in the below figure, a twisted-pair cable can pass a wide range of frequencies. However, with increasing frequency, the attenuation, measured in decibels per kilometre (dB/km), sharply increases with frequencies above 100kHz.

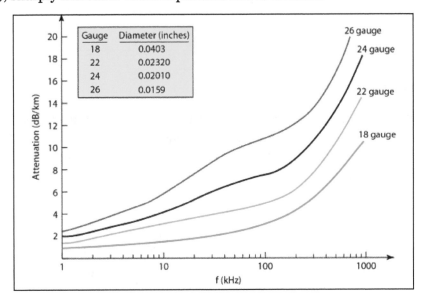

Applications of Shielded Twisted Pair Cable

- In telephone lines to provide voice and data channels. The DSL lines that are used by the telephone companies to provide high-data-rate connections also use the high-bandwidth capability of unshielded twisted-pair cables.

- Local Area Network, such as 10Base-T and 100Base-T, also use twisted-pair cables.

Coaxial Cable

Coaxial is called by this name because it contains two conductors that are parallel to each other. Copper is used in this as centre conductor which can be a solid wire or a standard one. It is surrounded by PVC installation, a sheath which is encased in an outer conductor of metal foil, barid or both.

Outer metallic wrapping is used as a shield against noise and as the second conductor which completes the circuit. The outer conductor is also encased in an insulating sheath. The outermost part is the plastic cover which protects the whole cable.

Here are the most common coaxial standards.

- 50-Ohm RG-7 or RG-11: used with thick Ethernet.

- 50-Ohm RG-58: used with thin Ethernet.

- 75-Ohm RG-59: used with cable television.

- 93-Ohm RG-62: used with ARCNET.

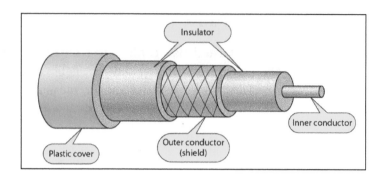

Coaxial Cable Standards

Coaxial cables are categorized by their Radio Government (RG) ratings. Each RG number denotes a unique set of physical specifications, including the wire gauge of the inner conductor, the thickness and the type of the inner insulator, the construction of the shield, and the size and type of the outer casing. Each cable defined by an RG rating is adapted for a specialized function, as shown in the table below:

Category	Impedance	Use
RG-59	75 Ω	Cable TV
RG-58	50 Ω	Thin Ethernet
RG-11	50 Ω	Thick Ethernet

Coaxial Cable Connectors

To connect coaxial cable to devices, we need coaxial connectors. The most common type of connector used today is the Bayonet Neill-Concelman (BNC) connector. The below figure shows 3 popular types of these connectors: the BNC Connector, the BNC T connector and the BNC terminator.

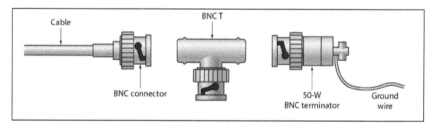

The BNC connector is used to connect the end of the cable to the device, such as a TV set. The BNC T connector is used in Ethernet networks to branch out to a connection to a computer or other device. The BNC terminator is used at the end of the cable to prevent the reflection of the signal.

There are two types of Coaxial cables:

- Baseband: This is a 50 ohm (Ω) coaxial cable which is used for digital transmission. It is mostly used for LAN's. Baseband transmits a single signal at a time with very high speed. The major drawback is that it needs amplification after every 1000 feet.

- Broadband: This uses analog transmission on standard cable television cabling. It transmits several simultaneous signal using different frequencies. It covers large area when compared with Baseband Coaxial Cable.

Advantages of Coaxial Cable

- Bandwidth is high.

- Used in long distance telephone lines.

- Transmits digital signals at a very high rate of 10Mbps.

- Much higher noise immunity.

- Data transmission without distortion.

- The can span to longer distance at higher speeds as they have better shielding when compared to twisted pair cable.

Disadvantages of Coaxial Cable

- Single cable failure can fail the entire network.

- Difficult to install and expensive when compared with twisted pair.

- If the shield is imperfect, it can lead to grounded loop.

Performance of Coaxial Cable

We can measure the performance of a coaxial cable in same way as that of Twisted Pair Cables. From the below figure, it can be seen that the attenuation is much higher in coaxial cable than in twisted-pair cable. In other words, although coaxial cable has a much higher bandwidth, the signal weakens rapidly and requires the frequent use of repeaters.

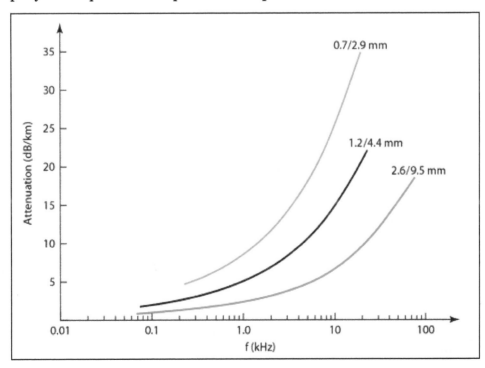

Applications of Coaxial Cable

- Coaxial cable was widely used in analog telephone networks, where a single coaxial network could carry 10,000 voice signals.

- Cable TV networks also use coaxial cables. In the traditional cable TV network, the entire network used coaxial cable. Cable TV uses RG-59 coaxial cable.

- In traditional Ethernet LANs. Because of it high bandwidth, and consequence high data rate, coaxial cable was chosen for digital transmission in early Ethernet LANs. The 10Base-2, or Thin Ethernet, uses RG-58 coaxial cable with BNC connectors to transmit data at 10Mbps with a range of 185 m.

Fiber Optic Cable

A fibre-optic cable is made of glass or plastic and transmits signals in the form of light. For better understanding we first need to explore several aspects of the nature of light. Light travels in a straight line as long as it is mobbing through a single uniform substance. If ray of light travelling through one substance suddenly enters another substance (of a different density), the ray changes direction.

The below figure shows how a ray of light changes direction when going from a more dense to a less dense substance.

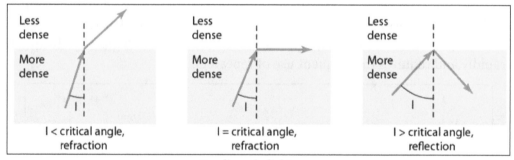

Bending of a light ray.

As the figure shows:

- If the angle of incidence I (the angle the ray makes with the line perpendicular to the interface between the two substances) is less than the critical angle, the ray refracts and moves closer to the surface.

- If the angle of incidence is greater than the critical angle, the ray reflects (makes a turn) and travels again in the denser substance.

- If the angle of incidence is equal to the critical angle, the ray refracts and moves parallel to the surface as shown.

Optical fibres use reflection to guide light through a channel. A glass or plastic core is surrounded by a cladding of less dense glass or plastic. The difference in density of the two materials must be such that a beam of light moving through the core is reflected off the cladding instead of being refracted into it.

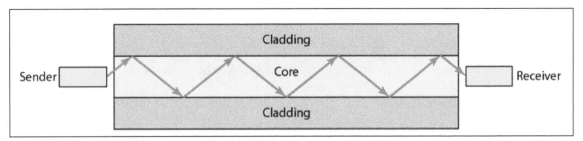

Internal view of an Optical fibre.

Propagation Modes of Fiber Optic Cable

Current technology supports two modes(Multimode and Single mode) for propagating light along optical channels, each requiring fibre with different physical characteristics. Multimode can be implemented in two forms: Step-index and Graded-index.

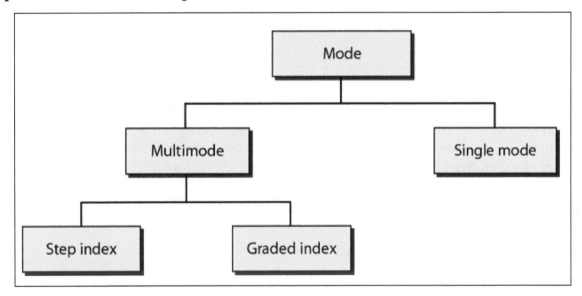

Multimode Propagation Mode

Multimode is so named because multiple beams from a light source move through the core in different paths. How these beams move within the cable depends on the structure of the core as shown in the figure.

- Inmultimode step-index fibre, the density of the core remains constant from the centre to the edges. A beam of light moves through this constant density in a straight line until it reaches the interface of the core and the cladding. The term step-index refers to the suddenness of this change, which contributes to the distortion of the signal as it passes through the fibre.

- Inmultimode graded-index fibre, this distortion gets decreases through the cable. The word index here refers to the index of refraction. This index of refraction is related to the density. A graded-index fibre, therefore, is one with varying densities. Density is highest at the centre of the core and decreases gradually to its lowest at the edge.

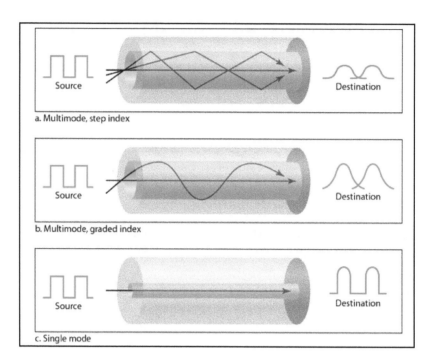

a. Multimode, step index

b. Multimode, graded index

c. Single mode

Single Mode

Single mode uses step-index fibre and a highly focused source of light that limits beams to a small range of angles, all close to the horizontal. The single-mode fibre itself is manufactured with a much smaller diameter than that of multimode fibre, and with substantially lower density.

The decrease in density results in a critical angle that is close enough to 90 degree to make the propagation of beams almost horizontal.

Fibre Sizes for Fiber Optic Cable

Optical fibres are defined by the ratio of the diameter or their core to the diameter of their cladding, both expressed in micrometers. The common sizes are shown in the figure below:

Type	Core (μm)	Cladding (μm)	Mode
50/125	50.0	125	Multimode, graded index
62.5/125	62.5	125	Multimode, graded index
100/125	100.0	125	Multimode, graded index
7/125	7.0	125	Single mod

Fibre Optic Cable Connectors

There are three types of connectors for fibre-optic cables, as shown in the figure below.

The Subscriber Channel (SC) connector is used for cable TV. It uses push/pull locking system. The Straight-Tip (ST) connector is used for connecting cable to the networking devices. MT-RJ is a connector that is the same size as RJ45.

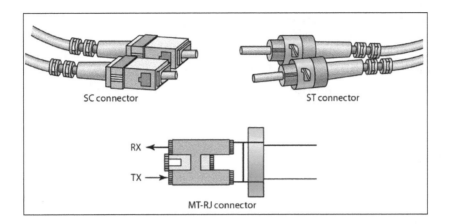

Advantages of Fibre Optic Cable

Fibre optic has several advantages over metallic cable:

- Higher bandwidth.
- Less signal attenuation.
- Immunity to electromagnetic interference.
- Resistance to corrosive materials.
- Light weight.
- Greater immunity to tapping.

Disadvantages of Fibre Optic Cable

There are some disadvantages in the use of optical fibre:

- Installation and maintenance.
- Unidirectional light propagation.
- High Cost.

Performance of Fibre Optic Cable

Attenuation is flatter than in the case of twisted-pair cable and coaxial cable. The performance is such that we need fewer (actually one tenth as many) repeaters when we use the fibre-optic cable.

Applications of Fibre Optic Cable

- Often found in backbone networks because its wide bandwidth is cost-effective.
- Some cable TV companies use a combination of optical fibre and coaxial cable thus creating a hybrid network.
- Local-area Networks such as 100Base-FX network and 1000Base-X also use fibre-optic cable.

Unbounded or Unguided Transmission Media

Unguided medium transport electromagnetic waves without using a physical conductor. This type of communication is often referred to as wireless communication. Signals are normally broadcast through free space and thus are available to anyone who has a device capable of receiving them.

The below figure shows the part of the electromagnetic spectrum, ranging from 3 kHz to 900 THz, used for wireless communication.

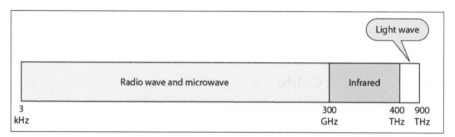

Unguided signals can travel from the source to the destination in several ways: Gound propagation, Sky propagation and Line-of-sight propagation as shown in figure.

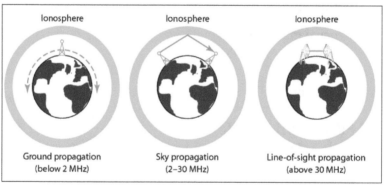

Propagation Modes.

- Ground Propagation: In this, radio waves travel through the lowest portion of the atmosphere, hugging the Earth. These low-frequency signals emanate in all directions from the transmitting antenna and follow the curvature of the planet.

- Sky Propagation: In this, higher-frequency radio waves radiate upward into the ionosphere where they are reflected back to Earth. This type of transmission allows for greater distances with lower output power.

- Line-of-sight Propagation: In this type, very high-frequency signals are transmitted in straight lines directly from antenna to antenna.

We can divide wireless transmission into three broad groups:

- Radio waves,

- Micro waves,

- Infrared waves.

Radio Waves

Electromagnetic waves ranging in frequencies between 3 KHz and 1 GHz are normally called radio waves.

Radio waves are omnidirectional. When an antenna transmits radio waves, they are propagated in all directions. This means that the sending and receiving antennas do not have to be aligned. A sending antenna send waves that can be received by any receiving antenna. The omnidirectional property has disadvantage, too. The radio waves transmitted by one antenna are susceptible to interference by another antenna that may send signal suing the same frequency or band.

Radio waves, particularly with those of low and medium frequencies, can penetrate walls. This characteristic can be both an advantage and a disadvantage. It is an advantage because, an AM radio can receive signals inside a building. It is a disadvantage because we cannot isolate a communication to just inside or outside a building.

Omnidirectional Antenna for Radio Waves

Radio waves use omnidirectional antennas that send out signals in all directions.

Applications of Radio Waves

- The omnidirectional characteristics of radio waves make them useful for multicasting in which there is one sender but many receivers.

- AM and FM radio, television, maritime radio, cordless phones, and paging are examples of multicasting.

Micro Waves

Electromagnetic waves having frequencies between 1 and 300 GHz are called micro waves. Micro waves are unidirectional. When an antenna transmits microwaves, they can be narrowly focused. This means that the sending and receiving antennas need to be aligned. The unidirectional property has an obvious advantage. A pair of antennas can be aligned without interfering with another pair of aligned antennas.

The following describes some characteristics of microwaves propagation:

- Microwave propagation is line-of-sight. Since the towers with the mounted antennas need to be in direct sight of each other, towers that are far apart need to be very tall.

- Very high-frequency microwaves cannot penetrate walls. This characteristic can be a disadvantage if receivers are inside the buildings.

- The microwave band is relatively wide, almost 299 GHz. Therefore, wider sub-bands can be assigned and a high date rate is possible.

- Use of certain portions of the band requires permission from authorities.

Unidirectional Antenna for Micro Waves

Microwaves need unidirectional antennas that send out signals in one direction. Two types of antennas are used for microwave communications: Parabolic Dish and Horn.

A parabolic antenna works as a funnel, catching a wide range of waves and directing them to a common point. In this way, more of the signal is recovered than would be possible with a single-point receiver.

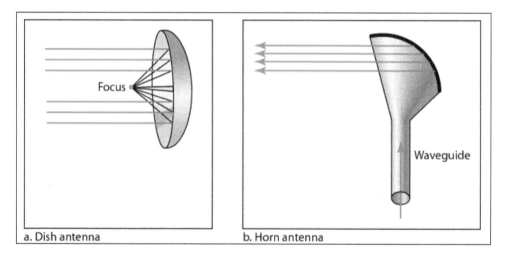

a. Dish antenna   b. Horn antenna

A horn antenna looks like a gigantic scoop. Outgoing transmissions are broadcast up a stem and deflected outward in a series of narrow parallel beams by the curved head. Received transmissions are collected by the scooped shape of the horn, in a manner similar to the parabolic dish, and are deflected down into the stem.

Applications of Micro Waves

Microwaves, due to their unidirectional properties, are very useful when unicast (one-to-one) communication is needed between the sender and the receiver. They are used in cellular phones, satellite networks and wireless LANs.

There are 2 types of Microwave Transmission:

- Terrestrial Microwave,

- Satellite Microwave.

Advantages of Microwave Transmission

- Used for long distance telephone communication,

- Carries 1000's of voice channels at the same time.

Disadvantages of Microwave Transmission

- It is very costly.

Terrestrial Microwave

For increasing the distance served by terrestrial microwave, repeaters can be installed with each antenna. The signal received by an antenna can be converted into transmittable form and relayed to next antenna as shown in below figure. It is an example of telephone systems all over the world

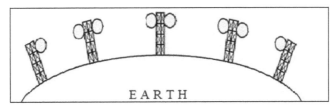

There are two types of antennas used for terrestrial microwave communication:

- Parabolic Dish Antenna: In this every line parallel to the line of symmetry reflects off the curve at angles in a way that they intersect at a common point called focus. This antenna is based on geometry of parabola.

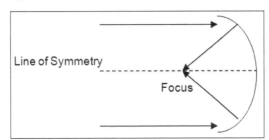

- Horn Antenna: It is a like gigantic scoop. The outgoing transmissions are broadcast up a stem and deflected outward in a series of narrow parallel beams by curved head.

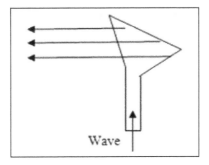

Satellite Microwave

This is a microwave relay station which is placed in outer space. The satellites are launched either by rockets or space shuttles carry them.

These are positioned 36000 Km above the equator with an orbit speed that exactly matches the rotation speed of the earth. As the satellite is positioned in a geo-synchronous orbit, it is stationery relative to earth and always stays over the same point on the ground. This is usually done to allow ground stations to aim antenna at a fixed point in the sky.

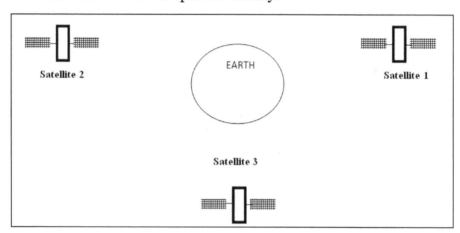

Features of Satellite Microwave

- Bandwidth capacity depends on the frequency used.
- Satellite microwave deployment for orbiting satellite is difficult.

Advantages of Satellite Microwave

- Transmitting station can receive back its own transmission and check whether the satellite has transmitted information correctly.
- A single microwave relay station which is visible from any point.

Disadvantages of Satellite Microwave

- Satellite manufacturing cost is very high.
- Cost of launching satellite is very expensive.
- Transmission highly depends on whether conditions, it can go down in bad weather.

Infrared Waves

Infrared waves, with frequencies from 300 GHz to 400 THz, can be used for short-range communication. Infrared waves, having high frequencies, cannot penetrate walls. This advantageous characteristic prevents interference between one system and another, a short-range communication system in on room cannot be affected by another system in the next room.

When we use infrared remote control, we do not interfere with the use of the remote by our neighbours. However, this same characteristic makes infrared signals useless for long-range communication. In addition, we cannot use infrared waves outside a building because the sun's rays contain infrared waves that can interfere with the communication.

Applications of Infrared Waves

- The infrared band, almost 400 THz, has an excellent potential for data transmission. Such a wide bandwidth can be used to transmit digital data with a very high data rate.

- The Infrared Data Association (IrDA), an association for sponsoring the use of infrared waves, has established standards for using these signals for communication between devices such as keyboards, mouse, PCs and printers.

- Infrared signals can be used for short-range communication in a closed area using line-of-sight propagation.

Wired and Wireless Technologies

Wired Technologies

- Coaxial cable is widely used for cable television systems, office buildings, and other worksites for local area networks. The cables consist of copper or aluminum wire surrounded by an insulating layer (typically a flexible material with a high dielectric constant), which itself is surrounded by a conductive layer. The insulation helps minimize interference and distortion. Transmission speed ranges from 200 million bits per second to more than 500 million bits per second.

Fiber optic cables are used to transmit light from one computer/network node to another.

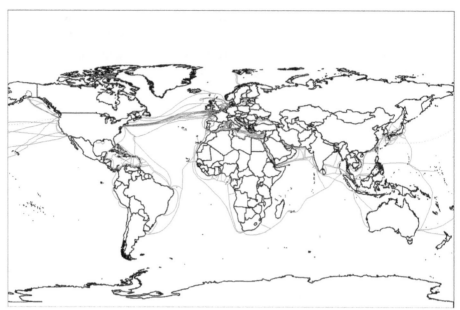

2007 map showing submarine optical fiber telecommunication cables around the world.

- ITU-T G.hn technology uses existing home wiring (coaxial cable, phone lines and power lines) to create a high-speed (up to 1 Gigabit/s) local area network.

- Signal traces on printed circuit boards are common for board-level serial communication, particularly between certain types integrated circuits, a common example being SPI.

- Ribbon cable (untwisted and possibly unshielded) has been a cost-effective media for serial protocols, especially within metallic enclosures or rolled within copper braid or foil, over short distances, or at lower data rates. Several serial network protocols can be deployed without shielded or twisted pair cabling, that is, with "flat" or "ribbon" cable, or a hybrid flat/twisted ribbon cable, should EMC, length, and bandwidth constraints permit: RS-232, RS-422, RS-485, CAN, GPIB, SCSI, etc.

- Twisted pair wire is the most widely used medium for all telecommunication. Twisted-pair cabling consist of copper wires that are twisted into pairs. Ordinary telephone wires consist of two insulated copper wires twisted into pairs. Computer network cabling (wired Ethernet as defined by IEEE 802.3) consists of 4 pairs of copper cabling that can be utilized for both voice and data transmission. The use of two wires twisted together helps to reduce crosstalk and electromagnetic induction. The transmission speed ranges from 2 million bits per second to 10 billion bits per second. Twisted pair cabling comes in two forms: unshielded twisted pair (UTP) and shielded twisted-pair (STP). Each form comes in several category ratings, designed for use in various scenarios.

- An optical fiber is a glass fiber. It carries pulses of light that represent data. Some advantages of optical fibers over metal wires are very low transmission loss and immunity from electrical interference. Optical fibers can simultaneously carry multiple wavelengths of light, which greatly increases the rate that data can be sent, and helps enable data rates of up to trillions of bits per second. Optic fibers can be used for long runs of cable carrying very high data rates, and are used for undersea cables to interconnect continents.

Price is a main factor distinguishing wired- and wireless-technology options in a business. Wireless options command a price premium that can make purchasing wired computers, printers and other devices a financial benefit. Before making the decision to purchase hard-wired technology products, a review of the restrictions and limitations of the selections is necessary. Business and employee needs may override any cost considerations.

Wireless Technologies

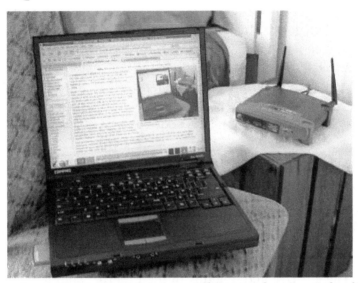

Personal computers are very often connected to networks using wireless links.

- Terrestrial microwave– Terrestrial microwave communication uses Earth-based transmitters and receivers resembling satellite dishes. Terrestrial microwaves are in the low gigahertz range, which limits all communications to line-of-sight. Relay stations are spaced approximately 50 km (30 mi) apart.

- Communications satellites– Satellites communicate via microwave radio waves, which are not deflected by the Earth's atmosphere. The satellites are stationed in space, typically in geostationary orbit 35,786 km (22,236 mi) above the equator. These Earth-orbiting systems are capable of receiving and relaying voice, data, and TV signals.

- Cellular and PCS systems use several radio communications technologies. The systems divide the region covered into multiple geographic areas. Each area has a low-power transmitter or radio relay antenna device to relay calls from one area to the next area.

- Radio and spread spectrum technologies– Wireless local area networks use a high-frequency radio technology similar to digital cellular and a low-frequency radio technology. Wireless LANs use spread spectrum technology to enable communication between multiple devices in a limited area. IEEE 802.11 defines a common flavor of open-standards wireless radio-wave technology known as Wi-Fi.

- Free-space optical communication uses visible or invisible light for communications. In most cases, line-of-sight propagation is used, which limits the physical positioning of communicating devices.

Nodes

Network nodes are the points of connection of the transmission medium to transmitters and receivers of the electrical, optical, or radio signals carried in the medium. Nodes may be associated with a computer, but certain types may have only a microcontroller at a node or possibly no programmable device at all. In the simplest of serial arrangements, one RS-232 transmitter can be connected by a pair of wires to one receiver, forming two nodes on one link, or a Point-to-Point topology. Some protocols permit a single node to only either transmit or receive (e.g., ARINC 429). Other protocols have nodes that can both transmit and receive into a single channel (e.g., CAN can have many transceivers connected to a single bus). While the conventional system building blocks of a computer network include network interface controllers (NICs), repeaters, hubs, bridges, switches, routers, modems, gateways, and firewalls, most address network concerns beyond the physical network topology and may be represented as single nodes on a particular physical network topology.

Network Interface Controller

A network interface controller (NIC, also known as a network interface card, network adapter, LAN adapter or physical network interface, and by similar terms) is a computer hardware component that connects a computer to a computer network.

Early network interface controllers were commonly implemented on expansion cards that plugged into a computer bus. The low cost and ubiquity of the Ethernet standard means that most newer computers have a network interface built into the motherboard.

Modern network interface controllers offer advanced features such as interrupt and DMA interfaces to the host processors, support for multiple receive and transmit queues, partitioning into multiple logical interfaces, and on-controller network traffic processing such as the TCP offload engine.

Purpose

The network controller implements the electronic circuitry required to communicate using a specific physical layer and data link layer standard such as Ethernet or Wi-Fi. This provides a base for a full network protocol stack, allowing communication among computers on the same local area network (LAN) and large-scale network communications through routable protocols, such as Internet Protocol (IP).

The NIC allows computers to communicate over a computer network, either by using cables or wirelessly. The NIC is both a physical layer and data link layer device, as it provides physical access to a networking medium and, for IEEE 802 and similar networks, provides a low-level addressing system through the use of MAC addresses that are uniquely assigned to network interfaces.

Implementation

Network controllers were originally implemented as expansion cards that plugged into a computer bus. The low cost and ubiquity of the Ethernet standard means that most new computers have a network interface controller built into the motherboard. Newer server motherboards may have multiple network interfaces built-in. The Ethernet capabilities are either integrated into the motherboard chipset or implemented via a low-cost dedicated Ethernet chip. A separate network card is typically no longer required unless additional independent network connections are needed or some non-Ethernet type of network is used. A general trend in computer hardware is towards integrating the various components of systems on a chip, and this is also applied to network interface cards.

12 early ISA 8 bit and 16 bit PC network cards. The lower right-most card is an early wireless network card, and the central card with partial beige plastic cover is a PSTN modem.

An Ethernet network controller typically has an 8P8C socket where the network cable is connected. Older NICs also supplied BNC, or AUI connections. Ethernet network controllers typically support 10 Mbit/s Ethernet, 100 Mbit/s Ethernet, and 1000 Mbit/s Ethernet varieties. Such controllers are designated as 10/100/1000, meaning that they can support data rates of 10, 100 or 1000 Mbit/s. 10 Gigabit Ethernet NICs are also available, and, as of November 2014, are beginning to be available on computer motherboards.

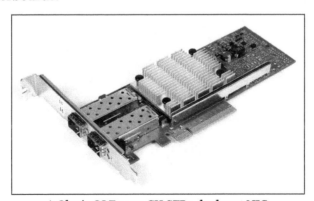

A Qlogic QLE3442-CU SFP+ dual port NIC.

Modular designs like SFP and SFP+ are highly popular, especially for fiber-optic communication. These define a standard receptacle for media-dependent transceivers, so users can easily adapt the network interface to their needs. LEDs adjacent to or integrated into the network connector inform the user of whether the network is connected, and when data activity occurs.

The NIC may use one or more of the following techniques to indicate the availability of packets to transfer:

- Polling is where the CPU examines the status of the peripheral under program control.

- Interrupt-driven I/O is where the peripheral alerts the CPU that it is ready to transfer data.

NICs may use one or more of the following techniques to transfer packet data:

- Programmed input/output, where the CPU moves the data to or from the NIC to memory.

- Direct memory access (DMA), where a device other than the CPU assumes control of the system bus to move data to or from the NIC to memory. This removes load from the CPU but requires more logic on the card. In addition, a packet buffer on the NIC may not be required and latency can be reduced.

Performance and Advanced Functionality

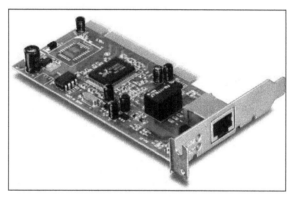

An ATM network interface.

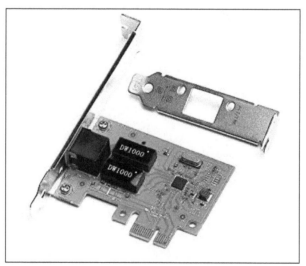

Intel 82574L Gigabit Ethernet NIC, a PCI Express ×1 card,
which provides two hardware receive queues.

Multiqueue NICs provide multiple transmit and receive queues, allowing packets received by the NIC to be assigned to one of its receive queues. The NIC may distribute incoming traffic between the receive queues using a hash function. Each receive queue is assigned to a separate interrupt; by routing each of those interrupts to different CPUs or CPU cores, processing of the interrupt requests triggered by the network traffic received by a single NIC can be distributed improving performance.

The hardware-based distribution of the interrupts, is referred to as receive-side scaling (RSS). Purely software implementations also exist, such as the receive packet steering (RPS) and receive flow steering (RFS). Further performance improvements can be achieved by routing the interrupt requests to the CPUs or cores executing the applications that are the ultimate destinations for network packets that generated the interrupts. This technique improves Locality of reference and results in higher overall performance, reduced latency and better hardware utilization because of the higher utilization of CPU caches and fewer required context switches. Examples of such implementations are the RFS and Intel Flow Director.

With multi-queue NICs, additional performance improvements can be achieved by distributing outgoing traffic among different transmit queues. By assigning different transmit queues to different CPUs or CPU cores, internal operating system contentions can be avoided. This approach is usually referred to as transmit packet steering (XPS).

Some products feature NIC partitioning (NPAR, also known as port partitioning) that uses SR-IOV to divide a single 10 Gigabit Ethernet NIC into multiple discrete virtual NICs with dedicated bandwidth, which are presented to the firmware and operating system as separate PCI device functions. TCP offload engine is a technology used in some NICs to offload processing of the entire TCP/IP stack to the network controller. It is primarily used with high-speed network interfaces, such as Gigabit Ethernet and 10 Gigabit Ethernet, for which the processing overhead of the network stack becomes significant.

Some NICs offer integrated field-programmable gate arrays (FPGAs) for user-programmable processing of network traffic before it reaches the host computer, allowing for significantly reduced latencies in time-sensitive workloads. Moreover, some NICs offer complete low-latency TCP/IP stacks running on integrated FPGAs in combination with userspace libraries that intercept networking operations usually performed by the operating system kernel; Solarflare's open-source OpenOnload network stack that runs on Linux is an example. This kind of functionality is usually referred to as user-level networking.

Repeaters and Hubs

A repeater is an electronic device that receives a network signal, cleans it of unnecessary noise and regenerates it. The signal may be reformed or retransmitted at a higher power level, to the other side of an obstruction possibly using a different transmission medium, so that the signal can cover longer distances without degradation. Commercial repeaters have extended RS-232 segments from 15 meters to over a kilometer. In most twisted pair Ethernet configurations, repeaters are required for cable that runs longer than 100 meters. With fiber optics, repeaters can be tens or even hundreds of kilometers apart.

Repeaters work within the physical layer of the OSI model, that is, there is no end-to-end change in the physical protocol across the repeater, or repeater pair, even if a different physical layer may be used between the ends of the repeater, or repeater pair. Repeaters require a small amount of time to regenerate the signal. This can cause a propagation delay that affects network performance and may affect proper function. As a result, many network architectures limit the number of repeaters that can be used in a row, e.g., the Ethernet 5-4-3 rule.

A repeater with multiple ports is known as hub, an Ethernet hub in Ethernet networks, a USB hub in USB networks.

- USB networks use hubs to form tiered-star topologies.

- Ethernet hubs and repeaters in LANs have been mostly obsoleted by modern switches.

Bridges

A network bridge is a computer networking device that creates a single aggregate network from multiple communication networks or network segments. This function is called network bridging. Bridging is distinct from routing. Routing allows multiple networks to communicate independently and yet remain separate, whereas bridging connects two separate networks as if they were a single network. In the OSI model, bridging is performed in the data link layer (layer 2). If one or more segments of the bridged network are wireless, the device is known as a wireless bridge.

There are three main types of network bridging technologies: simple bridging, multiport bridging, learning or transparent bridging.

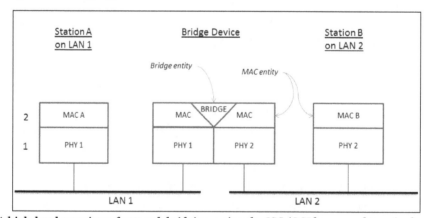

A high-level overview of network bridging, using the ISO/OSI layers and terminology.

Transparent Bridging

Transparent bridging uses a table called the forwarding information base to control the forwarding of frames between network segments. The table starts empty and entries are added as the bridge receives frames. If a destination address entry is not found in the table, the frame is flooded to all other ports of the bridge, flooding the frame to all segments except the one from which it was received. By means of these flooded frames, a host on the destination network will respond and a forwarding database entry will be created. Both source and destination addresses are used in this process: source addresses are recorded in entries in the table, while destination addresses are looked up in the table and matched to the proper segment to send the frame to. Digital Equipment Corporation (DEC) originally developed the technology in the 1980s.

In the context of a two-port bridge, one can think of the forwarding information base as a filtering database. A bridge reads a frame's destination address and decides to either forward or filter. If the bridge determines that the destination host is on another segment on the network, it forwards the frame to that segment. If the destination address belongs to the same segment as the source address, the bridge filters the frame, preventing it from reaching the other network where it is not needed.

Transparent bridging can also operate over devices with more than two ports. As an example, consider a bridge connected to three hosts, A, B, and C. The bridge has three ports. A is connected to bridge port 1, B is connected to bridge port 2, C is connected to bridge port 3. A sends a frame addressed to B to the bridge. The bridge examines the source address of the frame and creates an address and port number entry for A in its forwarding table. The bridge examines the destination address of the frame and does not find it in its forwarding table so it floods it to all other ports: 2 and 3. The frame is received by hosts B and C. Host C examines the destination address and ignores the frame. Host B recognizes a destination address match and generates a response to A. On the return path, the bridge adds an address and port number entry for B to its forwarding table. The bridge already has A's address in its forwarding table so it forwards the response only to port 1. Host C or any other hosts on port 3 are not burdened with the response. Two-way communication is now possible between A and B without any further flooding in network.

Simple Bridging

A simple bridge connects two network segments, typically by operating transparently and deciding on a frame-by-frame basis whether or not to forward from one network to the other. A store and forward technique is typically used so, as part of forwarding, the frame integrity is verified on the source network and CSMA/CD delays are accommodated on the destination network. In contrast to repeaters which simply extend the maximum span of a segment, bridges only forward frames that are required to cross the bridge. Additionally, bridges reduce collisions by creating a separate collision domain on either side of the bridge.

Multiport Bridging

A multiport bridge connects multiple networks and operates transparently to decide on a frame-by-frame basis whether to forward traffic. Additionally a multiport bridge must decide where to forward traffic. Like the simple bridge, a multiport bridge typically uses store and forward operation. The multiport bridge function serves as the basis for network switches.

Implementation

The forwarding information base stored in content-addressable memory (CAM) is initially empty. For each received ethernet frame the switch learns from the frame's source MAC address and adds this together with an ingress interface identifier to the forwarding information base. The switch then forwards the frame to the interface found in the CAM based on the frame's destination MAC address. If the destination address is unknown the switch sends the frame out on all interfaces (except the ingress interface). This behaviour is called unicast flooding.

Forwarding

Once a bridge learns the addresses of its connected nodes, it forwards data link layer frames using a layer-2 forwarding method. There are four forwarding methods a bridge can use, of which the second through fourth methods were performance-increasing methods when used on "switch" products with the same input and output port bandwidths:

1. Store and forward: The switch buffers and verifies each frame before forwarding it; a frame is received in its entirety before it is forwarded.

2. Cut through: The switch starts forwarding after the frame's destination address is received. There is no error checking with this method. When the outgoing port is busy at the time, the switch falls back to store-and-forward operation. Also, when the egress port is running at a faster data rate than the ingress port, store-and-forward is usually used.

3. Fragment free: A method that attempts to retain the benefits of both store and forward and cut through. Fragment free checks the first 64 bytes of the frame, where addressing information is stored. According to Ethernet specifications, collisions should be detected during the first 64 bytes of the frame, so frame transmissions that are aborted because of a collision will not be forwarded. Error checking of the actual data in the packet is left for the end device.

4. Adaptive switching: A method of automatically selecting between the other three modes.

Shortest Path Bridging

Shortest Path Bridging (SPB), specified in the IEEE 802.1aq standard, is a computer networking technology intended to simplify the creation and configuration of networks, while enabling multipath routing.

It is the replacement for the older spanning tree protocols: IEEE 802.1D, IEEE 802.1w, IEEE 802.1s. These blocked any redundant paths that could result in a layer 2 loop, whereas SPB allows all paths to be active with multiple equal cost paths, provides much larger layer 2 topologies, supports faster convergence times, and improves the efficiency by allowing traffic to load share across all paths of a mesh network. It is designed to virtually eliminate human error during configuration and preserves the plug-and-play nature that established Ethernet as the de facto protocol at layer 2.

The technology provides logical Ethernet networks on native Ethernet infrastructures using a link state protocol to advertise both topology and logical network membership. Packets are encapsulated at the edge either in media access control-in-media access control (MAC-in-MAC) 802.1ah or tagged 802.1Q/802.1ad frames and transported only to other members of the logical network. Unicast, multicast, and broadcast are supported and all routing is on symmetric shortest paths.

Switches

A network switch (also called switching hub, bridging hub, officially MAC bridge) is a computer networking device that connects devices on a computer network by using packet switching to receive, process, and forward data to the destination device.

A network switch is a multiport network bridge that uses hardware addresses to process and forward data at the data link layer (layer 2) of the OSI model. Some switches can also process data at the network layer (layer 3) by additionally incorporating routing functionality. Such switches are commonly known as layer-3 switches or multilayer switches.

Switches for Ethernet are the most common form of network switch. The first Ethernet switch was introduced by Kalpana in 1990. Switches also exist for other types of networks including Fibre Channel, Asynchronous Transfer Mode, and InfiniBand. Unlike less advanced repeater hubs, which broadcast the same data out of each of its ports and let the devices decide what data they need, a network switch forwards data only to the devices that need to receive it.

Avaya ERS 2550T-PWR, a 50-port Ethernet switch.

A switch is a device in a computer network that connects other devices together. Multiple data cables are plugged into a switch to enable communication between different networked devices. Switches manage the flow of data across a network by transmitting a received network packet only to the one or more devices for which the packet is intended. Each networked device connected to a switch can be identified by its network address, allowing the switch to direct the flow of traffic maximizing the security and efficiency of the network.

A switch is more intelligent than an Ethernet hub, which simply retransmits packets out of every port of the hub except the port on which the packet was received, unable to distinguish different recipients, and achieving an overall lower network efficiency.

An Ethernet switch operates at the data link layer (layer 2) of the OSI model to create a separate collision domain for each switch port. Each device connected to a switch port can transfer data to any of the other ports at any time and the transmissions will not interfere. Because broadcasts are still being forwarded to all connected devices by the switch, the newly formed network segment continues to be a broadcast domain. Switches may also operate at higher layers of the OSI model, including the network layer and above. A device that also operates at these higher layers is known as a multilayer switch.

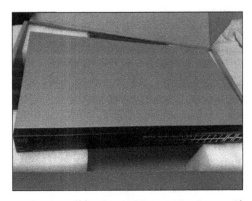 

Cisco small business SG300-28 28-port Gigabit Ethernet rackmount switch and its internals.

Segmentation involves the use of a switch to split a larger collision domain into smaller ones in order to reduce collision probability, and to improve overall network throughput. In the extreme case (i.e. micro-segmentation), each device is located on a dedicated switch port. In contrast to an Ethernet hub, there is a separate collision domain on each of the switch ports. This allows computers to have dedicated bandwidth on point-to-point connections to the network and also to run in full-duplex mode. Full-duplex mode has only one transmitter and one receiver per collision domain, making collisions impossible.

The network switch plays an integral role in most modern Ethernet local area networks (LANs). Mid-to-large sized LANs contain a number of linked managed switches. Small office/home office (SOHO) applications typically use a single switch, or an all-purpose device such as a residential gateway to access small office/home broadband services such as DSL or cable Internet. In most of these cases, the end-user device contains a router and components that interface to the particular physical broadband technology. User devices may also include a telephone interface for Voice over IP (VoIP).

Role in a Network

Switches are most commonly used as the network connection point for hosts at the edge of a network. In the hierarchical internetworking model and similar network architectures, switches are also used deeper in the network to provide connections between the switches at the edge.

In switches intended for commercial use, built-in or modular interfaces make it possible to connect different types of networks, including Ethernet, Fibre Channel, RapidIO, ATM, ITU-T G.hn and 802.11. This connectivity can be at any of the layers mentioned. While the layer-2 functionality is adequate for bandwidth-shifting within one technology, interconnecting technologies such as Ethernet and token ring is performed more easily at layer 3 or via routing. Devices that interconnect at the layer 3 are traditionally called routers, so layer 3 switches can also be regarded as relatively primitive and specialized routers.

Where there is a need for a great deal of analysis of network performance and security, switches may be connected between WAN routers as places for analytic modules. Some vendors provide firewall, network intrusion detection, and performance analysis modules that can plug into switch ports. Some of these functions may be on combined modules.

Through port mirroring, a switch can create a mirror image of data that can go to an external device such as intrusion detection systems and packet sniffers.

A modern switch may implement power over Ethernet (PoE), which avoids the need for attached devices, such as a VoIP phone or wireless access point, to have a separate power supply. Since switches can have redundant power circuits connected to uninterruptible power supplies, the connected device can continue operating even when regular office power fails.

Layer-specific Functionality

Modern commercial switches use primarily Ethernet interfaces. The core function of an Ethernet switch is to provide a multiport layer 2 bridging function. Many switches also perform operations at other layers. A device capable of more than bridging is known as a multilayer switch. Switches may learn about topologies at many layers and forward at one or more layers.

A modular network switch with three network modules
(a total of 24 Ethernet and 14 Fast Ethernet ports) and one power supply.

Layer 1

A layer 1 network device transfers data, but does not manage any of the traffic coming through it, an example is Ethernet hub. Any packet entering a port is repeated to the output of every other port except for the port of entry. Specifically, each bit or symbol is repeated as it flows in. A repeater hub can therefore only receive and forward at a single speed. Since every packet is repeated on every other port, packet collisions affect the entire network, limiting its overall capacity.

By the early 2000s, there was little price difference between a hub and a low-end switch. Hubs remained useful for a time for specialized applications, such supplying a copy of network traffic to a packet analyzer. A network tap may also be used for this purpose and many network switches now have a port mirroring feature that provides the same functionality.

Layer 2

Layer 2 switch without management functionality and 5 ports.

A layer 2 network device is a multiport device that uses hardware addresses, MAC address, to process and forward data at the data link layer (layer 2).

A switch operating as a network bridge may interconnect devices in a home or office. The bridge learns the MAC address of each connected device. Bridges also buffer an incoming packet and adapt the transmission speed to that of the outgoing port. While there are specialized applications, such as storage area networks, where the input and output interfaces are the same bandwidth, this is not always the case in general LAN applications. In LANs, a switch used for end user access typically concentrates lower bandwidth and uplinks into a higher bandwidth.

Interconnect between switches may be regulated using spanning tree protocol (STP) that disables links so that the resulting local area network is a tree without loops. In contrast to routers, spanning tree bridges must have topologies with only one active path between two points. Shortest path bridging is a layer 2 alternative to STP allows all paths to be active with multiple equal cost paths.

Layer 3

A layer-3 switch can perform some or all of the functions normally performed by a router. Most network switches, however, are limited to supporting a single type of physical network, typically Ethernet, whereas a router may support different kinds of physical networks on different ports.

A common layer-3 capability is awareness of IP multicast through IGMP snooping. With this awareness, a layer-3 switch can increase efficiency by delivering the traffic of a multicast group only to ports where the attached device has signalled that it wants to listen to that group.

Layer-3 switches typically support IP routing between VLANs configured on the switch. Some layer-3 switches support the routing protocols that routers use to exchange information about routes between networks.

Layer 4

While the exact meaning of the term layer-4 switch is vendor-dependent, it almost always starts with a capability for network address translation, and may add some type of load distribution based on TCP sessions or advanced QoS capabilities. The device may include a stateful firewall, a VPN concentrator, or be an IPSec security gateway.

Layer 7

Layer-7 switches may distribute the load based on uniform resource locators (URLs), or by using some installation-specific technique to recognize application-level transactions. A layer-7 switch may include a web cache and participate in a content delivery network (CDN).

Types

Form Factors

A rack-mounted 24-port 3Com switch.

Switches are available in many form factors, including stand-alone, desktop units which are typically intended to be used in a home or office environment outside a wiring closet; rack-mounted switches for use in an equipment rack or an enclosure; DIN rail mounted for use in industrial environments; and small installation switches, mounted into a cable duct, floor box or communications tower, as found, for example, in fibre to the office infrastructures.

Rack-mounted switches may be standalone units, stackable switches or large chassis units with swappable line cards.

Configuration Options

- Unmanaged switches have no configuration interface or options. They are plug and play. They are typically the least expensive switches, and therefore often used in a small office/ home office environment. Unmanaged switches can be desktop or rack mounted.

- Managed switches have one or more methods to modify the operation of the switch. Common management methods include: a command-line interface (CLI) accessed via serial console, telnet or Secure Shell, an embedded Simple Network Management Protocol (SNMP) agent allowing management from a remote console or management station, or a web interface for management from a web browser. Examples of configuration changes that one can do from a managed switch include: enabling features such as Spanning Tree Protocol or port mirroring, setting port bandwidth, creating or modifying virtual LANs (VLANs), etc. Two sub-classes of managed switches are smart and enterprise managed switches.

- Smart switches (aka intelligent switches) are managed switches with a limited set of management features. Likewise "web-managed" switches are switches which fall into a market niche between unmanaged and managed. For a price much lower than a fully managed switch they provide a web interface (and usually no CLI access) and allow configuration of basic settings, such as VLANs, port-bandwidth and duplex.

- Enterprise managed switches (aka managed switches) have a full set of management features, including CLI, SNMP agent, and web interface. They may have additional features to manipulate configurations, such as the ability to display, modify, backup and restore configurations. Compared with smart switches, enterprise switches have more features that can be customized or optimized, and are generally more expensive than smart switches. Enterprise switches are typically found in networks with larger number of switches and connections, where centralized management is a significant savings in administrative time and effort. A stackable switch is a version of enterprise-managed switch.

Typical Management Features

A couple of managed D-Link Gigabit Ethernet rackmount switches, connected to the Ethernet ports on a few patch panels using Category 6 patch cables (all equipment is installed in a standard 19-inch rack):

- Enable and disable ports.

- Link bandwidth and duplex settings.

- Quality of service configuration and monitoring.

- MAC filtering and other access control list features.

- Configuration of Spanning Tree Protocol (STP) and Shortest Path Bridging (SPB) features.

- Simple Network Management Protocol (SNMP) monitoring of device and link health.

- Port mirroring for monitoring traffic and troubleshooting.

- Link aggregation configuration to set up multiple ports for the same connection to achieve higher data transfer rates and reliability.

- VLAN configuration and port assignments including IEEE 802.1Q tagging.

- Network Access Control features such as IEEE 802.1X.

- IGMP snooping for control of multicast traffic.

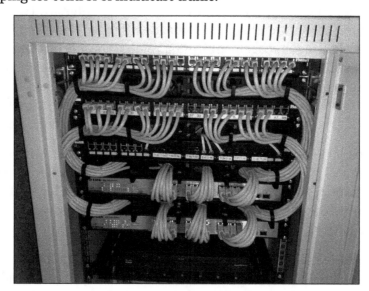

Traffic Monitoring

It is difficult to monitor traffic that is bridged using a switch because only the sending and receiving ports can see the traffic.

Methods that are specifically designed to allow a network analyst to monitor traffic include:

- Port mirroring– The switch sends a copy of network packets to a monitoring network connection.

- SMON– "Switch Monitoring" is described by RFC 2613 and is a protocol for controlling facilities such as port mirroring.

- RMON.

- sFlow.

These monitoring features are rarely present on consumer-grade switches. Other monitoring methods include connecting a layer-1 hub or network tap between the monitored device and its switch port.

Routers

A router is a networking device that forwards data packets between computer networks. Routers perform the traffic directing functions on the Internet. Data sent through the internet, such as a web page or email, is in the form of data packets. A packet is typically forwarded from one router to another router through the networks that constitute an internetwork (e.g. the Internet) until it reaches its destination node.

A router is connected to two or more data lines from different networks. When a data packet comes in on one of the lines, the router reads the network address information in the packet to determine the ultimate destination. Then, using information in its routing table or routing policy, it directs the packet to the next network on its journey.

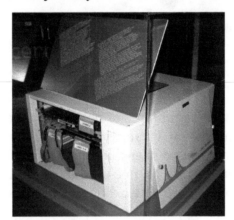

A ASM/2-32EM router deployed at CERN in 1987.

The most familiar type of routers are home and small office routers that simply forward IP packets between the home computers and the Internet. An example of a router would be the owner's cable or DSL router, which connects to the Internet through an Internet service provider (ISP). More sophisticated routers, such as enterprise routers, connect large business or ISP networks up to the powerful core routers that forward data at high speed along the optical fiber lines of the Internet backbone. Though routers are typically dedicated hardware devices, software-based routers also exist.

Operation

When multiple routers are used in interconnected networks, the routers can exchange information about destination addresses using a routing protocol. Each router builds up a routing table listing the preferred routes between any two systems on the interconnected networks.

A router has two types of network element components organized onto separate planes:

- Control plane: A router maintains a routing table that lists which route should be used to forward a data packet, and through which physical interface connection. It does this using internal preconfigured directives, called static routes, or by learning routes dynamically using a routing protocol. Static and dynamic routes are stored in the routing table. The control-plane logic then strips non-essential directives from the table and builds a forwarding information base (FIB) to be used by the forwarding plane.

- Forwarding plane: The router forwards data packets between incoming and outgoing interface connections. It forwards them to the correct network type using information that the packet header contains matched to entries in the FIB supplied by the control plane.

Applications

A typical home or small office DSL router showing the telephone socket (left, white) to connect it to the internet using ADSL, and Ethernet jacks (right, yellow) to connect it to home computers and printers.

A router may have interfaces for different types of physical layer connections, such as copper cables, fiber optic, or wireless transmission. It can also support different network layer transmission standards. Each network interface is used to enable data packets to be forwarded from one transmission system to another. Routers may also be used to connect two or more logical groups of computer devices known as subnets, each with a different network prefix.

Routers may provide connectivity within enterprises, between enterprises and the Internet, or between internet service providers' (ISPs') networks. The largest routers (such as the Cisco CRS-1 or Juniper PTX) interconnect the various ISPs, or may be used in large enterprise networks. Smaller routers usually provide connectivity for typical home and office networks.

All sizes of routers may be found inside enterprises. The most powerful routers are usually found in ISPs, academic and research facilities. Large businesses may also need more powerful routers to cope with ever-increasing demands of intranet data traffic. A hierarchical internetworking model for interconnecting routers in large networks is in common use.

Access, Core and Distribution

Access routers, including small office/home office (SOHO) models, are located at home and customer sites such as branch offices that do not need hierarchical routing of their own. Typically, they are optimized for low cost. Some SOHO routers are capable of running alternative free Linux-based firmware like Tomato, OpenWrt or DD-WRT.

Distribution routers aggregate traffic from multiple access routers. Distribution routers are often responsible for enforcing quality of service across a wide area network (WAN), so they may have considerable memory installed, multiple WAN interface connections, and substantial onboard data processing routines. They may also provide connectivity to groups of file servers or other external networks.

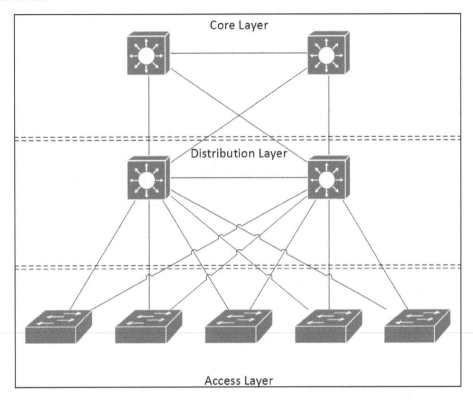

In enterprises, a core router may provide a collapsed backbone interconnecting the distribution tier routers from multiple buildings of a campus, or large enterprise locations. They tend to be optimized for high bandwidth, but lack some of the features of edge routers.

Security

External networks must be carefully considered as part of the overall security strategy of the local network. A router may include a firewall, VPN handling, and other security functions, or these may be handled by separate devices. Routers also commonly perform network address translation which restricts connections initiated from external connections but is not recognised as a security feature by all experts. Some experts argue that open source routers are more secure and reliable than closed source routers because open source routers allow mistakes to be quickly found and corrected.

Routing Different Networks

Routers are also often distinguished on the basis of the network in which they operate. A router in a local area network (LAN) of a single organisation is called an interior router. A router that is operated in the Internet backbone is described as exterior router. While a router that connects a LAN with the Internet or a wide area network (WAN) is called a border router, or gateway router.

Internet Connectivity and Internal Use

Routers intended for ISP and major enterprise connectivity usually exchange routing information using the Border Gateway Protocol (BGP). RFC 4098 defines the types of BGP routers according to their functions:

- Edge router: Also called a provider edge router, is placed at the edge of an ISP network. The router uses External Border Gateway Protocol to routers at other ISPs or large enterprise autonomous systems.

- Subscriber edge router: Also called a Customer Edge router, is located at the edge of the subscriber's network, it also uses EBGP to its provider's Autonomous System. It is typically used in an (enterprise) organization.

- Inter-provider border router: Interconnecting ISPs, is a BGP router that maintains BGP sessions with other BGP routers in ISP Autonomous Systems.

- Core router: A *core router* resides within an Autonomous System as a back bone to carry traffic between edge routers.

- Within an ISP: In the ISP's Autonomous System, a router uses internal BGP to communicate with other ISP edge routers, other intranet core routers, or the ISP's intranet provider border routers.

- Internet backbone: The Internet no longer has a clearly identifiable backbone, unlike its predecessor networks. The major ISPs' system routers make up what could be considered to be the current Internet backbone core. ISPs operate all four types of the BGP routers described here. An ISP "core" router is used to interconnect its edge and border routers. Core routers may also have specialized functions in virtual private networks based on a combination of BGP and Multi-Protocol Label Switching protocols.

- Port forwarding: Routers are also used for port forwarding between private Internet-connected servers.

- Voice/Data/Fax/Video Processing Routers: Commonly referred to as access servers or gateways, these devices are used to route and process voice, data, video and fax traffic on the Internet. Since 2005, most long-distance phone calls have been processed as IP traffic (VOIP) through a voice gateway. Use of access server type routers expanded with the advent of the Internet, first with dial-up access and another resurgence with voice phone service.

- Larger networks commonly use multilayer switches, with layer 3 devices being used to simply interconnect multiple subnets within the same security zone, and higher layer switches when filtering, translation, load balancing or other higher level functions are required, especially between zones.

Forwarding

The main purpose of a router is to connect multiple networks and forward packets destined either for its own networks or other networks. A router is considered a layer-3 device because its primary forwarding decision is based on the information in the layer-3 IP packet, specifically the destination IP address. When a router receives a packet, it searches its routing table to find the best match between the destination IP address of the packet and one of the addresses in the routing table.

Once a match is found, the packet is encapsulated in the layer-2 data link frame for the outgoing interface indicated in the table entry. A router typically does not look into the packet payload, but only at the layer-3 addresses to make a forwarding decision, plus optionally other information in the header for hints on, for example, quality of service (QoS). For pure IP forwarding, a router is designed to minimize the state information associated with individual packets. Once a packet is forwarded, the router does not retain any historical information about the packet.

The routing table itself can contain information derived from a variety of sources, such as a default or static routes that are configured manually, or dynamic routing protocols where the router learns routes from other routers. A default route is one that is used to route all traffic whose destination does not otherwise appear in the routing table; this is common – even necessary – in small networks, such as a home or small business where the default route simply sends all non-local traffic to the Internet service provider. The default route can be manually configured (as a static route), or learned by dynamic routing protocols, or be obtained by DHCP.

A router can run more than one routing protocol at a time, particularly if it serves as an autonomous system border router between parts of a network that run different routing protocols; if it does so, then redistribution may be used (usually selectively) to share information between the different protocols running on the same router.

Besides making a decision as to which interface a packet is forwarded to, which is handled primarily via the routing table, a router also has to manage congestion when packets arrive at a rate higher than the router can process. Three policies commonly used in the Internet are tail drop, random early detection (RED), and weighted random early detection (WRED). Tail drop is the simplest and most easily implemented; the router simply drops new incoming packets once the length of the queue exceeds the size of the buffers in the router. RED probabilistically drops datagrams early when the queue exceeds a pre-configured portion of the buffer, until a pre-determined max, when it becomes tail drop. WRED requires a weight on the average queue size to act upon when the traffic is about to exceed the pre-configured size, so that short bursts will not trigger random drops.

Another function a router performs is to decide which packet should be processed first when multiple queues exist. This is managed through QoS, which is critical when Voice over IP is deployed, so as not to introduce excessive latency.

Yet another function a router performs is called policy-based routing where special rules are constructed to override the rules derived from the routing table when a packet forwarding decision is made.

Router functions may be performed through the same internal paths that the packets travel inside the router. Some of the functions may be performed through an application-specific integrated circuit (ASIC) to avoid overhead of scheduling CPU time to process the packets. Others may have to be performed through the CPU as these packets need special attention that cannot be handled by an ASIC.

Modems

A modem (portmanteau of modulator-demodulator) is a hardware device that converts data into a format suitable for a transmission medium so that it can be transmitted from computer to computer (historically over telephone wires). A modem modulates one or more carrier wave signals to encode digital information for transmission and demodulates signals to decode the transmitted information. The goal is to produce a signal that can be transmitted easily and decoded to reproduce the original digital data. Modems can be used with almost any means of transmitting analog signals from light-emitting diodes to radio. A common type of modem is one that turns the digital data of a computer into modulated electrical signal for transmission over telephone lines and demodulated by another modem at the receiver side to recover the digital data.

Modems are generally classified by the maximum amount of data they can send in a given unit of time, usually expressed in bits per second (symbol bit(s), sometimes abbreviated "bps") or bytes per second (symbol B(s)). Modems can also be classified by their symbol rate, measured in baud. The baud unit denotes symbols per second, or the number of times per second the modem sends a new signal. For example, the ITU V.21 standard used audio frequency-shift keying with two possible frequencies, corresponding to two distinct symbols (or one bit per symbol), to carry 300 bits per second using 300 baud. By contrast, the original ITU V.22 standard, which could transmit and receive four distinct symbols (two bits per symbol), transmitted 1,200 bits by sending 600 symbols per second (600 baud) using phase-shift keying.

Acoustic coupler modem.

Dial-up Modem

TeleGuide terminal.

News wire services in the 1920s used multiplex devices that satisfied the definition of a modem. However, the modem function was incidental to the multiplexing function, so they are not commonly included in the history of modems. Modems grew out of the need to connect teleprinters over ordinary phone lines instead of the more expensive leased lines which had previously been used for current loop–based teleprinters and automated telegraphs.

In 1941, the Allies developed a voice encryption system called SIGSALY which used a vocoder to digitize speech, then encrypted the speech with one-time pad and encoded the digital data as tones using frequency shift keying.

Mass-produced modems in the United States began as part of the SAGE air-defense system in 1958 (the year the word modem was first used), connecting terminals at various airbases, radar sites, and command-and-control centers to the SAGE director centers scattered around the United States and Canada. SAGE modems were described by AT&T's Bell Labs as conforming to their newly published Bell 101 dataset standard. While they ran on dedicated telephone lines, the devices at each end were no different from commercial acoustically coupled Bell 101, 110 baud modems.

The 201A and 201B Data-Phones were synchronous modems using two-bit-per-baud phase-shift keying (PSK). The 201A operated half-duplex at 2,000 bit/s over normal phone lines, while the 201B provided full duplex 2,400 bit/s service on four-wire leased lines, the send and receive channels each running on their own set of two wires.

The famous Bell 103A dataset standard was also introduced by AT&T in 1962. It provided full-duplex service at 300 bit/s over normal phone lines. Frequency-shift keying was used, with the call originator transmitting at 1,070 or 1,270 Hz and the answering modem transmitting at 2,025 or 2,225 Hz. The readily available 103A2 gave an important boost to the use of remote low-speed terminals such as the Teletype Model 33 ASR and KSR, and the IBM 2741. AT&T reduced modem costs by introducing the originate-only 113D and the answer-only 113B/C modems.

Acoustic Couplers

The Novation CAT acoustically coupled modem.

For many years, the Bell System (AT&T) maintained a monopoly on the use of its phone lines and what devices could be connected to them. However, the FCC's seminal Carterfone Decision of 1968, the FCC concluded that electronic devices could be connected to the telephone system as long as they used an acoustic coupler. Since most handsets were supplied by Western Electric and thus of a standard design, acoustic couplers were relatively easy to build. Acoustically coupled Bell 103A-compatible 300 bit/s modems were common during the 1970s. Well-known models included the Novation CAT and the Anderson-Jacobson, the latter spun off from an in-house project at Stanford Research Institute (now SRI International). An even lower-cost option was the Pennywhistle modem, designed to be built using parts from electronics scrap and surplus stores.

In December 1972, Vadic introduced the VA3400, notable for full-duplex operation at 1,200 bit/s over the phone network. Like the 103A, it used different frequency bands for transmit and receive. In November 1976, AT&T introduced the 212A modem to compete with Vadic. It was similar in design, but used the lower frequency set for transmission. One could also use the 212A with a 103A modem at 300 bit/s. According to Vadic, the change in frequency assignments made the 212 intentionally incompatible with acoustic coupling, thereby locking out many potential modem manufacturers. In 1977, Vadic responded with the VA3467 triple modem, an answer-only modem sold to computer center operators that supported Vadic's 1,200-bit/s mode, AT&T's 212A mode, and 103A operation.

Carterfone and Direct Connection

The Hush-a-Phone decision applied only to mechanical connections, but the Carterfone decision of 1968, led to the FCC introducing a rule setting stringent AT&T designed tests for electronically coupling a device to the phone lines. This opened the door to direct-connect modems that plugged directly into the phone line rather than via a handset. However, the cost of passing the tests was considerable, and acoustically coupled modems remained common into the early 1980s.

The rapidly falling prices of electronics in the late 1970s led to an increasing number of direct-connect models around 1980. In spite of being directly connected, these modems were generally operated like their earlier acoustic versions – dialing and other phone-control operations were completed by hand, using an attached handset. A small number of modems added the ability to automatically answer incoming calls, or automatically place an outgoing call to a single number, but even these limited features were relatively rare or limited to special models in a lineup. When more flexible solutions were needed, third party "dialers" were used to automate calling, normally using a separate serial port to communicate with the dialer, which would then control the modem through a private electrical connection.

The introduction of microcomputer systems with internal expansion slots made the first software-controllable modems common. Slot connections gave the computer complete access to the modem's memory or input/output (I/O) channels, which allowed software to send commands to the modem, not just data. This led to a series of popular modems for the S-100 bus and Apple II computers that could directly dial the phone, answer incoming calls, and hang up the phone, the basic requirements of a bulletin board system (BBS). The seminal CBBS was created on an S-100 machine with a Hayes internal modem, and a number of similar systems followed.

Smartmodem and the Rise of BBSs

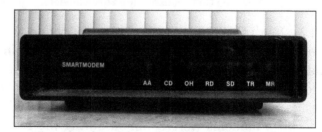

The original model 300-baud Hayes Smartmodem.

In later years, USRobotics Courier modems were common at many
BBSes because they had better compatibility with more brands of modems.

The next major advance in modems was the Hayes Smartmodem, introduced in 1981. The Smart-modem was an otherwise standard 103A 300 bit/s direct-connect modem, but it was attached to a small microcontroller that watched the data stream for certain character strings representing commands. This allowed both data and commands to be sent through a single serial port. The now-standard Hayes command set included instructions for picking up and hanging up the phone, dialing numbers, and answering calls, among others. This was similar to the commands offered by the internal modems, but unlike them, the Smartmodem could be connected to any computer with an RS-232 port, which was practically every microcomputer built.

The introduction of the Smartmodem made communications much simpler and more easily accessed. This provided a growing market for other vendors, who licensed the Hayes patents and competed on price or by adding features. Through the 1980s, a number of new higher-speed modems, first 1,200 and then 2,400 bit/s, greatly improved the responsiveness of the online systems, and made file transfer practical. This led to rapid growth of online services with their large file libraries, which in turn gave more reason to own a modem. The rapid update of modems led to a similar rapid increase in BBS use, which was helped by the fact that BBSs could control the modem simply by sending strings, rather than talking to a device driver that was different for every direct-connect modem.

1200 and 2400 Bit/s

The 300 bit/s modems used audio frequency-shift keying to send data. In this system, the stream of 1s and 0s in computer data is translated into sounds which can be easily sent on the phone lines. In the Bell 103 system, the originating modem sends 0s by playing a 1,070 Hz tone, and 1s at 1,270 Hz, with the answering modem transmitting its 0s on 2,025 Hz and 1s on 2,225 Hz. These frequencies were chosen carefully; they are in the range that suffers minimum distortion on the phone system and are not harmonics of each other.

In the 1,200 bit/s and faster systems, phase-shift keying was used. In this system the two tones for any one side of the connection are sent at similar frequencies as in the 300 bit/s systems, but slightly out of phase. Voiceband modems generally remained at 300 and 1,200 bit/s (V.21 and V.22) into the mid-1980s. A V.22bis 2,400-bit/s system similar in concept to the 1,200-bit/s Bell 212 signaling was introduced in the U.S., and a slightly different one in Europe. The limited available frequency range meant the symbol rate of 1,200 bit/s modems was still only 600 baud (symbols per second). The bit rate increases were achieved by defining four or eight distinct symbols, which allowed the encoding of two or three bits per symbol instead of only 1. The use of smaller shifts had the drawback of making each symbol more vulnerable to interference, but improvements in phone line quality at the same time helped compensate for this. By the late 1980s, most modems could support all of these standards and 2,400-bit/s operation was becoming common.

Proprietary Standards

Many other standards were also introduced for special purposes, commonly using a high-speed channel for receiving, and a lower-speed channel for sending. One typical example was used in the French Minitel system, in which the user's terminals spent the majority of their time receiving information. The modem in the Minitel terminal thus operated at 1,200 bit/s for reception, and 75 bit/s for sending commands back to the servers.

Three U.S. companies became famous for high-speed versions of the same concept. Telebit introduced its Trailblazer modem in 1984, which used a large number of 36 bit/s channels to send data one-way at rates up to 18,432 bit/s. A single additional channel in the reverse direction allowed the two modems to communicate how much data was waiting at either end of the link, and the modems could change direction on the fly. The Trailblazer modems also supported a feature that allowed them to spoof the UUCP g protocol, commonly used on Unix systems to send e-mail, and thereby speed UUCP up by a tremendous amount. Trailblazers thus became extremely common on Unix systems, and maintained their dominance in this market well into the 1990s.

USRobotics (USR) introduced a similar system, known as HST, although this supplied only 9,600 bit/s (in early versions at least) and provided for a larger backchannel. Rather than offer spoofing, USR instead created a large market among FidoNet users by offering its modems to BBS sysops at a much lower price, resulting in sales to end users who wanted faster file transfers. Hayes was forced to compete, and introduced its own 9,600 bit/s standard, Express 96 (also known as Ping-Pong), which was generally similar to Telebit's PEP. Hayes, however, offered neither protocol spoofing nor sysop discounts, and its high-speed modems remained rare.

A common feature of these high-speed modems was the concept of fallback, or speed hunting, allowing them to communicate with less-capable modems. During the call initiation, the modem would transmit a series of signals and wait for the remote modem to respond. They would start at high speeds and get progressively slower until there was a response. Thus, two USR modems would be able to connect at 9,600 bit/s, but, when a user with a 2,400 bit/s modem called in, the USR would fall back to the common 2,400 bit/s speed. This would also happen if a V.32 modem and a HST modem were connected. Because they used a different standard at 9,600 bit/s, they would fall back to their highest commonly supported standard at 2,400 bit/s. The same applies to V.32bis and 14,400 bit/s HST modem, which would still be able to communicate with each other at 2,400 bit/s.

Echo Cancellation

Fax modem.

Echo cancellation was the next major advance in modem design. Local telephone lines use the same wires to send and receive data, which results in a small amount of the outgoing signal being reflected back. This is useful for people talking on the phone, as it provides a signal to the speaker that their voice is making it through the system. However, this reflected signal causes problems for the modem, which is unable to distinguish between a signal from the remote modem and the echo of its own signal. This was why earlier modems split the signal frequencies into "answer" and "originate"; the modem could then ignore any signals in the frequency range it was using for transmission. Even with improvements to the phone system allowing higher speeds, this splitting of available phone signal bandwidth still imposed a half-speed limit on modems.

Echo cancellation eliminated this problem. During the call setup and negotiation period, both modems send a series of unique tones and then listen for them to return through the phone system. They measure the total delay time and then set up a local delay loop to the same time. Once the connection is completed, they send their signals into the phone lines as normal, but also into the delay, which is inverted. The signal returning through the echo meets the inverted version coming from the delay line, and cancels out the echo. This allowed both modems to use the full spectrum available, doubling the speed.

Additional improvements were introduced via the quadrature amplitude modulation (QAM) encoding system. Previous systems using phase shift keying (PSK) encoded two bits (or sometimes three) per symbol by slightly delaying or advancing the signal's phase relative to a set carrier tone. QAM used a combination of phase shift and amplitude to encode four bits per symbol. Transmitting at 1,200 baud produced the 4,800 bit/s V.27ter standard, the same working at a base rate of 2,400 baud produced the 9,600 bit/s V.32. The carrier frequency was 1,650 Hz in both systems. For many years, most engineers considered this rate to be the limit of data communications over telephone networks.

The introduction of these higher-speed systems also led to the digital fax machine during the 1980s. Digital faxes are simply an image format sent over a high-speed (commonly 14.4 kbit/s) modem. Software running on the host computer can convert any image into fax format, which can then be sent using the modem. Such software was at one time an add-on, but has since become largely universal.

Breaking the 9.6 kbit/s Barrier

The first 9,600 bit/s modem was developed in 1968, and sold for more than $20,000, but had high error rates.

In 1980, Gottfried Ungerboeck from IBM Zurich Research Laboratory applied channel coding techniques to search for new ways to increase the speed of modems. His results were astonishing but only conveyed to a few colleagues. In 1982, he agreed to publish what is now a landmark paper in the theory of information coding. By applying parity check coding to the bits in each symbol, and mapping the encoded bits into a two-dimensional diamond pattern, Ungerboeck showed that it was possible to increase the speed by a factor of two with the same error rate. The new technique was called mapping by set partitions, now known as trellis modulation.

Error correcting codes, which encode code words (sets of bits) in such a way that they are far from each other, so that in case of error they are still closest to the original word (and not confused with another) can be thought of as analogous to sphere packing or packing pennies on a surface: the further two bit sequences are from one another, the easier it is to correct minor errors.

Dave Forney introduced the trellis diagram in a landmark 1973 paper that popularized the Viterbi algorithm. Practically all modems operating faster than 9600 bit/s decode trellis-modulated data using the Viterbi algorithm.

V.32 modems operating at 9600 bit/s were expensive and were only starting to enter the market in the early 1990s when V.32bis was standardized. Rockwell International's chip division developed a new driver chip set incorporating the standard and aggressively priced it. Supra, Inc. arranged a short-term exclusivity arrangement with Rockwell, and developed the SupraFAXModem 14400 based on it. Introduced in January 1992 at $399 (or less), it was half the price of the slower V.32 modems already on the market. This led to a price war, and by the end of the year V.32 was dead, never having been really established, and V.32bis modems were widely available for $250.

V.32bis was so successful that the older high-speed standards had little to recommend them. USR fought back with a 16,800 bit/s version of HST, while AT&T introduced a one-off 19,200 bit/s method they referred to as V.32ter, but neither non-standard modem sold well.

V.34/28.8 kbit/s and 33.6 kbit/s

V.34 modem in the shape of an internal ISA card.

V.34 data/fax modem as PC card for notebooks.

Any interest in these proprietary improvements was destroyed during the lengthy introduction of the 28,800 bit/s V.34 standard. While waiting, several companies decided to release hardware and introduced modems they referred to as V.FAST. In order to guarantee compatibility with V.34 modems once the standard was ratified (1994), the manufacturers were forced to use more flexible parts, generally a DSP and microcontroller, as opposed to purpose-designed ASIC modem chips.

The ITU standard V.34 represents the culmination of the joint efforts. It employs the most powerful coding techniques including channel encoding and shape encoding. From the mere four bits per symbol (9.6 kbit/s), the new standards used the functional equivalent of 6 to 10 bits per symbol, plus increasing baud rates from 2,400 to 3,429, to create 14.4, 28.8, and 33.6 kbit/s modems. This rate is near the theoretical Shannon limit. When calculated, the Shannon capacity of a narrowband line is $\text{bandwidth} \times \log_2(1 + P_u / P_n)$, with P_u / P_n the (linear) signal-to-noise ratio. Narrowband phone lines have a bandwidth of 3,000 Hz so using $P_u / P_n = 1000$ (SNR = 30 dB), the capacity is approximately 30 kbit/s.

Using Digital Lines and PCM

Modem bank at an ISP.

During the late 1990s, Rockwell-Lucent and USRobotics introduced competing technologies based upon the digital transmission used in telephony networks. The standard digital transmission in modern networks is 64 kbit/s but some networks use a part of the bandwidth for remote office sig-naling (e.g. to hang up the phone), limiting the effective rate to 56 kbit/s DS0. This new technology was adopted into ITU standards V.90 and is common in modern computers. The 56 kbit/s rate is only possible from the central office to the user site (downlink). In the United States, government regulation limits the maximum power output, resulting in a maximum data rate of 53.3 kbit/s. The uplink (from the user to the central office) still uses V.34 technology at 33.6 kbit/s. USRobotics be-gan work on the technology first, calling theirs X2 because 56k was twice the speed of 28k modems. USRobotics held a 40-percent share of the retail modem market, and Rockwell International held an 80-percent share of the modem chipset market. Concerned with being shut out of the market, Rockwell began work on a rival 56k technology and joined with Lucent and Motorola on what it called K56Flex or Flex. Both technologies reached the market around February 1997; although problems with K56Flex modems were noted in product reviews through July, within six months they worked equally well with variations dependent on local connection characteristics. The retail price of the 56K modems was about US$200, compared to $100 for 33K modems. Separate equip-ment was required by Internet service providers (ISPs) to support the incompatible technologies, with costs varying depending on whether their current equipment could be upgraded. About half of all ISPs offered 56K support by October 1997. Consumer sales were relatively low, which US-Robotics and Rockwell attributed to conflicting standards.

The International Telecommunication Union (ITU) announced the draft of a new 56 kbit/s stan-dard, V.90, in February 1998, with strong industry support. Incompatible with either existing standard, it was an amalgam of both which was designed to allow both types of modem to be converted to it by a firmware upgrade. This V.90 standard was approved in September 1998, and widely adopted by ISPs and consumers.

Later in V.92, the digital PCM technique was applied to increase the upload speed to a maximum of 48 kbit/s, but at the expense of download rates. A 48 kbit/s upstream rate would reduce the down-stream as low as 40 kbit/s due to echo on the telephone line. To avoid this problem, V.92 modems offer the option to turn off the digital upstream and instead use a 33.6 kbit/s analog connection, in order to maintain a high digital downstream of 50 kbit/s or higher. V.92 also adds two other features. The first is the ability for users who have call waiting to put their dial-up Internet connection on hold for extended periods of time while they answer a call. The second feature is the ability to quickly connect to one's ISP. This is achieved by remembering the analog and digital characteristics of the telephone line, and using this saved information when reconnecting.

Using Compression to Exceed 56 kbit/S

V.42, V.42bis and V.44 standards allow the modem to transmit data faster than its basic rate would imply. For instance, a 53.3 kbit/s connection with V.44 can transmit up to $53.3 \times 6 = 320$ kbit/s using pure text. However, the compression ratio tends to vary due to noise on the line, or due to the transfer of already-compressed files (ZIP files, JPEG images, MP3 audio, MPEG video). At some points the modem will be sending compressed files at approximately 50 kbit/s, uncompressed files at 160 kbit/s, and pure text at 320 kbit/s, or any value in between.

In such situations, a small amount of memory in the modem, a buffer, is used to hold the data while it is being compressed and sent across the phone line, but in order to prevent overflow of the buffer, it sometimes becomes necessary to tell the computer to pause the datastream. This is accomplished through hardware flow control using extra lines on the modem–computer connection. The computer is then set to supply the modem at some higher rate, such as 320 kbit/s, and the modem will tell the computer when to start or stop sending data.

Compression by the ISP

As telephone-based 56k modems began losing popularity, some Internet service providers such as Netzero/Juno, Netscape, and others started using pre-compression to increase the throughput and maintain their customer base. The server-side compression operates much more efficiently than the on-the-fly compression done by modems because these compression techniques are application-specific (JPEG, text, EXE, etc.). The website text, images, and Flash executables are compacted to approximately 4%, 12%, and 30%, respectively. The drawback of this approach is a loss in quality, which causes image content to become pixelated and smeared. ISPs employing this approach often advertise it as "accelerated dial-up".

These accelerated downloads are now integrated into the Opera and Amazon Silk web browsers, using their own server-side text and image compression.

Softmodem

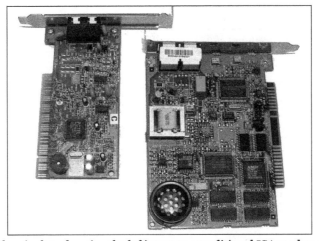

A PCI Winmodem/softmodem (on the left) next to a traditional ISA modem (on the right).

A Winmodem or SoftModem is a stripped-down modem that replaces tasks traditionally handled in hardware with software. In this case the modem is a simple interface and codec to code and decode the digital signal. Softmodems are cheaper than traditional modems because they have fewer hardware components. However, the software interpreting the modem tones to be sent to the softmodem uses some system resources. For online gaming, this can be a real concern. Another problem is the lack of cross-platform compatibility, meaning that non-Windows operating systems (such as Linux) often do not have an equivalent driver to operate the modem.

List of Dial-up Speeds

These values are maximum values, and actual values may be slower under certain conditions (for example, noisy phone lines). A baud is one symbol per second; each symbol may encode one or more data bits.

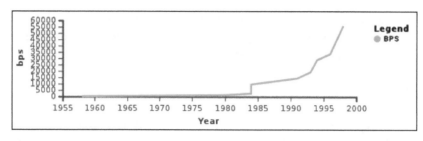

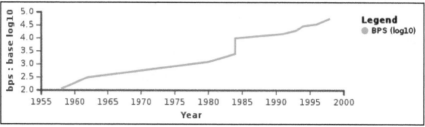

Connection	Modula-tion	Bitrate [kbit/s]	Year released
110 baud Bell 101 modem	FSK	0.1	1958
300 baud (Bell 103 or V.21)	FSK	0.3	1962
1200 modem (1200 baud) (Bell 202)	FSK	1.2	
1200 modem (600 baud) (Bell 212A or V.22)	QPSK	1.2	1980
2400 modem (600 baud) (V.22bis)	QAM	2.4	1984
2400 modem (1200 baud) (V.26bis)	PSK	2.4	
4800 modem (1600 baud) (V.27ter)	PSK	4.8	
9600 modem (2400 baud) (V.32)	QAM	9.6	1984
14.4k modem (2400 baud) (V.32bis)	trellis	14.4	1991
19.2k modem (2400 baud) (V.32terbo)	trellis	19.2	1993
28.8k modem (3200 baud) (V.34)	trellis	28.8	1994
33.6k modem (3429 baud) (V.34)	trellis	33.6	1996
56k modem (8000/3429 baud) (V.90)	digital	56.0/33.6	1998
56k modem (8000/8000 baud) (V.92)	digital	56.0/48.0	2000
Bonding modem (two 56k modems) (V.92)		112.0/96.0	
Hardware compression (variable) (V.90/V.42bis)		56.0–220.0	
Hardware compression (variable) (V.92/V.44)		56.0–320.0	
Server-side web compression (variable) (Netscape ISP)		100.0–1,000.0	

Popularity

A 1994 Software Publishers Association found that although 60% of computers in US households had a modem, only 7% of households went online. A CEA study in 2006 found that dial-up Internet access is declining in the U.S. In 2000, dial-up Internet connections accounted for 74% of all U.S. residential Internet connections. The United States demographic pattern for dial-up modem users per capita has been more or less mirrored in Canada and Australia for the past 20 years.

Dial-up modem use in the U.S. had dropped to 60% by 2003, and in 2006, stood at 36%. Voiceband modems were once the most popular means of Internet access in the U.S., but with the advent of new ways of accessing the Internet, the traditional 56K modem is losing popularity. The dial-up modem is still widely used by customers in rural areas, where DSL, cable, satellite, or fiber optic service is not available, or they are unwilling to pay what these companies charge. In its 2012 annual report, AOL showed it still collects around US$700 million in fees from dial-up users: about three million people.

Broadband

ADSL (asymmetric digital subscriber line) modems, a more recent development, are not limited to the telephone's voiceband audio frequencies. Standard twisted-pair telephone cable can, for short distances, carry signals with much higher frequencies than the cable's maximum frequency rating. ADSL broadband takes advantage of this capability. However, ADSL's performance gradually declines as the telephone cable's length increases. This limits ADSL broadband service to subscribers within a relatively short distance of the telephone exchange.

DSL modem.

Cable modems use infrastructure originally intended to carry television signals and therefore designed from the outset to carry higher frequencies. A single cable can carry radio and television signals at the same time as broadband internet service without interference. Newer types of broadband modems are also available, including satellite modems and power line modems.

Most consumers did not know about networking and routers when broadband became available. However, many people knew that a modem connected a computer to the Internet over a telephone line. To take advantage of consumers' familiarity with modems, companies called these devices broadband modems rather than using less familiar terms such as adapter, interface, transceiver, or bridge. In fact, broadband modems fit the definition of modem because they use complex waveforms to carry digital data. They use more advanced technology than dial-up modems: typically they can modulate and demodulate hundreds of channels simultaneously or use much wider channels than dial-up modems.

Radio

Direct broadcast satellite, WiFi, and mobile phones all use modems to communicate, as do most other wireless services today. Modern telecommunications and data networks also make extensive use of radio modems where long distance data links are required. Such systems are an important part of the PSTN, and are also in common use for high-speed computer network links to outlying areas where fibre is not economical.

Even where a cable is installed, it is often possible to get better performance or make other parts of the system simpler by using radio frequencies and modulation techniques through a cable. Coaxial cable has a very large bandwidth, but signal attenuation becomes a major problem at high data rates if a baseband digital signal is used. By using a modem, a much larger amount of digital data can be transmitted through a single wire. Digital cable television and cable Internet services use radio frequency modems to provide the increasing bandwidth needs of modern households. Using a modem also allows for frequency-division multiple access to be used, making full-duplex digital communication with many users possible using a single wire.

Wireless modems come in a variety of types, bandwidths, and speeds. Wireless modems are often referred to as transparent or smart. They transmit information that is modulated onto a carrier frequency to allow many simultaneous wireless communication links to work simultaneously on different frequencies.

Transparent modems operate in a manner similar to their phone line modem cousins. Typically, they were half duplex, meaning that they could not send and receive data at the same time. Typically, transparent modems are polled in a round robin manner to collect small amounts of data from scattered locations that do not have easy access to wired infrastructure. Transparent modems are most commonly used by utility companies for data collection.

Smart modems come with media access controllers inside, which prevents random data from colliding and resends data that is not correctly received. Smart modems typically require more bandwidth than transparent modems, and typically achieve higher data rates.

WiFi and WiMax

The WiFi and WiMax standards use wireless mobile broadband modems operating at microwave frequencies.

Mobile Broadband

Modems which use a mobile telephone system (GPRS, UMTS, HSPA, EVDO, WiMax, etc.), are known as mobile broadband modems (sometimes also called wireless modems). Wireless modems can be embedded inside a laptop or appliance, or be external to it. External wireless modems are connect cards, USB modems for mobile broadband and cellular routers. A connect card is a PC Card or ExpressCard which slides into a PCMCIA/PC card/ExpressCard slot on a computer. USB wireless modems use a USB port on the laptop instead of a PC card or Express-Card slot. A USB modem used for mobile broadband Internet is also sometimes referred to as a dongle. A cellular router may have an external datacard (AirCard) that slides into it. Most cellular routers do allow such datacards or USB modems. Cellular routers may not be modems by definition, but they contain modems or allow modems to be slid into them. The difference between a cellular router and a wireless modem is that a cellular router normally allows multiple people to connect to it (since it can route data or support multi-point to multi-point connections), while a modem is designed for one connection.

USB wireless modem.

Most of GSM wireless modems come with an integrated SIM cardholder (i.e., Huawei E220, Sierra 881, etc.) and some models are also provided with a microSD memory slot and jack for additional external antenna such as Huawei E1762 and Sierra Wireless Compass 885. The CDMA (EVDO) versions do not use R-UIM cards, but use Electronic Serial Number (ESN) instead.

The cost of using a wireless modem varies from country to country. Some carriers implement flat rate plans for unlimited data transfers. Some have caps (or maximum limits) on the amount of data that can be transferred per month. Other countries have plans that charge a fixed rate per data transferred—per megabyte or even kilobyte of data downloaded; this tends to add up quickly in today's content-filled world, which is why many people are pushing for flat data rates.

The faster data rates of the newest wireless modem technologies (UMTS, HSPA, EVDO, WiMax) are also considered to be broadband wireless modems and compete with other broadband modems.

Until the end of April 2011, worldwide shipments of USB modems surpassed embedded 3G and 4G modules by 3:1 because USB modems can be easily discarded, but embedded modems could start to gain popularity as tablet sales grow and as the incremental cost of the modems shrinks, so by 2016, the ratio may change to 1:1.

Like mobile phones, mobile broadband modems can be SIM locked to a particular network provider. Unlocking a modem is achieved the same way as unlocking a phone, by using an 'unlock code'.

Residential Gateways

Some devices referred to as "broadband modems" are residential gateways, integrating the functions of a modem, network address translation (NAT) router, Ethernet switch, WiFi access point, DHCP server, firewall, among others. Some residential gateway offer a so-called "bridged mode", which disables the built-in routing function and makes the device function similarly to a plain modem. This bridged mode is separate from RFC 1483 bridging.

DC Powerline

DC-BUS powerline modem provide communication over noisy power lines at speeds up to 1.3Mbit/s using ordinary UART, LIN, SPI and CAN protocols.

Optical Modem

Modems that are used to connect to a fiber optic network are known as optical network units (ONUs). Fiber optic systems can be upgraded by the use of quadrature amplitude modulation. The modulator and demodulator are separate components rather than a single assembly as with most modems.

QAM16

16QAM uses a 16-point constellation to send four bits per symbol. Speeds are usually on the order of 200 or 400 gigabits per second.

QAM64

64QAM uses a 64-point constellation to send six bits per symbol. Although suppliers have announced components, announcements of installation are rare. Speeds of 65 terabits per second have been observed.

Firewalls

In computing, a firewall is a network security system that monitors and controls incoming and outgoing network traffic based on predetermined security rules. A firewall typically establishes a barrier between a trusted internal network and untrusted external network, such as the Internet.

Firewalls are often categorized as either network firewalls or host-based firewalls. Network firewalls filter traffic between two or more networks and run on network hardware. Host-based firewalls run on host computers and control network traffic in and out of those machines.

The term firewall originally referred to a wall intended to confine a fire within a building. Later uses refer to similar structures, such as the metal sheet separating the engine compartment of a vehicle or aircraft from the passenger compartment. The term was applied in the late 1980s to network technology that emerged when the Internet was fairly new in terms of its global use and connectivity. The predecessors to firewalls for network security were the routers used in the late 1980s, because they separated networks from one another, thus halting the spread of problems from one network to another.

First Generation: Packet Filters

The firewall shows its settings for incoming and outgoing traffic.

The first reported type of network firewall is called a packet filter. Packet filters act by inspecting packets transferred between computers. When a packet does not match the packet filter's set of filtering rules, the packet filter either drops (silently discards) the packet, or rejects the packet (discards it and generates an Internet Control Message Protocol notification for the sender) else it is allowed to pass. Packets may be filtered by source and destination network addresses, protocol, source and destination port numbers. The bulk of Internet communication in 20th and early 21st century used either Transmission Control Protocol (TCP) or User Datagram Protocol (UDP) in conjunction with well-known ports, enabling firewalls of that era to distinguish between, and thus control, specific types of traffic (such as web browsing, remote printing, email transmission, file transfer), unless the machines on each side of the packet filter used the same non-standard ports.

The first paper published on firewall technology was in 1988, when engineers from Digital Equipment Corporation (DEC) developed filter systems known as packet filter firewalls. At AT&T Bell Labs, Bill Cheswick and Steve Bellovin continued their research in packet filtering and developed a working model for their own company based on their original first generation architecture.

Second Generation: Stateful Filters

From 1989–1990, three colleagues from AT&T Bell Laboratories, Dave Presotto, Janardan Sharma, and Kshitij Nigam, developed the second generation of firewalls, calling them circuit-level gateways.

Second-generation firewalls perform the work of their first-generation predecessors but also maintain knowledge of specific conversations between endpoints by remembering which port number the two IP addresses are using at layer 4 (transport layer) of the OSI model for their conversation, allowing examination of the overall exchange between the nodes.

This type of firewall is potentially vulnerable to denial-of-service attacks that bombard the firewall with fake connections in an attempt to overwhelm the firewall by filling its connection state memory.

Third Generation: Application Layer

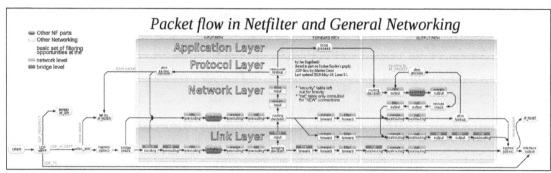

Flow of network packets through Netfilter.

Marcus Ranum, Wei Xu, and Peter Churchyard released an application firewall known as Firewall Toolkit (FWTK) in October 1993. This became the basis for Gauntlet firewall at Trusted Information Systems.

The key benefit of application layer filtering is that it can understand certain applications and protocols (such as File Transfer Protocol (FTP), Domain Name System (DNS), or Hypertext Transfer Protocol (HTTP)). This is useful as it is able to detect if an unwanted application or service is attempting to bypass the firewall using a disallowed protocol on an allowed port, or detect if a protocol is being abused in any harmful way.

As of 2012, the so-called next-generation firewall (NGFW) is a wider or deeper inspection at the application layer. For example, the existing deep packet inspection functionality of modern firewalls can be extended to include:

- Intrusion prevention systems (IPS).

- User identity management integration (by binding user IDs to IP or MAC addresses for "reputation").

- Web application firewall (WAF): WAF attacks may be implemented in the tool "WAF Fingerprinting utilizing timing side channels" (WAFFle).

Types

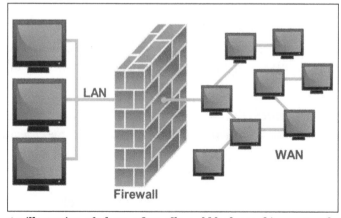

An illustration of where a firewall would be located in a network.

Firewalls are generally categorized as network-based or host-based. Network-based firewalls are positioned on the gateway computers of LANs, WANs and intranets. They are either software appliances running on general-purpose hardware, or hardware-based firewall computer appliances. Firewall appliances may also offer other functionality to the internal network they protect, such as acting as a DHCPor VPN server for that network. Host-based firewalls are positioned on the network node itself and control network traffic in and out of those machines. The host-based firewall may be a daemon or service as a part of the operating system or an agent application such as endpoint security or protection. Each has advantages and disadvantages. However, each has a role in layered security.

Firewalls also vary in type depending on where communication originates, where it is intercepted, and the state of communication being traced.

Network Layer or Packet Filters

Network layer firewalls, also called packet filters, operate at a relatively low level of the TCP/IP protocol stack, not allowing packets to pass through the firewall unless they match the established rule set. The firewall administrator may define the rules; or default rules may apply. The term "packet filter" originated in the context of BSD operating systems.

Network layer firewalls generally fall into two sub-categories, stateful and stateless.

Commonly used packet filters on various versions of Unix are ipfw (FreeBSD, Mac OS X (< 10.7)), NPF (NetBSD), PF (Mac OS X (> 10.4), OpenBSD, and some other BSDs), iptables/ipchains (Linux) and IPFilter.

Application-layer

Application-layer firewalls work on the application level of the TCP/IP stack (i.e., all browser traffic, or all telnet or FTP traffic), and may intercept all packets traveling to or from an application.

Application firewalls function by determining whether a process should accept any given connection. Application firewalls accomplish their function by hooking into socket calls to filter the connections between the application layer and the lower layers of the OSI model. Application firewalls that hook into socket calls are also referred to as socket filters. Application firewalls work much like a packet filter but application filters apply filtering rules (allow/block) on a per process basis instead of filtering connections on a per port basis. Generally, prompts are used to define rules for processes that have not yet received a connection. It is rare to find application firewalls not combined or used in conjunction with a packet filter.

Also, application firewalls further filter connections by examining the process ID of data packets against a rule set for the local process involved in the data transmission. The extent of the filtering that occurs is defined by the provided rule set. Given the variety of software that exists, application firewalls only have more complex rule sets for the standard services, such as sharing services. These per-process rule sets have limited efficacy in filtering every possible association that may occur with other processes. Also, these per-process rule sets cannot defend against modification of the process via exploitation, such as memory corruption exploits. Because of these limitations, application firewalls are beginning to be supplanted by a new generation of application firewalls that rely on mandatory access control (MAC), also referred to as sandboxing, to protect vulnerable services.

Proxies

A proxy server (running either on dedicated hardware or as software on a general-purpose machine) may act as a firewall by responding to input packets (connection requests, for example) in the manner of an application, while blocking other packets. A proxy server is a gateway from one network to another for a specific network application, in the sense that it functions as a proxy on behalf of the network user.

Proxies make tampering with an internal system from the external network more difficult, so that misuse of one internal system would not necessarily cause a security breach exploitable from outside the firewall (as long as the application proxy remains intact and properly configured). Conversely, intruders may hijack a publicly reachable system and use it as a proxy for their own purposes; the proxy then masquerades as that system to other internal machines. While use of internal address spaces enhances security, crackers may still employ methods such as IP spoofing to attempt to pass packets to a target network.

Network Address Translation

Firewalls often have network address translation (NAT) functionality, and the hosts protected behind a firewall commonly have addresses in the "private address range", as defined in RFC 1918. Firewalls often have such functionality to hide the true address of computer which is connected to the network. Originally, the NAT function was developed to address the limited number of IPv4 routable addresses that could be used or assigned to companies or individuals as well as reduce both the amount and therefore cost of obtaining enough public addresses for every computer in an organization. Although NAT on its own is not considered a security feature, hiding the addresses of protected devices has become an often used defense against network reconnaissance.

References

- Different-types-of-network-topologies: instrumentationtools.com, Retrieved 13 March, 2019

- Groth, david; toby skandier (2005). Network+ study guide, fourth edition. Sybex, inc. Isbn 0-7821-4406-3

- Network-topology-types, computer-networks: studytonight.com, Retrieved 30 January, 2019

- Atis committee prqc. "mesh topology". Atis telecom glossary 2007. Alliance for telecommunications industry solutions. Retrieved 2008-10-10

- Computer-network-topologies, data-communication-computer-network: tutorialspoint.com, Retrieved 31 March, 2019

- Bicsi, b. (2002). Network design basics for cabling professionals. Mcgraw-hill professional. Isbn 9780071782968

- Different-types-of-network-topologies: instrumentationtools.com, Retrieved 29 June, 2019

- Urs von burg (2001). The triumph of ethernet: technological communities and the battle for the lan standard. Stanford university press. Pp. 175–176, 255–256. Isbn 978-0-8047-4095-1

- Transmission-mode, computer-networks: studytonight.com, Retrieved 17 May, 2019

- "overview of key routing protocol concepts: architectures, protocol types, algorithms and metrics". Tcpipguide. com. Archived from the original on 20 december 2010. Retrieved 15 january 2011

- Network-topologies-advantages-disadvantages, Retrieved 14 July, 2019

- "Windows small business server 2008: router setup". Microsoft technet nov 2010. Archived from the original on 30 december 2010. Retrieved 15 january 2011

- Greenstein, shane; stango, victor (2006). Standards and public policy. Cambridge university press. Pp. 129–132. Isbn 978-1-139-46075-0. Archived from the original on 2017-03-24

4

Security of Computer Networks

Network security refers to the policies and practices that are used to prevent and monitor unauthorized access of a computer network. Some of its diverse types are access control, antivirus and antimalware software, application security, behavioral analytics, data loss prevention, email security, firewalls, mobile device security, etc. This chapter closely examines these key types of network security to provide an extensive understanding of the subject.

Network Security Threats

Viruses and Worms

Computer viruses and worms are destructive malicious programs designed to infect core systems, destroying essential system data and making networks inoperable. Viruses are attached to a system or host file and can lay dormant until inadvertently activated by a timer or event. Worms are more general – infecting documents, spreadsheets and other files, sometimes by utilizing macros. Once either one enters your system, it will immediately begin replicating itself, infecting networked systems and inadequately-protected computers. Viruses and worms form the building blocks for many more advanced cyber threats.

Installing anti-malware solutions on all networked devices and systems can significantly reduce the possibility of contracting these viruses or allowing them to spread. By recognizing the threats early and containing them, these solutions enable admins to detect malicious programs and remove them before they inflict any damage. In addition, IT professionals must aggressively keep software up to date, both on the end-user systems and on core system computers. With more infrastructure in the cloud, protective strategies must be extended to protect both local and cloud-resident data. And users must be trained to avoid the human engineering aspects of attacks, such as phishing attacks. This multi-faceted approach is known as defense-in-depth.

Drive-by Download Attacks

In the past, a simple way to ensure that you didn't contract a computer virus was to not download files from any source you didn't trust. Easy right? Unfortunately, today it's not that easy. Adrive-by downloadis a form of attack that allows malicious code to be downloaded from an internet site through a browser, app, or integrated operating system without any action on the user's part. These URLs are designed to look and act like real websites, but in fact, they are breeding grounds for several different types of malicious code in hopes that one of them will get through your system's security.

Keeping your browser up-to-date is one of the best ways to help identify these malicious sites before you visit them. You can also use a safe search tool, designed to filter potential threats and ensure you're not able to navigate to them.

Botnets

Botnets are powerful networks of compromised machines that can be remotely controlled and used to launch attacks of massive scale, sometimes including millions of Zombie computers. Botnets are controlled by Command and Control (C&C) networks, which are run by the hacker. They can be used to launch Distributed Denial of Service (DDOS) attacks, to make a target website so busy that it can't process legitimate requests. In fact, DDOS attacks are sometimes able to completely crash the targeted site, and relief may be offered only if the target website owner pays a ransom. Botnets can also be used to attack secure systems, with each bot operating at a low attack frequency to evade detection, but the aggregate performing a large brute-force attack.

The first defense against botnets is to keep your own machines from becoming botnet "Zombies," by using techniques for preventing infection from worms and viruses, including using antivirus software and keeping operating software up to date. But even if all machines in your enterprise are kept clean, you can be attacked when outside machines are directed to attack your web server or infrastructure. Because of the scale, defense in this case requires a cooperative approach including working with your ISP, system software vendors, and law enforcement agencies.

Phishing Attacks

Phishing attacks are a form of social engineering attack that is designed to steal user logins, credit card credentials, and other types of personal financial information. In most cases, these attacks come from a perceived trusted source, when in fact they're designed to impersonate reputable websites, banking institutions, and personal contacts. Once you reply to these messages and use your credentials or enter your financial details, the information is then sent directly to the malicious source.

To adequately combat phishing attacks, vigilance is critical. Unfortunately, these attempted attacks are hard to avoid, but as a rule of thumb, you should train your users to always be cautious when reading and opening all emails. Before clicking an external email link, you should look at the actual URL, as it may be different than the text in the email. Enter the URL manually, or be 100% sure of the source and delete any emails that seem to be fraudulent.

Exploit Kits

Over the years, hackers have looked for more automated ways to exploit users systems. These kits are self-contained and sold on the dark web. The attack is planned to work in several stages starting with a scan of the user's system once they navigate to a landing page. If vulnerabilities are discovered, the compromised website will then divert web traffic to an exploit and eventually the malicious payload.

Exploit kits are designed to be discreet, so discovering them as they are executed requires the same techniques used to defend against other sources of worms and viruses. Software solutions include anti-virus and intrusion preventions systems, and human solutions include anti-phishing training for users.

Distributed Denial of Service

A very damaging form of cyber attack that is regularly being used against businesses today is DDoS (Distributed Denial of Service) attacks. The purpose of these attacks is to overwhelm the hosted servers of their targets with requests for data, making them completely inoperable. This form of attack can be disastrous for companies that sell their products and services online, causing thousands if not millions of dollars in lost revenue a day.

Early detection is vital to protect your network effectively against a DDoS attack. WAFs (Web Application Firewalls) are a great tool to use against these attacks as they give you more control over your web traffic while recognizing malicious web exploits. Using these security solutions, you can create custom rules that enable you to block common attack patterns and can deploy countermeasures within minutes of recognizing network discrepancies.

Because DDOS attacks can be so large they can overwhelm your connection to the Internet, a cooperative approach including your service provider is often required. When your site is hosted in the cloud, some measure of protection should be included in your cloud service.

Ransomware

Among all of the latest cybersecurity threats that have been discovered over the years, none create as much fear and uncertainty as ransomware attacks. 67% of businesses attacked by ransomware have permanently lost part of or all of their company data. By infecting secure database systems, encrypting data, and threatening deletion or corruption of files unless a hefty ransom is paid, ransomware is a very dangerous form of malware. The massive increase in ransomware was triggered by the creation of crypto-currencies like Bitcoin, which allow ransom demands to be paid anonymously.

As ransomware is a form of malware, the same defensive strategies are required – antivirus software, keeping software updated with the latest security patches, and training employees to recognize phishing attacks. But there is an additional protection which is essential – reducing the impact of a loss of data by having a backup and ransomware recovery strategy or by keeping data in multiple, replicated locations. This way, the business can continue uninterrupted, without needing to pay ransom.

Cryptojacking

With the rise in popularity of cryptocurrency mining, hackers have found ingenious ways of utilizing hardware resources from unsuspecting victims for their financial gain. By tricking their victims into loading mining codes onto their computers, hackers can use their target's CPU processing resources to mine for cryptocurrency, significantly impacting the performance of their systems. Without understanding the cause of these performance slowdowns, companies can incur real costs trying to source performance solutions or replacing system hardware to resolve the issues.

To defend against these malicious resource attacks, IT teams should have methods to continuously monitor and diagnose CPU usage and alert to changes over time. Cryptojacking attacks are similar to worms and viruses, except that the end goal is to steal CPU resources not to corrupt data. As such, the same preventative measures are required as with other malware attacks.

APT Threats

APTs (Advanced Persistent Threats) are a form of cyber attack where an unauthorized attacker code enters an unsuspecting system network and remains there for an extended period undetected. Rather than inflicting damage to these systems, APTs will quietly sit, stealing financial information and other critical security information. APTs use a variety of techniques to gain initial access, including malware, exploit kits, and other sophisticated means. Once login credentials are discovered, APTs can scan and infect deeper parts of the infected system, inevitably compromising all forms of data and easily navigating between connected networks.

While these forms of attack are difficult to detect, there are some key indicators that system administrators can notice to help identify and counter APTs, including looking for unusual patterns in network activity or large amounts of data access, outside the normal range for the business. In addition, IT professionals can improve defense by segmenting the network to isolate critical data, using honeypots to trap internal attacks, and using application-specific white lists to limit data access to only the few applications that should be allowed.

Cyberattack

In computers and computer networks an attack is any attempt to expose, alter, disable, destroy, steal or gain unauthorized access to or make unauthorized use of an asset. A cyberattack is any type of offensive maneuver that targets computer information systems, infrastructures, computer networks, or personal computer devices. An attacker is a person or process that attempts to access data, functions or other restricted areas of the system without authorization, potentially with malicious intent. Depending on context, cyberattacks can be part of cyberwarfare or cyberterrorism. A cyberattack can be employed by nation-states, individuals, groups, society or organizations. A cyberattack may originate from an anonymous source.

A cyberattack may steal, alter, or destroy a specified target by hacking into a susceptible system. Cyberattacks can range from installing spyware on a personal computer to attempting to destroy the infrastructure of entire nations. Legal experts are seeking to limit the use of the term to incidents causing physical damage, distinguishing it from the more routine data breaches and broader hacking activities.

Cyberattacks have become increasingly sophisticated and dangerous.

User behavior analytics and SIEM can be used to help prevent these attacks.

Since the late 1980s cyberattacks have evolved several times to use innovations in information technology as vectors for committing cybercrimes. In recent years, the scale and robustness of cyberattacks has increased rapidly, as observed by the World Economic Forum in its 2018 report: "Offensive cyber capabilities are developing more rapidly than our ability to deal with hostile incidents."

In May 2000, the Internet Engineering Task Force defined attack in RFC 2828 as:

> An assault on system security that derives from an intelligent threat, i.e., an intelligent act that is a deliberate attempt (especially in the sense of a method or technique) to evade security services and violate the security policy of a system.

CNSS Instruction No. 4009 dated 26 April 2010 by Committee on National Security Systems of United States of America defines an attack as:

> Any kind of malicious activity that attempts to collect, disrupt, deny, degrade, or destroy information system resources or the information itself.

The increasing dependencies of modern society on information and computers networks (both in private and public sectors, including military) has led to new terms like cyber attack and cyberwarfare.

CNSS Instruction No. 4009 define a cyber attack as:

> An attack, via cyberspace, targeting an enterprise's use of cyberspace for the purpose of disrupting, disabling, destroying, or maliciously controlling a computing environment/infrastructure; or destroying the integrity of the data or stealing controlled information.

Prevalence

In the first six months of 2017, two billion data records were stolen or impacted by cyberattacks, and ransomware payments reached US$2 billion, double that in 2016.

Cyberwarfare and Cyberterrorism

Cyberwarfare utilizes techniques of defending and attacking information and computer networks that inhabit cyberspace, often through a prolonged cyber campaign or series of related campaigns. It denies an opponent's ability to do the same, while employing technological instruments of war to attack an opponent's critical computer systems. Cyberterrorism, on the other hand, is "the use of computer network tools to shut down critical national infrastructures (such as energy, transportation, government operations) or to coerce or intimidate a government or civilian population". That means the end result of both cyberwarfare and cyberterrorism is the same, to damage critical infrastructures and computer systems linked together within the confines of cyberspace.

Factors

Three factors contribute to why cyber-attacks are launched against a state or an individual: the fear factor, spectacularity factor, and vulnerability factor.

Spectacularity Factor

The spectacularity factor is a measure of the actual damage achieved by an attack, meaning that the attack creates direct losses (usually loss of availability or loss of income) and garners negative publicity. On February 8, 2000, a Denial of Service attack severely reduced traffic to many major sites, including Amazon, Buy.com, CNN, and eBay (the attack continued to affect still other sites the next day). Amazon reportedly estimated the loss of business at $600,000.

Vulnerability Factor

Vulnerability factor exploits how vulnerable an organization or government establishment is to cyber-attacks. Organizations without maintenance systems might be running on old servers which are more vulnerable than updated systems. An organization can be vulnerable to a denial of service attack and a government establishment can be defaced on a web page. A computer network attack disrupts the integrity or authenticity of data, usually through malicious code that alters program logic that controls data, leading to errors in output.

Professional Hackers to Cyberterrorists

Professional hackers, either working on their own or employed by the government or military service, can find computer systems with vulnerabilities lacking the appropriate security software. Once those vulnerabilities are found, they can infect systems with malicious code and then remotely control the system or computer by sending commands to view content or to disrupt other computers. There needs to be a pre-existing system flaw within the computer such as no antivirus protection or faulty system configuration for the viral code to work. Many professional hackers will promote themselves to cyberterrorists where a new set of rules govern their actions. Cyberterrorists have premeditated plans and their attacks are not born of rage. They need to develop their plans step-by-step and acquire the appropriate software to carry out an attack. They usually have political agendas, targeting political structures. Cyber terrorists are hackers with a political motivation, their attacks can impact political structure through this corruption and destruction. They also target civilians, civilian interests and civilian installations. As previously stated cyberterrorists attack persons or property and cause enough harm to generate fear.

Types of Attack

An attack can be active or passive. An "active attack" attempts to alter system resources or affect their operation. A "passive attack" attempts to learn or make use of information from the system but does not affect system resources (e.g., wiretapping).

An attack can be perpetrated by an insider or from outside the organization.

An "inside attack" is an attack initiated by an entity inside the security perimeter (an "insider"), i.e., an entity that is authorized to access system resources but uses them in a way not approved by those who granted the authorization.

An "outside attack" is initiated from outside the perimeter, by an unauthorized or illegitimate user of the system (an "outsider"). In the Internet, potential outside attackers range from amateur pranksters to organized criminals, international terrorists, and hostile governments.

The term "attack" relates to some other basic security terms as shown in the following diagram:

```
+ - - - - - - - - - - - - +  + - - - - +  + - - - - - - - - - - - -+
| An Attack:              |  |Counter- |  | A System Resource:     |
| i.e., A Threat Action   |  | measure |  | Target of the Attack   |
| +----------+            |  |         |  | +------------------+   |
| | Attacker |<================||<=========                        |
| |  i.e.,   |    Passive  |  |         |  | | Vulnerability    |   |
| | A Threat |<================>||<========>                       |
| |  Agent   |   or Active |  |         |  | +-------|||-------+   |
| +----------+    Attack   |  |         |  |         VVV           |
|                          |  |         |  | Threat Consequences   |
+ - - - - - - - - - - - - +  + - - - - +  + - - - - - - - - - - - -+
```

A resource (both physical or logical), called an asset, can have one or more vulnerabilities that can be exploited by a threat agent in a threat action. As a result, the confidentiality, integrity or availability of resources may be compromised. Potentially, the damage may extend to resources in addition to the one initially identified as vulnerable, including further resources of the organization, and the resources of other involved parties (customers, suppliers).

The so-called CIA triad is the basis of information security.

The attack can be active when it attempts to alter system resources or affect their operation: so it compromises integrity or availability. A "passive attack" attempts to learn or make use of information from the system but does not affect system resources: so it compromises confidentiality.

A threat is a potential for violation of security, which exists when there is a circumstance, capability, action or event that could breach security and cause harm. That is, a threat is a possible danger that might exploit a vulnerability. A threat can be either "intentional" (i.e., intelligent; e.g., an individual cracker or a criminal organization) or "accidental" (e.g., the possibility of a computer malfunctioning, or the possibility of an "act of God" such as an earthquake, a fire, or a tornado).

A set of policies concerned with information security management, the information security management systems (ISMS), has been developed to manage, according to risk management principles, the countermeasures in order to accomplish to a security strategy set up following rules and regulations applicable in a country.

An attack should led to a security incident i.e. a security event that involves a security violation. In other words, a security-relevant system event in which the system's security policy is disobeyed or otherwise breached.

The overall picture represents the risk factors of the risk scenario.

An organization should make steps to detect, classify and manage security incidents. The first logical step is to set up an incident response plan and eventually a computer emergency response team.

In order to detect attacks, a number of countermeasures can be set up at organizational, procedural and technical levels. Computer emergency response team, information technology security audit and intrusion detection system are example of these.

An attack usually is perpetrated by someone with bad intentions: black hatted attacks falls in this category, while other perform penetration testing on an organization information system to find out if all foreseen controls are in place.

The attacks can be classified according to their origin: i.e. if it is conducted using one or more computers: in the last case is called a distributed attack. Botnets are used to conduct distributed attacks.

Other classifications are according to the procedures used or the type of vulnerabilities exploited: attacks can be concentrated on network mechanisms or host features.

Some attacks are physical: i.e. theft or damage of computers and other equipment. Others are attempts to force changes in the logic used by computers or network protocols in order to achieve unforeseen (by the original designer) result but useful for the attacker. Software used to for logical attacks on computers is called malware.

The following is a partial short list of attacks:

- Passive:

    ○ Computer and network surveillance.

    ○ Network:

        □ Wiretapping,

        □ Fiber tapping,

        □ Port scan,

        □ Idle scan,

    ○ Host:

        □ Keystroke logging,

        □ Data scraping,

        □ Backdoor.

- Active:

    ○ Denial-of-service attack:

- DDos or Distributed Denial or service attack is an attempt made by the hacker to block access to a server or a website that is connected to the Internet. This is achieved using multiple computerized systems, which overloads the target system with requests,making it incapable of responding to any query.

○ Spoofing.

○ Network:

- Man-in-the-middle,

- Man-in-the-browser,

- ARP poisoning,

- Ping flood,

- Ping of death,

- Smurf attack.

○ Host:

- Buffer overflow,

- Heap overflow,

- Stack overflow,

- Format string attack.

Intrusion kill chain for information security.

In detail, there are a number of techniques to utilize in cyber-attacks and a variety of ways to administer them to individuals or establishments on a broader scale. Attacks are broken down into two categories: syntactic attacks and semantic attacks. Syntactic attacks are straightforward; it is considered malicious software which includes viruses, worms, and Trojan horses.

Syntactic Attacks

Viruses

A virus is a self-replicating program that can attach itself to another program or file in order to reproduce. The virus can hide in unlikely locations in the memory of a computer system and attach itself to whatever file it sees fit to execute its code. It can also change its digital footprint each time it replicates making it harder to track down in the computer.

Worms

A worm does not need another file or program to copy itself; it is a self-sustaining running program. Worms replicate over a network using protocols. The latest incarnation of worms make use of known vulnerabilities in systems to penetrate, execute their code, and replicate to other systems such as the Code Red II worm that infected more than 259 000 systems in less than 14 hours. On a much larger scale, worms can be designed for industrial espionage to monitor and collect server and traffic activities then transmit it back to its creator.

Trojan Horses

A Trojan horse is designed to perform legitimate tasks but it also performs unknown and unwanted activity. It can be the basis of many viruses and worms installing onto the computer as keyboard loggers and backdoor software. In a commercial sense, Trojans can be imbedded in trial versions of software and can gather additional intelligence about the target without the person even knowing it happening. All three of these are likely to attack an individual and establishment through emails, web browsers, chat clients, remote software, and updates.

Semantic Attacks

Semantic attack is the modification and dissemination of correct and incorrect information. Information modified could have been done without the use of computers even though new opportunities can be found by using them. To set someone into the wrong direction or to cover your tracks, the dissemination of incorrect information can be utilized.

Consequence of a Potential Attack

A whole industry is working trying to minimize the likelihood and the consequence of an information attack.

They offer different products and services, aimed at:

- Study all possible attacks category.
- Publish books and articles about the subject.
- Discovering vulnerabilities.
- Evaluating the risks.
- Fixing vulnerabilities.

- Invent, design and deploy countermeasures.

- Set up contingency plan in order to be ready to respond.

Many organizations are trying to classify vulnerability and their consequence: the most famous vulnerability database is the Common Vulnerabilities and Exposures.

Computer emergency response teams are set up by government and large organization to handle computer security incidents.

Infrastructures as Targets

Once a cyber-attack has been initiated, there are certain targets that need to be attacked to cripple the opponent. Certain infrastructures as targets have been highlighted as critical infrastructures in time of conflict that can severely cripple a nation. Control systems, energy resources, finance, tele-communications, transportation, and water facilities are seen as critical infrastructure targets during conflict. A new report on the industrial cybersecurity problems, produced by the British Columbia Institute of Technology, and the PA Consulting Group, using data from as far back as 1981, reportedly has found a 10-fold increase in the number of successful cyber-attacks on infrastructure Supervisory Control and Data Acquisition (SCADA) systems since 2000. Cyberattacks that have an adverse physical effect are known as cyber-physical attacks.

Control Systems

Control systems are responsible for activating and monitoring industrial or mechanical controls. Many devices are integrated with computer platforms to control valves and gates to certain physical infrastructures. Control systems are usually designed as remote telemetry devices that link to other physical devices through internet access or modems. Little security can be offered when dealing with these devices, enabling many hackers or cyberterrorists to seek out systematic vulnerabilities. Paul Blomgren, manager of sales engineering at cybersecurity firm explained how his people drove to a remote substation, saw a wireless network antenna and immediately plugged in their wireless LAN cards. They took out their laptops and connected to the system because it wasn't using passwords. "Within 10 minutes, they had mapped every piece of equipment in the facility," Blomgren said. "Within 15 minutes, they mapped every piece of equipment in the operational control network. Within 20 minutes, they were talking to the business network and had pulled off several business reports. They never even left the vehicle."

Energy

Energy is seen as the second infrastructure that could be attacked. It is broken down into two categories, electricity and natural gas. Electricity also known as electric grids power cities, regions, and households; it powers machines and other mechanisms used in day-to-day life. Using U.S. as an example, in a conflict cyberterrorists can access data through the Daily Report of System Status that shows power flows throughout the system and can pinpoint the busiest sections of the grid. By shutting those grids down, they can cause mass hysteria, backlog, and confusion; also being able to locate critical areas of operation to further attacks in a more direct method. Cyberterrorists can access instructions on how to connect to the Bonneville Power Administration which helps direct them on how to not fault the system in the process. This is a major advantage that can be utilized when cyber-attacks are being made because foreign attackers with no prior knowledge of the system can attack with the highest accuracy without drawbacks. Cyberattacks on natural gas installations go much the same way as it would with attacks on electrical grids. Cyberterrorists can shutdown these installations stopping the flow or they can even reroute gas flows to another section that can be occupied by one of their allies. There was a case in Russia with a gas supplier known as Gazprom, they lost control of their central switchboard which routes gas flow, after an inside operator and Trojan horse program bypassed security.

Finance

Financial infrastructures could be hit hard by cyber-attacks as the financial system is linked by computer systems. is constant money being exchanged in these institutions and if cyberterrorists were to attack and if transactions were rerouted and large amounts of money stolen, financial industries would collapse and civilians would be without jobs and security. Operations would stall from region to region causing nationwide economical degradation. In the U.S. alone, the average daily volume of transactions hit $3 trillion and 99% of it is non-cash flow. To be able to disrupt that amount of money for one day or for a period of days can cause lasting damage making investors pull out of funding and erode public confidence.

A cyberattack on a financial institution or transactions may be referred to as a cyberheist. These attacks may start with phishing that targets employees, using social engineering to coax information from them. They may allow attackers to hack into the network and put keyloggers on the accounting systems. In time, the cybercriminals are able to obtain password and keys information. An organization's bank accounts can then be accessed via the information they have stolen using the keyloggers. In May 2013, a gang carried out a US$40 million cyberheist from the Bank of Muscat.

Telecommunications

Cyberattacking telecommunication infrastructures have straightforward results. Telecommunication integration is becoming common practice, systems such as voice and IP networks are merging. Everything is being run through the internet because the speeds and storage capabilities are endless. Denial-of-service attacks can be administered as previously mentioned, but more complex attacks can be made on BGP routing protocols or DNS infrastructures. It is less likely that an attack would target or compromise the traditional telephony network of SS7 switches, or an attempted attack on physical devices such as microwave stations or satellite facilities. The ability would still be there to shut down those physical facilities to disrupt telephony networks. The whole idea on these cyber-attacks is to cut people off from one another, to disrupt communication, and by doing so, to impede critical information being sent and received. In cyberwarfare, this is a critical way of gaining the upper-hand in a conflict. By controlling the flow of information and communication, a nation can plan more accurate strikes and enact better counter-attack measures on their enemies.

Transportation

Transportation infrastructure mirrors telecommunication facilities; by impeding transportation for individuals in a city or region, the economy will slightly degrade over time. Successful cyber attacks can impact scheduling and accessibility, creating a disruption in the economic chain. Carrying methods will be impacted, making it hard for cargo to be sent from one place to another. In January 2003 during the "slammer" virus, Continental Airlines was forced to shut down flights due to computer problems. Cyberterrorists can target railroads by disrupting switches, target flight software to impede airplanes, and target road usage to impede more conventional transportation methods. In May 2015, a man, Chris Roberts, who was a cyberconsultant, revealed to the FBI that he had repeatedly, from 2011 to 2014, managed to hack into Boeing and Airbus flights' controls via the onboard entertainment system, allegedly, and had at least once ordered a flight to climb. The FBI, after detaining him in April 2015 in Syracuse, had interviewed him about the allegations.

Water

Water as an infrastructure could be one of the most critical infrastructures to be attacked. It is seen as one of the greatest security hazards among all of the computer-controlled systems. There is the potential to have massive amounts of water unleashed into an area which could be unprotected causing loss of life and property damage. It is not even water supplies that could be attacked; sewer systems can be compromised too. There was no calculation given to the cost of damages, but the estimated cost to replace critical water systems could be in the hundreds of billions of dollars. Most of these water infrastructures are well developed making it hard for cyber-attacks to cause any significant damage, at most, equipment failure can occur causing power outlets to be disrupted for a short time.

Network security is an integration of multiple layers of defenses in the network and at the network. Policies and controls are implemented by each network security layer. Access to networks is gained by authorized users, whereas, malicious actors are indeed blocked from executing threats and exploits.

Risks to Computer security

Backdoor

A backdoor in a computer system, a cryptosystem or an algorithm, is any secret method of bypassing normal authentication or security controls. They may exist for a number of reasons, including by original design or from poor configuration. They may have been added by an authorized party to allow some legitimate access, or by an attacker for malicious reasons; but regardless of the motives for their existence, they create a vulnerability.

Denial-of-Service Attack

Denial of service attacks (DoS) are designed to make a machine or network resource unavailable to its intended users. Attackers can deny service to individual victims, such as by deliberately entering a wrong password enough consecutive times to cause the victims account to be locked, or they may overload the capabilities of a machine or network and block all users at once. While a network attack from a single IP address can be blocked by adding a new firewall rule, many forms of Distributed denial of service (DDoS) attacks are possible, where the attack comes from a large number of points – and defending is much more difficult. Such attacks can originate from the zombie computers of a botnet, but a range of other techniques are possible including reflection and amplification attacks, where innocent systems are fooled into sending traffic to the victim.

Direct-access Attacks

An unauthorized user gaining physical access to a computer is most likely able to directly copy data from it. They may also compromise security by making operating system modifications, installing software worms, keyloggers, covert listening devices or using wireless mice. Even when the system is protected by standard security measures, these may be able to be by-passed by booting another operating system or tool from a CD-ROM or other bootable media. Disk encryption and Trusted Platform Module are designed to prevent these attacks.

Eavesdropping

Eavesdropping is the act of surreptitiously listening to a private conversation, typically between hosts on a network. For instance, programs such as Carnivore and NarusInSight have been used by the FBI and NSA to eavesdrop on the systems of internet service providers. Even machines that operate as a closed system (i.e., with no contact to the outside world) can be eavesdropped upon via monitoring the faint electromagnetic transmissions generated by the hardware; TEMPEST is a specification by the NSA referring to these attacks.

Multi-vector and Polymorphic Attacks

Surfacing in 2017, a new class of multi-vector, polymorphic cyber threats surfaced that combined several types of attacks and changed form to avoid cyber security controls as they spread. These threats have been classified as fifth generation cyber attacks.

Phishing

Phishing is the attempt to acquire sensitive information such as usernames, passwords, and credit card details directly from users. Phishing is typically carried out by email spoofing or instant messaging, and it often directs users to enter details at a fake website whose look and feel are almost identical to the legitimate one. The fake website often ask for personal information, such as log-in and passwords. This information can then be used to gain access to the individual's real account on the real website. Preying on a victim's trust, phishing can be classified as a form of social engineering.

Privilege Escalation

Privilege escalation describes a situation where an attacker with some level of restricted access is able to, without authorization, elevate their privileges or access level. For example, a standard computer user may be able to exploit a vulnerability in the system to gain access to restricted data; or even become "root" and have full unrestricted access to a system.

Social Engineering

Social engineering aims to convince a user to disclose secrets such as passwords, card numbers, etc. by, for example, impersonating a bank, a contractor, or a customer. A common scam involves fake CEO emails sent to accounting and finance departments. In early 2016, the FBI reported that the scam has cost US businesses more than $2bn in about two years.

In May 2016, the Milwaukee Bucks NBA team was the victim of this type of cyber scam with a perpetrator impersonating the team's president Peter Feigin, resulting in the handover of all the team's employees' 2015 W-2 tax forms.

Spoofing

Spoofing is the act of masquerading as a valid entity through falsification of data (such as an IP address or username), in order to gain access to information or resources that one is otherwise unauthorized to obtain. There are several types of spoofing, including:

- Email spoofing, where an attacker forges the sending (From, or source) address of an email.

- IP address spoofing, where an attacker alters the source IP address in a network packet to hide their identity or impersonate another computing system.

- MAC spoofing, where an attacker modifies the Media Access Control (MAC) address of their network interface to pose as a valid user on a network.

- Biometric spoofing, where an attacker produces a fake biometric sample to pose as another user.

Tampering

Tampering describes a malicious modification of products. So-called "Evil Maid" attacks and security services planting of surveillance capability into routers are examples.

Security by Design

Security by design, or alternately secure by design, means that the software has been designed from the ground up to be secure. In this case, security is considered as a main feature.

Some of the techniques in this approach include:

- The principle of least privilege, where each part of the system has only the privileges that are needed for its function. That way even if an attacker gains access to that part, they have only limited access to the whole system.

- Automated theorem proving to prove the correctness of crucial software subsystems.

- Code reviews and unit testing, approaches to make modules more secure where formal correctness proofs are not possible.

- Defense in depth, where the design is such that more than one subsystem needs to be violated to compromise the integrity of the system and the information it holds.

- Default secure settings, and design to "fail secure" rather than "fail insecure". Ideally, a secure system should require a deliberate, conscious, knowledgeable and free decision on the part of legitimate authorities in order to make it insecure.

- Audit trails tracking system activity, so that when a security breach occurs, the mechanism and extent of the breach can be determined. Storing audit trails remotely, where they can only be appended to, can keep intruders from covering their tracks.

- Full disclosure of all vulnerabilities, to ensure that the "window of vulnerability" is kept as short as possible when bugs are discovered.

Security Architecture

The Open Security Architecture organization defines IT security architecture as "the design artifacts that describe how the security controls (security countermeasures) are positioned, and how they relate to the overall information technology architecture. These controls serve the purpose to maintain the system's quality attributes: confidentiality, integrity, availability, accountability and assurance services".

Techopedia defines security architecture as "a unified security design that addresses the necessities and potential risks involved in a certain scenario or environment. It also specifies when and where to apply security controls. The design process is generally reproducible." The key attributes of security architecture are:

- The relationship of different components and how they depend on each other.

- The determination of controls based on risk assessment, good practice, finances, and legal matters.

- The standardization of controls.

Security Measures

A state of computer "security" is the conceptual ideal, attained by the use of the three processes: threat prevention, detection, and response. These processes are based on various policies and system components, which include the following:

- User account access controls and cryptography can protect systems files and data, respectively.

- Firewalls are by far the most common prevention systems from a network security perspective as they can (if properly configured) shield access to internal network services, and block certain kinds of attacks through packet filtering. Firewalls can be both hardware- or software-based.

- Intrusion Detection System (IDS) products are designed to detect network attacks in-progress and assist in post-attack forensics, while audit trails and logs serve a similar function for individual systems.

- "Response" is necessarily defined by the assessed security requirements of an individual system and may cover the range from simple upgrade of protections to notification of legal authorities, counter-attacks, and the like. In some special cases, a complete destruction of the compromised system is favored, as it may happen that not all the compromised resources are detected.

Today, computer security comprises mainly "preventive" measures, like firewalls or an exit procedure. A firewall can be defined as a way of filtering network data between a host or a network and another network, such as the Internet, and can be implemented as software running on the machine, hooking into the network stack (or, in the case of most UNIX-based operating systems such as Linux, built into the operating system kernel) to provide real-time filtering and blocking. Another implementation is a so-called "physical firewall", which consists of a separate machine filtering network traffic. Firewalls are common amongst machines that are permanently connected to the Internet.

Some organizations are turning to big data platforms, such as Apache Hadoop, to extend data accessibility and machine learning to detect advanced persistent threats.

However, relatively few organisations maintain computer systems with effective detection systems, and fewer still have organized response mechanisms in place. As a result, as Reuters points out: "Companies for the first time report they are losing more through electronic theft of data than physical stealing of assets". The primary obstacle to effective eradication of cyber crime could be traced to excessive reliance on firewalls and other automated "detection" systems. Yet it is basic evidence gathering by using packet capture appliances that puts criminals behind bars.

Vulnerability Management

Vulnerability management is the cycle of identifying, and remediating or mitigating vulnerabilities, especially in software and firmware. Vulnerability management is integral to computer security and network security.

Vulnerabilities can be discovered with a vulnerability scanner, which analyzes a computer system in search of known vulnerabilities, such as open ports, insecure software configuration, and susceptibility to malware.

Beyond vulnerability scanning, many organizations contract outside security auditors to run regular penetration tests against their systems to identify vulnerabilities. In some sectors, this is a contractual requirement.

Reducing Vulnerabilities

While formal verification of the correctness of computer systems is possible, it is not yet common. Operating systems formally verified include seL4, and SYSGO's PikeOS – but these make up a very small percentage of the market.

Two factor authentication is a method for mitigating unauthorized access to a system or sensitive information. It requires "something you know"; a password or PIN, and "something you have"; a card, dongle, cellphone, or other piece of hardware. This increases security as an unauthorized person needs both of these to gain access.

Social engineering and direct computer access (physical) attacks can only be prevented by non-computer means, which can be difficult to enforce, relative to the sensitivity of the information. Training is often involved to help mitigate this risk, but even in a highly disciplined environments (e.g. military organizations), social engineering attacks can still be difficult to foresee and prevent.

Enoculation, derived from inoculation theory, seeks to prevent social engineering and other fraudulent tricks or traps by instilling a resistance to persuasion attempts through exposure to similar or related attempts.

It is possible to reduce an attacker's chances by keeping systems up to date with security patches and updates, using a security scanner[definition needed] or/and hiring competent people responsible for security.(This statement is ambiguous. Even systems developed by "competent" people get penetrated) The effects of data loss/damage can be reduced by careful backing up and insurance.

Hardware Protection Mechanisms

While hardware may be a source of insecurity, such as with microchip vulnerabilities maliciously introduced during the manufacturing process, hardware-based or assisted computer security also offers an alternative to software-only computer security. Using devices and methods such as dongles, trusted platform modules, intrusion-aware cases, drive locks, disabling USB ports, and mobile-enabled access may be considered more secure due to the physical access (or sophisticated backdoor access) required in order to be compromised. Each of these is covered in more detail below.

- USB dongles are typically used in software licensing schemes to unlock software capabilities, but they can also be seen as a way to prevent unauthorized access to a computer or other device's software. The dongle, or key, essentially creates a secure encrypted tunnel between the software application and the key. The principle is that an encryption scheme on the dongle, such as Advanced Encryption Standard (AES) provides a stronger measure of security, since it is harder to hack and replicate the dongle than to simply copy the native software to another machine and use it. Another security application for dongles is to use them for accessing web-based content such as cloud software or Virtual Private Networks (VPNs). In addition, a USB dongle can be configured to lock or unlock a computer.

- Trusted platform modules (TPMs) secure devices by integrating cryptographic capabilities onto access devices, through the use of microprocessors, or so-called computers-on-a-chip. TPMs used in conjunction with server-side software offer a way to detect and authenticate hardware devices, preventing unauthorized network and data access.

- Computer case intrusion detection refers to a device, typically a push-button switch, which detects when a computer case is opened. The firmware or BIOS is programmed to show an alert to the operator when the computer is booted up the next time.

- Drive locks are essentially software tools to encrypt hard drives, making them inaccessible to thieves. Tools exist specifically for encrypting external drives as well.

- Disabling USB ports is a security option for preventing unauthorized and malicious access to an otherwise secure computer. Infected USB dongles connected to a network from a computer inside the firewall are considered by the magazine Network World as the most common hardware threat facing computer networks.

- Disconnecting or disabling peripheral devices (like camera, GPS, removable storage etc.), that are not in use.

- Mobile-enabled access devices are growing in popularity due to the ubiquitous nature of cell phones. Built-in capabilities such as Bluetooth, the newer Bluetooth low energy (LE), Near field communication (NFC) on non-iOS devices and biometric validation such as thumb print readers, as well as QR code reader software designed for mobile devices, offer new, secure ways for mobile phones to connect to access control systems. These control systems provide computer security and can also be used for controlling access to secure buildings.

Secure Operating Systems

One use of the term "computer security" refers to technology that is used to implement secure operating systems. In the 1980s the United States Department of Defense (DoD) used the "Orange Book" standards, but the current international standard ISO/IEC 15408, "Common Criteria" defines a number of progressively more stringent Evaluation Assurance Levels. Many common operating systems meet the EAL4 standard of being "Methodically Designed, Tested and Reviewed", but the formal verification required for the highest levels means that they are uncommon. An example of an EAL6 ("Semiformally Verified Design and Tested") system is Integrity-178B, which is used in the Airbus A380 and several military jets.

Secure Coding

In software engineering, secure coding aims to guard against the accidental introduction of security vulnerabilities. It is also possible to create software designed from the ground up to be secure. Such systems are "secure by design". Beyond this, formal verification aims to prove the correctness of the algorithms underlying a system; important for cryptographic protocols for example.

Capabilities and Access Control Lists

Within computer systems, two of many security models capable of enforcing privilege separation are access control lists (ACLs) and capability-based security. Using ACLs to confine programs has been proven to be insecure in many situations, such as if the host computer can be tricked into indirectly allowing restricted file access, an issue known as the confused deputy problem. It has also been shown that the promise of ACLs of giving access to an object to only one person can never be guaranteed in practice. Both of these problems are resolved by capabilities. This does not mean practical flaws exist in all ACL-based systems, but only that the designers of certain utilities must take responsibility to ensure that they do not introduce flaws.

Capabilities have been mostly restricted to research operating systems, while commercial OSs still use ACLs. Capabilities can, however, also be implemented at the language level, leading to a style of programming that is essentially a refinement of standard object-oriented design. An open source project in the area is the E language.

End User Security Training

The end-user is widely recognized as the weakest link in the security chain and it is estimated that more than 90% of security incidents and breaches involve some kind of human error. Among the most commonly recorded forms of errors and misjudgment are poor password management, the inability to recognize misleading URLs and to identify fake websites and dangerous email attachments.

As the human component of cyber risk is particularly relevant in determining the global cyber risk an organization is facing, security awareness training, at all levels, not only provides formal compliance with regulatory and industry mandates but is considered essential in reducing cyber risk and protecting individuals and companies from the great majority of cyber threats.

The focus on the end-user represents a profound cultural change for many security practitioners, who have traditionally approached cybersecurity exclusively from a technical perspective, and moves along the lines suggested by major security centers to develop a culture of cyber awareness within the organization, recognizing that a security aware user provides an important line of defense against cyber attacks.

Sniffing Attack

Sniffing in general terms refers to investigate something covertly in order to find confidential information. From an information security perspective, sniffing refers to tapping the traffic or routing the traffic to a target where it can be captured, analyzed and monitored. Sniffing is usually performed to analyze the network usage, troubleshooting network issues, monitoring the session for development and testing purpose. Since we have understood what basically sniffing is, let's move on to know how it can be used to perform attacks.

Remember back in some movies, law agencies, and criminals used to bug the telephone lines in order to hear the calls that a person receives in order to get some information. This is a perfect example of sniffing attacks. This technology can be used to test the telephone lines and determine the quality of the call but criminals used it for their own illegitimate purpose. In the world of internet, sniffing can be performed using an application, hardware devices at both the network and host level. Any network packet having information in plain text can be intercepted and read by the attackers. This information can be usernames, passwords, secret codes, banking details or any information which is of value to the attacker. This attack is just the technical equivalent of a physical spy.

Sniffing motives:

- Getting username an passwords,
- Stealing bank related/transaction related information,
- Spying on email and chat messages,
- Identity theft.

Types of Sniffing

There are two types of sniffing- active and passive. As the name suggests, active involves some activity or interaction by the attacker in order to gain information. In passive the attacker is just hiding dormant and getting the information. Let's discuss passive sniffing first.

Passive Sniffing

This kind of sniffing occurs at the hub. A hub is a device that received the traffic on one port and then retransmits that traffic on all other ports. It does not take into account that the traffic is not meant for other destinations. In this case, if a sniffer device is placed at the hub then all the network traffic can be directly captured by the sniffer. The sniffer can sit there undetected for a long time and spy on the network. Since hubs are not used these days much, this kind of attack will be an old-school trick to perform. Hubs are being replaced by switches and that is where active sniffing comes into the picture.

Active Sniffing

In a nutshell, a switch learns a CAM table that has the mac addresses of the destinations. Basis this table the switch is able to decide what network packet is to be sent where. In active sniffing, the sniffer will flood the switch with bogus requests so that the CAM table gets full. Once the CAM is full the switch will act as a switch and send the network traffic to all ports. Now, this is legitimate traffic that gets distributed to all the ports. This way the attacker can sniff the traffic from the switch.

Attack Implementations in the Network

MAC Flooding

Flooding the switch with MAC addresses so that the CAM table is overflowed and sniffing can be done.

DNS Cache Poisoning

Altering the DNS cache records so that it redirects the request to a malicious website where the attacker can capture the traffic. The malicious website may be a genuine looking website which has been set up by the attacker so that the victims trust the website. The user may enter the login details and they are sniffed right away.

Evil Twin Attack

The attacker uses malicious software to change the DNS of the victim. The attacker has a twin DNS set up already (evil twin), which will respond to the requests. This can be easily used to sniff the traffic and reroute it to the website that the attacker wishes.

MAC Spoofing

The attacker can gather the MAC address(s) that are being connected to the switch. The sniffing device is set with the same MAC address so that the messages that are intended for the original machine are delivered to the sniffer machine since it has the same MAC address set.

Identify a Sniffer

Identifying the type of sniffer can depend on how sophisticated the attack is. It is possible that the sniffer may go undetected for a large amount of time hiding in the network. There is some anti-sniffer software available in the market to catch the intruders but it may be possible that the sniffers get away with it creating a false sense of security. A sniffer can be software installed onto your system, a hardware device plugged in, sniffer at a DNS level or other network nodes etc.

Practical networks are complex and so it becomes difficult to identify sniffers. Since identification is tough, we will be discussing ways to render the sniffed information useless to the attacker.

Protocols Vulnerable to Sniffing Attacks

As we are aware that the network follows a layered approach, each layer has a dedicated task that the next layer adds up to it. Till now we have not discussed that on what layer sniffing attacks happen. Sniffing attacks work on various layers depending on the motive of the attack. Sniffers can capture the PDU's from various layers but layer 3 (Network) and 7 (Application) are of key importance. Out of all the protocols, some are susceptible to sniffing attacks. Secured version of protocols are also available but if some systems are still using the unsecured versions then the risk of information leakage becomes considerable.

HTTP

Hypertext transfer protocol is used at layer 7 of the OSI model. This is an application layer protocol that transmits the information in plain text. This was fine, when there were static websites or websites that did not required any input from the user. Anyone can set up a MITM proxy in between and listen to all the traffic or modify that traffic for personal gains. Now when we have entered into the web 2.O world, we need to ensure that the user's interaction is secured. This is ensured by using the secured version of HTTP i.e. HTTPS. Using https, the traffic is encrypted as soon as it leaves layer 7.

TELNET

Telnet is a client-server protocol that provides communication facility through virtual terminal. Telnet does not encrypt the traffic by default. Anyone having access to a switch or hub that connects the client and the server can sniff the telnet traffic for username and password. SSH is used as an alternate to the unsecured telnet. SSH uses cryptography to encrypt the traffic and provides confidentiality and integrity to the traffic.

FTP

FTP is used to transfer files between client and server. For authentication FTP used plain text username and password mechanism. Like telnet, an attacker can sniff the traffic to gain credentials and access all the files on the server. FTP can be secured by sung SSL/TLS or can be replaced by a more secured version called SFTP (SSH file transfer protocol).

POP

It stands for Post office protocol and is used by email clients to download the emails form the mail server. It also used plain text mechanism for communication hence it is also vulnerable to sniffing attacks. POP is followed by POP2 and POP3 which are little bit more secure than the original version.

SNMP

Simple network management protocol is used for communication with managed network devices on the network. SNMP uses various messages for communication and community strings for performing client authentication. Community strings in effect are just like password that is transmitted in clear text. SNMP has been superseded by SNMPV2 and V3, v3 being the latest and most secure.

Top Sniffing Tools

Wireshark

An opensource packet capturer and analyzer. It supports Windows, Linux etc. and is a GUI based tool (alternate to Tcpdump). It used pcap to monitor and capture the packets from the network interface. The packets can be filtered basis IP, protocol and many other parameters. The packets can be grouped or marked basis relevance. Each packet can be selected and dissected as per need.

Sniff

It is used for network analysis and password sniffing from various network protocols. It can analyze a variety of protocols (FTP, Telnet, POP, rLogin, Microsoft SMB, SNMP, IMAP etc) for getting the information.

Microsoft network monitor: As the name suggests it is used for capturing and analyzing the network. It is used for troubleshooting the network. Some of the features of the software are Grouping, a Large pool of protocol support(300+), Wireless monitor mode, reassembly of fragmented messages etc.

Debookee

It is a paid tool that can be used to monitor and analyze the network. It is able to intercept and analyze the traffic from devices that are in that subnet, irrespective of the device type (Laptop, devices, TV etc). It offers various modules:

- Network analysis module: Scan for connected devices, Intercept traffic in a subnet, TCP port scanner, Network analysis and monitoring of HTTP, DNS, TCP, DHCP protocols, Analyse VoIP calls etc.

- WiFi monitoring module: Details of access points in radio range, wireless client details, wifi statistics etc.

- SSL/TLS decryption module: Support for monitoring and analyzing secured protocols.

Precautionary Measures against Sniffing Attacks

- Connect to trusted networks: Do you trust a free Wi-Fi offered by the coffee shop next door? Connecting to any public network will have a risk that the traffic might be sniffed. Attackers choose these public places exploiting the user's lack of knowledge. Public networks are setup and then may or may not be monitored for any intrusions or bugs. Attackers can either sniff that network or create a new network of their own with similar names so that the users get tricked into joining that network. An attacker sitting at an airport can create a Wi-Fi with the name of "Free Airport Wi-Fi" and the nearby users may connect to it sending all the data through the attackers' sniffer node. The word of caution here is that you should only connect to the network you trust – home network, office network etc.

- Encrypt: Encrypt all the traffic that leaves your system. This will ensure that even if the traffic is being sniffed, the attacker will not be able to make sense of it. One thing here to be noted is that security work on defense in depth principle. Encrypting he data does not mean that now everything is safe. The attacker might be able to capture a lot of data and run crypto attacks to get something out of it. Use of secured protocols ensures that the traffic is encrypted and renders security for the traffic. Websites using https protocol are more secure than the ones that use HTTP – how is that achieved? Encryption.

- Network scanning and monitoring: Networks must be scanned for any kind of intrusion attempt or rogue devices that may be setup in span mode to capture traffic. Network admins must monitor the network as well so as to ensure the device hygiene. IT team can use various techniques to determine the presence of sniffers in the network. Bandwidth monitoring is one, an audit of devices which are set to promiscuous mode etc.

Cracking of Wireless Networks

Cracking a wireless network is defeating the security of a wireless local-area network (back-jack wireless LAN). A commonly used wireless LAN is a Wi-Fi network. Wireless LANs have inherent security weaknesses from which wired networks are exempt.

Wireless cracking is an information network attack similar to a direct intrusion. Two frequent types of vulnerabilities in wireless LANs are those caused by poor configuration, and those caused by weak or flawed security protocols.

Wireless Network Basics

- Wireless local-area networks are based on IEEE 802.11. This is a set of standards defined by the Institute of Electrical and Electronics Engineers.

- 802.11 networks are either infrastructure networks or ad hoc networks. By default, people refer to infrastructure networks. Infrastructure networks are composed of one or more access points that coordinate the wireless traffic between the nodes and often connect the nodes to a wired network, acting as a bridge or a router:

  - Each access point constitutes a network that is named a *basic service set* or BSS. A BSS is identified by a BSSID, usually the MAC address of the access point.

  - Each access point is part of an *extended service set* or ESS, which is identified by an ESSID or SSID in short, usually a character string.

  - A basic service set consists of one access point and several wireless *clients*. An extended service set is a configuration with multiple access points and roaming capabilities for the clients. An independent basic service set or IBSS is the ad hoc configuration. This configuration allows wireless clients to connect to each other directly, without an access point as a central manager.

  - Access points broadcast a signal regularly to make the network known to clients. They relay traffic from one wireless client to another. Access points may determine which clients may connect, and when clients do, they are said to be *associated* with the access point. To obtain access to an access point, both the BSSID and the SSID are required.

- Ad hoc networks have no access point for central coordination. Each node connects in a peer-to-peer way. This configuration is an *independent basic service set* or IBSS. Ad hoc networks also have an SSID.

Wireless Network Frames

802.11 networks use *data frames*, *management frames*, and *control frames*. Data frames convey the real data, and are similar to those of Ethernet. Management frames maintain both network configuration and connectivity. Control frames manage access to the ether and prevent access points and clients from interfering with each other in the ether. Some information on management frames will be helpful to better understand what programs for *reconnaissance* do.

- Beacon frames are used primarily in reconnaissance. They advertise the existence and basic configuration of the network. Each frame contains the BSSID, the SSID, and some information on basic authentication and encryption. Clients use the flow of beacon frames to monitor the signal strength of their access point.

- Probe request frames are almost the same as the beacon frames. A probe request frame is sent from a client when it wants to connect to a wireless network. It contains information about the requested network.

- Probe response frames are sent to clients to answer probe request frames. One response frame answers each request frame, and it contains information on the capabilities and configurations of the network. Useful for reconnaissance.

- Authentication request frames are sent by clients when they want to connect to a network. Authentication precedes association in infrastructure networks. Either open authentication or shared key authentication is possible. After serious flaws were found in shared key authentication, most networks switched to open authentication, combined with a stronger authentication method applied after the association phase.

- Authentication response frames are sent to clients to answer authentication request frames. There is one answer to each request, and it contains either status information or a challenge related to shared key authentication.

- Association request frames are sent by clients to associate with the network. An association request frame contains much of the same information as the probe request contains, and it must have the SSID. This can be used to obtain the SSID when a network is configured to hide the SSID in beacon frames.

- Association response frames are sent to clients to answer an association request frame. They contain a bit of network information and indicate whether the association was successful.

- Deauthentication and disassociation frames are sent to a node to notify that an authentication or an association has failed and must be established anew.

Reconnaissance of Wireless Networks

Wardriving is a common method of wireless network reconnaissance. A well-equipped wardriver uses a laptop computer with a wireless card, an antenna mounted on the car, a power inverter, a connected GPS receiver, and a way to connect to the internet wirelessly. The purpose of wardriving is to locate a wireless network and to collect information about its configuration and associated clients. The laptop computer and the wireless card must support a mode called monitor or rfmon.

Netstumbler

Netstumbler is a network discovery program for Windows. It is free. Netstumbler has become one of the most popular programs for wardriving and wireless reconnaissance, although it has a disadvantage. It can be detected easily by most wireless intrusion detection systems, because it actively probes a network to collect information. Netstumbler has integrated support for a GPS unit. With this support, Netstumbler displays GPS coordinate information next to the information about each discovered network, which can be useful for finding specific networks again after having sorted out collected data. The latest release of Netstumbler is of 1 April 2004. It does not work well with 64-bit Windows XP or Windows Vista.

Insider

The inSSIDer is a Wi-Fi network scanner for the 32-bit and 64-bit versions of Windows XP, Vista, 7, Windows 8 and Android. It is free and open source. The software uses the current wireless card or a wireless USB adapter and supports most GPS devices (namely those that use NMEA 2.3 or higher). Its graphical user interface shows MAC address, SSID, signal strength, hardware brand, security, and network type of nearby Wi-Fi networks. It can also track the strength of the signals and show them in a time graph.

Kismet

Kismet is a wireless network traffic analyser for OS X, Linux, OpenBSD, NetBSD, and FreeBSD.

Wireshark

Wireshark is a packet sniffer and network traffic analyser that can run on all popular operating systems, but support for the capture of wireless traffic is limited. It is free and open source. Decoding and analysing wireless traffic is not the foremost function of Wireshark, but it can give results that cannot be obtained with programs. Wireshark requires sufficient knowledge of the network protocols to obtain a full analysis of the traffic, however.

Analysers of AirMagnet

AirMagnet Laptop Analyser and AirMagnet Handheld Analyser are wireless network analysis tools made by AirMagnet. The company started with the Handheld Analyser, which was very suitable for surveying sites where wireless networks were deployed as well as for finding rogue access points. The Laptop Analyser was released because the hand-held product was impractical for the reconnaissance of wide areas. These commercial analysers probably offer the best combination of powerful analysis and simple user interface. However, they are not as well adapted to the needs of a wardriver as some of the free programs.

Androdumpper

Androdumpper is an Android APK that is used to test and hack WPS Wireless routers which have a vulnerability by using algorithms to hack into that WIFI network. It runs best on Android version 5.0+.

Airopeek

Airopeek is a packet sniffer and network traffic analyser made by Wildpackets. This commercial program supports Windows and works with most wireless network interface cards. It has become the industrial standard for capturing and analysing wireless traffic. However, like Wireshark, Airopeek requires thorough knowledge of the protocols to use it to its ability.

KisMac

KisMac is a program for the discovery of wireless networks that runs on the OS X operating system. The functionality of KisMac includes GPS support with mapping, SSID decloaking, deauthentication attacks, and WEP cracking.

Penetration of a Wireless Network

There are two basic types of vulnerabilities associated with WLANs: those caused by poor configuration and those caused by poor encryption. Poor configuration causes many vulnerabilities. Wireless networks are often put into use with no or insufficient security settings. With no security settings – the default configuration – access is obtained simply by association. Without sufficient security settings, networks can easily be defeated by cloaking and MAC address filtering. Poor encryption causes the remaining vulnerabilities. Wired Equivalent Privacy (WEP) is defective and can be defeated in several ways. Wi-Fi Protected Access (WPA) and Cisco's Lightweight Extensible Authentication Protocol (LEAP) are vulnerable to dictionary attacks.

Encryption Types and their Attacks

Wired Equivalent Privacy

WEP was the encryption standard firstly available for wireless networks. It can be deployed in 64 and 128 bit strength. 64 bit WEP has a secret key of 40 bits and an initialisation vector of 24 bits, and is often called 40 bit WEP. 128 bit WEP has a secret key of 104 bits and an initialisation vector of 24 bits, and is called 104 bit WEP. Association is possible using a password, an ASCII key. The FMS attack – named after Fluhrer, Mantin, and Shamir – is based on a weakness of the RC4 encryption algorithm. The researchers found that 9000 of the possible 16 million initialisation vectors can be considered weak, and collecting enough of them allows the determination of the encryption key. To crack the WEP key in most cases, 5 million encrypted packets must be captured to collect about 3000 weak initialisation vectors. The weak initialisation vectors are supplied to the Key Scheduling Algorithm (KSA) and the Pseudo Random Generator (PRNG) to determine the first byte of the WEP key. This procedure is then repeated for the remaining bytes of the key. The chopping attack chops the last byte off from the captured encrypted packets. This breaks the Cyclic Redundancy Check/Integrity Check Value (CRC/ICV). When all 8 bits of the removed byte were zero, the CRC of the shortened packet is made valid again by manipulation of the last four bytes. This manipulation is: result = original XOR certain value. The manipulated packet can then be retransmitted. This method enables the determination of the key by collecting unique initialisation vectors. The main problem with both the FMS attack and the chopping attack is that capturing enough packets can take weeks or sometimes months. Fortunately, the speed of capturing packets can be increased by injecting packets into the network. One or more Address Resolution Protocol (ARP) packets are usually collected to this end, and then transmitted to the access point repeatedly until enough response packets have been captured. ARP packets are a good choice because they have a recognizable size of 28 bytes. Waiting for a legitimate ARP packet can take awhile. ARP packets are most commonly transmitted during an authentication process. Rather than waiting for that, sending a deauthentication frame that pushes a client off the network will require that client to reauthenticate. This often creates an ARP packet.

Wi-Fi Protected Access

WPA was developed because of the vulnerabilities of WEP. WPA uses either a pre-shared key (WPA-PSK) or is used in combination with a RADIUS server (WPA-RADIUS). For its encryption algorithm, WPA uses either the Temporal Key Integrity Protocol (TKIP) or the Advanced Encryption Standard (AES). WPA2 was developed because of some vulnerabilities of WPA-PSK and to strengthen the encryption further. WPA2 uses both TKIP and AES, and requires not only an encryption piece but also an authentication piece. A form of the Extensible Authentication Protocol (EAP) is deployed for this piece. WPA-PSK can be attacked when the PSK is shorter than 21 characters. Firstly, the four-way EAP Over LAN (EAPOL) handshake must be captured. This can be captured during a legitimate authentication, or a reauthentication can be forced by sending deauthentication packets to clients. Secondly, each word of a word-list must be hashed with the Hashed Message Authentication Code – Secure Hash Algorithm 1 and two so called nonce values, along with the MAC address of the client that asked for authentication and the MAC address of the access point that gave authentication. Word-lists can be found at. LEAP uses a variation of Microsoft Challenge Handshake Protocol version 2 (MS-CHAPv2). This handshake uses the Data Encryption Standard (DES) for key selection. LEAP can be cracked with a dictionary attack. The attack involves capturing an authentication sequence and then comparing the last two bytes of a captured response with those generated with a word-list. WPA-RADIUS cannot be cracked. However, if the RADIUS authentication server itself can be cracked, then the whole network is imperilled. The security of authentication servers is often neglected. WPA2 can be attacked by using the WPA-PSK attack, but is largely ineffective.

Aircrack-ng

Aircrack-ng runs on Windows and Linux, and can crack WEP and WPA-PSK. It can use the Pychkine-Tews-Weinmann and KoreK attacks, both are statistical methods that are more efficient than the traditional FMS attack. Aircrack-ng consists of components. Airmon-ng configures the wireless network card. Airodump-ng captures the frames. Aireplay-ng generates traffic. Aircrack-ng does the cracking, using the data collected by airodump-ng. Finally, airdecap-ng decrypts all packets that were captured. Thus, aircrack-ng is the name of the suite and also of one of the components.

CoWPAtty

CoWPAtty automates the dictionary attack for WPA-PSK. It runs on Linux. The program is started using a command-line interface, specifying a word-list that contains the passphrase, a dump file that contains the four-way EAPOL handshake, and the SSID of the network.

Void11

Void11 is a program that deauthenticates clients. It runs on Linux.

MAC Address Filtering and its Attack

MAC address filtering can be used alone as an ineffective security measure, or in combination with encryption. The attack is determining an allowed MAC address, and then changing the MAC address of the attacker to that address. EtherChange is one of the many programs available to change the MAC address of network adapters. It runs on Windows.

Penetration testing of a wireless network is often a stepping stone for penetration testing of the internal network. The wireless network then serves as a so-called *entry vector*. If WPA-RADIUS is in use at a target site, another entry vector must be investigated.

Reconnaissance of the Local-area Network

Sniffing

A 'wireless' sniffer can find IP addresses, which is helpful for network mapping. Access points usually connect the nodes of a wireless network to a wired network as a bridge or a router. Both a bridge and a router use a routing table to forward packets.

Footprinting

Finding relevant and reachable IP addresses is the objective of the reconnaissance phase of attacking an organization over the Internet. The relevant IP addresses are determined by collecting as many DNS host names as possible and translating them to IP addresses and IP address ranges. This is called footprinting.

A search engine is the key for finding as much information as possible about a target. In many cases, organizations do not want to protect all their resources from internet access. For instance, a web server must be accessible. Many organizations additionally have email servers, FTP servers, and other systems that must be accessible over the internet. The IP addresses of an organization are often grouped together. If one IP address has been found, the rest probably can be found around it.

Name servers store tables that show how domain names must be translated to IP addresses and vice versa. With Windows, the command NSLookup can be used to query DNS servers. When the word help is entered at NSLookup's prompt, a list of all commands is given. With Linux, the command dig can be used to query DNS servers. It displays a list of options when invoked with the option -h only. And the command host reverses IP addresses to hostnames. The program nmap can be used as a reverse DNS walker: nmap -sL 1.1.1.1-30 gives the reverse entries for the given range.

ARIN, RIPE, APNIC, LACNIC, and AFRINIC are the five Regional Internet Registries that are responsible for the assignment and registration of IP addresses. All have a website with which their databases can be searched for the owner of an IP address. Some of the Registries respond to a search for the name of an organization with a list of all IP address ranges that are assigned to the name. However, the records of the Registries are not always correct and are in most cases useless.

Probably most computers with access to the internet receive their IP address dynamically by DHCP. This protocol has become more popular over the last years because of a decrease of available IP addresses and an increase of large networks that are dynamic. DHCP is particularly important when many employees take a portable computer from one office to another. The router/firewall device that people use at home to connect to the internet probably also functions as a DHCP server.

Nowadays many router/DHCP devices perform Network Address Translation (NAT). The NAT device is a gateway between the local network and the internet. Seen from the internet, the NAT device seems to be a single host. With NAT, the local network can use any IP address space. Some IP address ranges are reserved for private networks. These ranges are typically used for the local area network behind a NAT device, and they are: 10.0.0.0 - 10.255.255.255, 172.16.0.0 - 172.31.255.255, and 192.168.0.0 - 192.168.255.255.

The relevant IP addresses must be narrowed down to those that are reachable. For this purpose, the process of scanning enters on the scene.

Host Scanning

Once access to a wireless network has been gained, it is helpful to determine the network's topology, including the names of the computers connected to the network. Nmap can be used for this, which is available in a Windows and a Linux version. However, Nmap does not provide the user with a network diagram. The network scanner Network View that runs on Windows does. The program asks for one IP address or an IP address range. When the program has finished scanning, it displays a map of the network using different pictures for routers, workstations, servers, and laptops, all with their names added.

The most direct method for finding hosts on a LAN is using the program ping. When using a modern flavour of Unix, shell commands can be combined to produce custom ping-sweeps. When using Windows, the command-line can also be used to create a ping-sweep. Nmap can be used for a host scan when the option -sP is added: nmap -n -sP 10.160.9.1-30 scans the first 30 addresses of the subnet 10.160.9, where the -n option prevents reverse DNS lookups.

Ping packets could reliably determine whether a computer was on line at a specified IP address. Nowadays these ICMP echo request packets are sometimes blocked by the firewall of an operating system. Although Nmap also probes TCP port 80, specifying more TCP ports to probe is recommended when pings are blocked. Consequently, nmap -sP -PS21, 22, 23, 25, 80, 139, 445, 3389 10.160.9.1-30 can achieve better results. And by combining various options as in nmap -sP -PS21, 22, 23, 25, 80, 135, 139, 445, 1025, 3389 -PU53, 67, 68, 69, 111, 161, 445, 514 -PE -PP -PM 10.160.9.1-30, superb host scanning is achieved.

Nmap is available for Windows and most Unix operating systems, and offers graphical and command-line interfaces.

Port Scanning

The purpose of port scanning is finding the open ports on the computers that were found with a host scan. When a port scan is started on a network without making use of the results of a host scan, much time is wasted when many IP addresses in the address range are vacant.

Open Ports

Most programs that communicate over the Internet use either the TCP or the UDP protocol. Both protocols support 65536 so called ports that programs can choose to bind to. This allows programs to run concurrently on one IP address. Most programs have default ports that are most often used. For example, HTTP servers commonly use TCP port 80.

Network scanners try to connect to TCP or UDP ports. When a port accepts a connection, it can be assumed that the commonly bound program is running.

TCP connections begin with a SYN packet being sent from client to server. The server responds with a SYN/ACK packet. Finally, the client sends an ACK packet. When the scanner sends a SYN packet and gets the SYN/ACK packet back, the port is considered open. When a RST packet is received instead, the port is considered closed. When no response is received the port is either considered filtered by a firewall or there is no running host at the IP address.

Scanning UDP ports is more difficult because UDP does not use handshakes and programs tend to discard UDP packets that they cannot process. When an UDP packet is sent to a port that has no program bound to it, an ICMP error packet is returned. That port can then be considered closed. When no answer is received, the port can be considered either filtered by a firewall or open. Many people abandoned UDP scanning because simple UDP scanners cannot distinguish between filtered and open ports.

Common Ports

Although it is most thorough to scan all 65536 ports, this would take more time than scanning only the most common ports. Therefore, Nmap scans 1667 TCP ports by default.

Specifying Ports

The -p option instructs Nmap to scan specified ports, as in nmap -p 21-25,80,100-160 10.150.9.46. Specifying TCP and UDP ports is also possible, as in nmap -pT:21-25, 80, U:5000-5500 10.150.9.46.

Specifying Targets

Nmap always requires the specification of a host or hosts to scan. A single host can be specified with an IP address or a domain name. Multiple hosts can be specified with IP address ranges. Examples are 1.1.1.1, www.company.com, and 10.1.50.1-5, 250-254.

Specifying Scan Type

TCP SYN Scan

Nmap performs a TCP SYN scan by default. In this scan, the packets have only their SYN flag set. The -sS option specifies the default explicitly. When Nmap is started with administrator privileges, this default scan takes effect. When Nmap is started with user privileges, a connect scan is performed.

TCP Connect Scan

The -sT option instructs Nmap to establish a full connection. This scan is inferior to the previous because an additional packet must be sent and logging by the target is more likely. The connect scan is performed when Nmap is executed with user privileges or when IPv6 addresses are scanned.

TCP Null Scan

The -sN option instructs Nmap to send packets that have none of the SYN, RST, and ACK flags set. When the TCP port is closed, a RST packet is sent in return. When the TCP port is open or filtered, there is no response. The null scan can often bypass a stateless firewall, but is not useful when a stateful firewall is employed.

UDP Empty Packet Scan

The -sU option instructs Nmap to send UDP packets with no data. When an ICMP error is returned, the port can be assumed closed. When no response is received, the port can be assumed open or filtered. No differentiation between open and filtered ports is a severe limitation.

UDP Application Data Scan

The -sU -sV options instruct Nmap to use application data for application identification. This combination of options can lead to very slow scanning.

Specifying Scan Speed

When packets are sent to a network faster than it can cope with they will be dropped. This leads to inaccurate scanning results. When an intrusion detection system or intrusion prevention system is present on the target network, detection becomes more likely as speed increases. Many IPS devices and firewalls respond to a storm of SYN packets by enabling SYN cookies that make appear every port to be open. Full speed scans can even wreak havoc on stateful network devices.

Nmap provides five templates for adjusting speed and also adapts itself. The -T0 option makes it wait for 5 minutes before the next packet is sent, the -T1 option makes it wait for 15 seconds, -T2 inserts 0.4 seconds, -T3 is the default (which leaves timing settings unchanged), -T4 reduces time-outs and retransmissions to speed things up slightly, and -T5 reduces time-outs and retransmissions even more to speed things up significantly. Modern IDS/IPS devices can detect scans that use the -T1 option. The user can also define a new template of settings and use it instead of a provided one.

Application Identification

The -sV option instructs Nmap to also determine the version of a running application.

Operating System Identification

The -O option instructs Nmap to try to determine the operating systems of the targets. Specially crafted packets are sent to open and closed ports and the responses are compared with a database.

Saving Output

The -oX <filename> option instructs Nmap to save the output to a file in XML format.

Vulnerability Scanning

A vulnerability is a bug in an application program that affects security. They are made public on places such as the BugTraq and the Full-Disclosure mailing lists. The Computer Emergency Response Team (CERT) brings out a statistical report every year. There were 8064 vulnerabilities counted in 2006 alone.

Vulnerability scanning is determining whether known vulnerabilities are present on a target.

Exploitation of a Vulnerability

An exploit takes advantage of a bug in an application. This can take effect in the execution of arbitrary commands by inserting them in the execution path of the program. Escalation of privileges, bypass of authentication, or infringement of confidentiality can be the result.

Metasploit

The Metasploit framework was released in 2003. This framework provided for the first time:

- A single exploit database with easy updating,
- Freely combining of an exploit with a payload,
- A consistent interface for setting options,
- Integrated encoding and evasion.

Where,

- An exploit is a code module that uses a particular vulnerability,
- A payload is code that is sent along with the exploit to take some action, such as providing a command-line interface,
- Options are used to select variants of exploits and payloads,
- Encoding is modifying the payload to circumvent limitations, whether they are caused by the logic of the vulnerability or an inadequate ips,
- Evasion is bypassing security devices by employing evasion techniques.

The basic procedure of using Metasploit is: choose an exploit, choose a payload, set the IP address and port of the target, start the exploit, evaluate, and stop or repeat the procedure.

Metasploit is not suited for finding the vulnerabilities of a host; a vulnerability scanner is. Alternatively, when a port scanner has found an open port, all exploits for that port may be tried.

Metasploit 3.0 provides the following payloads:

- VNC injection: This payload for targets that run Windows gives a graphical user interface to the target that is synchronized with the graphical user interface of the target.

- File execution: This payload for targets that run Windows uploads a file and executes it.

- Interactive shell: This payload gives a command-line interface to the target.

- Add user: This payload adds a user with specified name and password that has administrator access.

- Meterpreter: This payload gives a rich command-line interface to targets that run Windows.

VNC connections need a relatively large bandwidth to be usable, and if someone is in front of the compromised computer then any interaction will be seen very quickly. The command-line interfaces of Linux and OS X are powerful, but that of Windows is not. The Meterpreter payload remedies these shortcomings. The reference gives a list of Meterpreter commands.

Maintaining Control

The ultimate gratification for a network intruder always is to obtain administrator privileges for a network. When an intruder is inside, one of his or her first undertakings is often to install a so-called rootkit on a target computer. This is a collection of programs to facilitate durable influence on a system. Some of these programs are used to compromise new user accounts or new computers on the network. Other programs are to obscure the presence of the intruder. These obscuring programs may include false versions of standard network utilities such as netstat, or programs that can remove all data from the log files of a computer that relate to the intruder. Yet other programs of a rootkit may be used to survey the network or to overhear more passwords that are travelling over it. Rootkits may also give the means to change the very operating system of the computer it is installed on.

The network intruder then proceeds with creating one or more so called back doors. These are access provisions that are hard to find for system administrators, and they serve to prevent the logging and monitoring that results from normal use of the network. A back door may be a concealed account or an account of which the privileges have been escalated. Or it may be a utility for remote access, such as Telnet, that has been configured to operate with a port number that is not customary.

The network intruder then proceeds with stealing files, or stealing credit card information, or preparing a computer to send spam emails at will. Another goal is to prepare for the next intrusion. A cautious intruder is protective against discovery of his or her location. The method of choice is to use a computer that already has been attacked as an intermediary. Some intruders use a series of intermediate computers, making it impracticable to locate them.

Back Doors

The purpose of a back door is to maintain a communication channel and having methods to control a host that has been gained entry to. These methods include those for file transfer and the execution of programs. It is often important to make sure that the access or communication remains secret. And access control is desirable in order to prevent others from using the back door.

Back Orifice 2000 was designed as a back door. The server runs on Windows, and there are clients for Windows, Linux and other operating systems. The server is configured easily with a utility. After configuration, the server needs to be uploaded to the target and then started. Back Orifice 2000 supports file transfer, file execution, logging of keystrokes, and control of connections. There is also an AES plug-in for traffic encryption and an STCPIO plug-in for further obfuscation of the traffic. The first plug-in adds security and the combination of these plug-ins makes it much harder for an IDS to relate the traffic to a back door.

Rootkits

Rootkits specialize in hiding themselves and other programs.

Hacker Defender (hxdef) is an open source rootkit for Windows. It can hide its files, its process, its registry entries, and its port in multiple DLLs. Although it has a simple command-line interface as a back door, it is often better to use its ability to hide a more appropriate tool.

Prevention and Protection

An unprotected wireless network is extremely insecure. From anywhere within broadcast range, someone can eavesdrop or start using the network. Therefore, the IEEE 802.11 standard for wireless networks was accompanied with Wired Equivalent Privacy (WEP). This security protocol takes care of the following:

- Authentication: Assurance that all participants are who they state they are, and are authorized to use the network.

- Confidentiality: Protection against eavesdropping.

- Integrity: Assurance of data being unaltered.

WEP has been criticized by security experts. Most experts regard it as ineffective by now.

In 2004 a draft for a better security protocol appeared, and it was included in the IEEE 802.11 standard in 2007. This new protocol, WPA2, uses an AES block cipher instead of the RC4 algorithm and has better procedures for authentication and key distribution. WPA2 is much more secure than WEP, but WEP was still in wide use in 2009.

Many wireless routers also support controlling the MAC addresses of computers that are authorized to use a wireless network. This measure can effectively stop a neighbour from using the network, but experienced intruders will not be stopped. MAC filtering can be attacked because a MAC address can be faked easily.

In the past, turning off the broadcasting of the SSID has also been thought to give security to a wireless network. This is not the case however. Freely available tools exist that quickly discover an SSID that is not broadcast. Microsoft has also determined that switching off the broadcasting of the SSID leads to less security. Details can be found in Non-broadcast Wireless Networks with Microsoft Windows.

Returning to encryption, the WEP specification at any encryption strength is unable to withstand determined hacking. Therefore, Wi-Fi Protected Access (WPA) was derived from WEP. Software upgrades are often available. The latest devices that conform to the 802.11g or 802.11n standards also support WPA2. (WPA uses the TKIP encryption, WPA2 uses the stronger AES method.) It is recommended to use only hardware that supports WPA or WPA2.

Installing updates regularly, disabling WPS, setting a custom SSID, requiring WPA2, and using a strong password make a wireless router more difficult to crack. Even so, unpatched security flaws in a router's software or firmware may still be used by an attacker to bypass encryption and gain control of the device. Many router manufacturers do not always provide security updates in a timely manner, or at all, especially for more inexpensive models.

WPS currently has a severe vulnerability in which the 8 pin numbered (0-9) passwords being used can easily be split into two halves, this means that each half can be brute-forced individually and so the possible combinations are greatly lessened ($10^4 + 10^4$, as opposed to 10^8). This vulnerability has been addressed by most manufacturers these days by using a lock down mechanism where the router will automatically lock its WPS after a number of failed pin attempts (it can take a number of hours before the router will automatically unlock, some even have to be rebooted which can make WPS attacks completely obsolete). Without a lock down feature, a WPA2 router with WPS enabled can easily be cracked in 5 hours using a brute force WPS attack.

SSID's are used in routers not only to identify them within the mass of 2.4, 3.6, 5 and 60 GHz frequencies which are currently flying around our cities, but are also used as a "seed" for the router's password hashes. Standard and popular SSID's such as "Netgear" can be brute forced through the use of rainbow tables, however the use of a salt greatly improves security against rainbow tables. The most popular method of WPA and WPA2 cracking is through obtaining what's known as a "4 way handshake". When a device is connecting with a network there is a 4-stage authorization process referred to as a 4 way handshake. When a wireless device undergoes this process this handshake is sent through the air and can easily be monitored and saved by an external system. The handshake will be encrypted by the router's password, this means that as opposed to communicating with the router directly (which can be quite slow), the cracker can attempt to brute force the handshake itself using dictionary attacks. A device that is connected directly with the router will still undergo this very process, however, the handshake will be sent through the connected wire as opposed to the air so it cannot be intercepted. If a 4 way handshake has already been intercepted, it does not mean that the cracker will be granted immediate access however. If the password used contains at least 12 characters consisting of both random upper and lower case letters and numbers that do not spell a word, name or have any pattern then the password will be essentially uncrackable. Just to give an example of this, let's just take the minimum of 8 characters for WPA2 and suppose we take upper case and lower case letters, digits from 0-9 and a small selection of symbols, we can avail of a hefty choice of 64 characters. In an 8 character length password this is a grand total of 64^8 possible combinations. Taking a single machine that could attempt 500 passwords per second, this gives us just about 17,900 years to attempt every possible combination. Not even to mention the amount of space necessary to store each combination in a dictionary.

Detection

A network scanner or sniffer is an application program that makes use of a wireless network interface card. It repeatedly tunes the wireless card successively to a number of radio channels. With a passive scanner this pertains only to the receiver of the wireless card, and therefore the scanning cannot be detected.

An attacker can obtain a considerable amount of information with a passive scanner, but more information may be obtained by sending crafted frames that provoke useful responses. This is called active scanning or probing. Active scanning also involves the use of the transmitter of the wireless card. The activity can therefore be detected and the wireless card can be located.

Detection is possible with an intrusion detection system for wireless networks, and locating is possible with suitable equipment.

Wireless intrusion detection systems are designed to detect anomalous behaviour. They have one or more sensors that collect SSIDs, radio channels, beacon intervals, encryption, MAC addresses, transmission speeds, and signal-to-noise ratios. Wireless intrusion detection systems maintain a registry of MAC addresses with which unknown clients are detected.

Legality

Making use of someone else's wireless access point or wireless router to connect to the internet – without the owner's consent in any way – is not punishable by criminal law in The Netherlands. This is true even if the device uses some form of access protection. To penetrate someone else's computer without the owner's consent is punishable by criminal law though.

Crackers and Society

There is consensus that computer attackers can be divided in the following groups:

- Adolescent amateurs: They often have a basic knowledge of computer systems and apply scripts and techniques that are available on the internet.

- Adult amateurs: Most of them are motivated by the intellectual challenge.

- Professionals: They know much about computers. They are motivated by the financial reward but they are also fond of their activity.

Naming of Crackers

The term hacker was originally used for someone who could modify a computer for his or her own purposes. Hacking is an intrusion combined with direct alteration of the security or data structures of the breached system. The word hacking is often confused with cracking in popular media discourse, and obfuscates the fact that hacking is less about eavesdropping and more related to interference and alteration. However, because of the consistent abuse by the news media, in 2007 the term hacker was commonly used for someone who accesses a network or a computer without authorization of the owner.

In 2011, Collins Dictionary stated that the word hacker can mean a computer fanatic, in particular one who by means of a personal computer breaks into the computer system of a company, government, or the like. It also denoted that in that sense the word hacker is slang. Slang words are not appropriate in formal writing or speech.

Computer experts reserve the word hacker for a very clever programmer. They call someone who breaks into computers an intruder, attacker, or cracker.

Types of Network Security

Access Control

Not every user should have access to your network. To keep out potential attackers, you need to recognize each user and each device. Then you can enforce your security policies. You can block noncompliant endpoint devices or give them only limited access. This process is network access control (NAC).

Antivirus and Antimalware Software

"Malware," short for "malicious software," includes viruses, worms, Trojans, ransomware, and spyware. Sometimes malware will infect a network but lie dormant for days or even weeks. The best antimalware programs not only scan for malware upon entry, but also continuously track files afterward to find anomalies, remove malware, and fix damage.

Application Security

Any software you use to run your business needs to be protected, whether your IT staff builds it or whether you buy it. Unfortunately, any application may contain holes, or vulnerabilities, that attackers can use to infiltrate your network. Application security encompasses the hardware, software, and processes you use to close those holes.

Behavioral Analytics

To detect abnormal network behavior, you must know what normal behavior looks like. Behavioral analytics tools automatically discern activities that deviate from the norm. Your security team can then better identify indicators of compromise that pose a potential problem and quickly remediate threats.

Data Loss Prevention

Organizations must make sure that their staff does not send sensitive information outside the network. Data loss prevention, or DLP, technologies can stop people from uploading, forwarding, or even printing critical information in an unsafe manner.

Email Security

Email gateways are the number one threat vector for a security breach. Attackers use personal information and social engineering tactics to build sophisticated phishing campaigns to deceive recipients and send them to sites serving up malware. An email security application blocks incoming attacks and controls outbound messages to prevent the loss of sensitive data.

Firewalls

Firewalls put up a barrier between your trusted internal network and untrusted outside networks, such as the Internet. They use a set of defined rules to allow or block traffic. A firewall can be hardware, software, or both. Cisco offers unified threat management (UTM) devices and threat-focused next-generation firewalls.

Intrusion Prevention Systems

An intrusion prevention system (IPS) scans network traffic to actively block attacks. Cisco Next-Generation IPS (NGIPS) appliances do this by correlating huge amounts of global threat intelligence to not only block malicious activity but also track the progression of suspect files and malware across the network to prevent the spread of outbreaks and reinfection.

Mobile Device Security

Cybercriminals are increasingly targeting mobile devices and apps. Within the next 3 years, 90 percent of IT organizations may support corporate applications on personal mobile devices. Of course, you need to control which devices can access your network. You will also need to configure their connections to keep network traffic private.

Network Segmentation

Software-defined segmentation puts network traffic into different classifications and makes enforcing security policies easier. Ideally, the classifications are based on endpoint identity, not mere IP addresses. You can assign access rights based on role, location, and more so that the right level of access is given to the right people and suspicious devices are contained and remediated.

Security Information and Event Management

SIEM products pull together the information that your security staff needs to identify and respond to threats. These products come in various forms, including physical and virtual appliances and server software.

VPN

A virtual private network encrypts the connection from an endpoint to a network, often over the Internet. Typically, a remote-access VPN uses IPsec or Secure Sockets Layer to authenticate the communication between device and network.

Web Security

A web security solution will control your staff's web use, block web-based threats, and deny access to malicious websites. It will protect your web gateway on site or in the cloud. "Web security" also refers to the steps you take to protect your own website.

Wireless Security

Wireless networks are not as secure as wired ones. Without stringent security measures, installing a wireless LAN can be like putting Ethernet ports everywhere, including the parking lot. To prevent an exploit from taking hold, you need products specifically designed to protect a wireless network.

Endpoint Security

Endpoint Security, also known Endpoint Protection or Network Security, is a methodology used for protecting corporate networks when accessed through remote devices such as laptops or several other wireless devices and mobile devices. For instance, Comodo Advanced Endpoint Protection software presents seven layers of defense that include viruscope, file reputation, auto-sandbox, host intrusion prevention, web URL filtering, firewall, and antivirus software. All this is offered under a single offering in order to protect them from both unknown and known threats.

Countermeasures

Network Surveillance

Network surveillance is the monitoring of data being transferred over computer networks such as the Internet. The monitoring is often done surreptitiously and may be done by or at the behest of governments, by corporations, criminal organizations, or individuals. It may or may not be legal and may or may not require authorization from a court or other independent agency.

Computer and network surveillance programs are widespread today, and almost all Internet traffic is or could potentially be monitored for clues to illegal activity.

Surveillance is very useful to governments and law enforcement to maintain social control, recognize and monitor threats, and prevent/investigate criminal activity. With the advent of programs such as the Total Information Awareness program, technologies such as high speed surveillance computers and biometrics software, and laws such as the Communications Assistance For Law Enforcement Act, governments now possess an unprecedented ability to monitor the activities of citizens.

However, many civil rights and privacy groups—such as Reporters Without Borders, the Electronic Frontier Foundation, and the American Civil Liberties Union—have expressed concern that increasing surveillance of citizens may lead to a mass surveillance society, with limited political and personal freedoms. Fears such as this have led to numerous lawsuits such as Hepting v. AT&T. The hacktivist group Anonymous has hacked into government websites in protest of what it considers "draconian surveillance".

End-to-end Encryption

End-to-end encryption (E2EE) is a digital communications paradigm of uninterrupted protection of data traveling between two communicating parties. It involves the originating party encrypting data so only the intended recipient can decrypt it, with no dependency on third parties. End-to-end encryption prevents intermediaries, such as Internet providers or application service providers, from discovering or tampering with communications. End-to-end encryption generally protects both confidentiality and integrity.

Examples of end-to-end encryption include HTTPS for web traffic, PGP for email, OTR for instant messaging, ZRTP for telephony, and TETRA for radio.

Typical server-based communications systems do not include end-to-end encryption. These systems can only guarantee protection of communications between clients and servers, not between the communicating parties themselves. Examples of non-E2EE systems are Google Talk, Yahoo Messenger, Facebook, and Dropbox. Some such systems, for example LavaBit and SecretInk, have even described themselves as offering "end-to-end" encryption when they do not. Some systems that normally offer end-to-end encryption have turned out to contain a back door that subverts negotiation of the encryption key between the communicating parties, for example Skype or Hushmail.

The end-to-end encryption paradigm does not directly address risks at the communications endpoints themselves, such as the technical exploitation of clients, poor quality random number generators, or key escrow. E2EE also does not address traffic analysis, which relates to things such as the identities of the end points and the times and quantities of messages that are sent.

SSL and TLS

The introduction and rapid growth of e-commerce on the world wide web in the mid-1990s made it obvious that some form of authentication and encryption was needed. Netscape took the first shot at a new standard. At the time, the dominant web browser was Netscape Navigator. Netscape created a standard called secure socket layer (SSL). SSL requires a server with a certificate. When a client requests access to an SSL-secured server, the server sends a copy of the certificate to the client. The SSL client checks this certificate (all web browsers come with an exhaustive list of CA root certificates preloaded), and if the certificate checks out, the server is authenticated and the client negotiates a symmetric-key cipher for use in the session. The session is now in a very secure encrypted tunnel between the SSL server and the SSL client.

Communication Protocols

A communication protocol is a set of rules for exchanging information over a network. In a protocol stack, each protocol leverages the services of the protocol layer below it, until the lowest layer controls the hardware which sends information across the media. The use of protocol layering is today ubiquitous across the field of computer networking. An important example of a protocol stack is HTTP (the World Wide Web protocol) running over TCP over IP (the Internet protocols) over IEEE 802.11 (the Wi-Fi protocol). This stack is used between the wireless router and the home user's personal computer when the user is surfing the web.

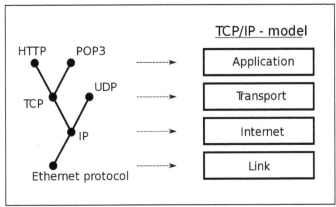

The TCP/IP model or Internet layering scheme and its relation to common protocols often layered on top of it.

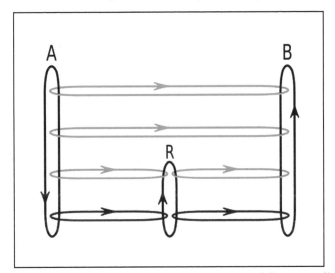

Message flows (A-B) in the presence of a router (R), red flows are effective communication paths, black paths are across the actual network links.

Communication protocols have various characteristics. They may be connection-oriented or connectionless, they may use circuit mode or packet switching, and they may use hierarchical addressing or flat addressing.

IEEE 802

IEEE 802 is a family of IEEE standards dealing with local area networks and metropolitan area networks. The complete IEEE 802 protocol suite provides a diverse set of networking capabilities. The protocols have a flat addressing scheme. They operate mostly at levels 1 and 2 of the OSI model.

For example, MAC bridging (IEEE 802.1D) deals with the routing of Ethernet packets using a

Spanning Tree Protocol. IEEE 802.1Q describes VLANs, and IEEE 802.1X defines a port-based Network Access Control protocol, which forms the basis for the authentication mechanisms used in VLANs (but it is also found in WLANs) – it is what the home user sees when the user has to enter a "wireless access key".

Ethernet

Ethernet, sometimes simply called LAN, is a family of protocols used in wired LANs, described by a set of standards together called IEEE 802.3 published by the Institute of Electrical and Electronics Engineers.

Wireless LAN

Wireless LAN, also widely known as WLAN or WiFi, is probably the most well-known member of the IEEE 802 protocol family for home users today. It is standardized by IEEE 802.11 and shares many properties with wired Ethernet.

Internet Protocol Suite

The Internet Protocol Suite, also called TCP/IP, is the foundation of all modern networking. It offers connection-less as well as connection-oriented services over an inherently unreliable network traversed by data-gram transmission at the Internet protocol (IP) level. At its core, the protocol suite defines the addressing, identification, and routing specifications for Internet Protocol Version 4 (IPv4) and for IPv6, the next generation of the protocol with a much enlarged addressing capability.

SONET and SDH

Synchronous optical networking (SONET) and Synchronous Digital Hierarchy (SDH) are standardized multiplexing protocols that transfer multiple digital bit streams over optical fiber using lasers. They were originally designed to transport circuit mode communications from a variety of different sources, primarily to support real-time, uncompressed, circuit-switched voice encoded in PCM (Pulse-Code Modulation) format. However, due to its protocol neutrality and transport-oriented features, SONET/SDH also was the obvious choice for transporting Asynchronous Transfer Mode (ATM) frames.

Asynchronous Transfer Mode

Asynchronous Transfer Mode (ATM) is a switching technique for telecommunication networks. It uses asynchronous time-division multiplexing and encodes data into small, fixed-sized cells. This differs from other protocols such as the Internet Protocol Suite or Ethernet that use variable sized packets or frames. ATM has similarity with both circuit and packet switched networking. This makes it a good choice for a network that must handle both traditional high-throughput data traffic, and real-time, low-latency content such as voice and video. ATM uses a connection-oriented model in which a virtual circuit must be established between two endpoints before the actual data exchange begins.

While the role of ATM is diminishing in favor of next-generation networks, it still plays a role in the last mile, which is the connection between an Internet service provider and the home user.

Cellular Standards

There are a number of different digital cellular standards, including: Global System for Mobile Communications (GSM), General Packet Radio Service (GPRS), cdmaOne, CDMA2000, Evolution-Data Optimized (EV-DO), Enhanced Data Rates for GSM Evolution (EDGE), Universal Mobile Telecommunications System (UMTS), Digital Enhanced Cordless Telecommunications (DECT), Digital AMPS (IS-136/TDMA), and Integrated Digital Enhanced Network (iDEN).

Cyber Security

Cyber security refers to the body of technologies, processes, and practices designed to protect networks, devices, programs, and data from attack, damage, or unauthorized access. Cyber security may also be referred to as information technology security.

Cyber security is important because government, military, corporate, financial, and medical organizations collect, process, and store unprecedented amounts of data on computers and other devices. A significant portion of that data can be sensitive information, whether that be intellectual property, financial data, personal information, or other types of data for which unauthorized access or exposure could have negative consequences. Organizations transmit sensitive data across networks and to other devices in the course of doing businesses, and cyber security describes the discipline dedicated to protecting that information and the systems used to process or store it. As the volume and sophistication of cyber attacks grow, companies and organizations, especially those that are tasked with safeguarding information relating to national security, health, or financial records, need to take steps to protect their sensitive business and personnel information. As early as March 2013, the nation's top intelligence officials cautioned that cyber attacks and digital spying are the top threat to national security, eclipsing even terrorism.

For an effective cyber security, an organization needs to coordinate its efforts throughout its entire information system. Elements of cyber encompass all of the following:

- Network security,
- Application security,
- Endpoint security,
- Data security,
- Identity management,
- Database and infrastructure security,
- Cloud security,
- Mobile security,
- Disaster recovery/business continuity planning,
- End-user education.

Mobile IP in Computer Network

Mobile IP is a communication protocol (created by extending Internet Protocol, IP) that allows the users to move from one network to another with the same IP address. It ensures that the communication will continue without user's sessions or connections being dropped.

References

- The-top-9-network-security-threats-of-2019: securityfirstcorp.com, Retrieved 6 January, 2019

- Satter, raphael (28 march 2017). "what makes a cyberattack? Experts lobby to restrict the term". Retrieved 7 july 2017

- Computer-network-mobile-ip: geeksforgeeks.org, Retrieved 2 July, 2019

- "Computer security and mobile security challenges". Researchgate.net. 3 december 2015. Archived from the original on 12 october 2016. Retrieved 4 august 2016

- Scannell, kara (24 february 2016). "ceo email scam costs companies $2bn". Financial times (25 feb 2016). Archived from the original on 23 june 2016. Retrieved 7 may 2016

- What-is-network-security: comodo.com, Retrieved 19 May, 2019

- Spoofing. Oxford reference. Oxford university press. 21 january 201 6. Doi:10.1093/acref/9780199688975.001.-0001. Isbn 9780199688975. Retrieved 8 october 2017

- What-is-a-sniffing-attack-and-how-can-you-defend-it, information-security: greycampus.com, Retrieved 14 July, 2019

- Omura, yasuhisa; mallik, abhijit; matsuo, naoto (2017). Mos devices for low-voltage and low-energy applications. John wiley & sons. P. 53. Isbn 9781119107354

- What-cyber-security: digitalguardian.com, Retrieved 5 August, 2019

- Asif, saad (2018). 5g mobile communications: concepts and technologies. Crc press. Pp. 128–134. Isbn 9780429881343

5

Applications of Computer Networks

Computer networks are used in numerous fields and systems such as ethernet, world wide web, intranet, internet, extranet, deep web and cloud computing. The diverse applications of networks in these areas have been thoroughly discussed in this chapter.

Ethernet

Ethernet is the traditional technology for connecting wired local area networks (LANs), enabling devices to communicate with each other via a protocol - a set of rules or common network language.

As a data-link layer protocol in the TCP/IP stack, Ethernet describes how network devices can format and transmit data packets so other devices on the same local or campus area network segment can recognize, receive and process them. An Ethernet cable is the physical, encased wiring over which the data travels.

Any device accessing a geographically localized network using a cable, i.e., with a wired rather than wireless connection, likely uses Ethernet - whether in a home, school or office setting. From businesses to gamers, diverse end users depend on the benefits of Ethernet connectivity, including reliability and security.

Compared to wireless LAN technology, Ethernet is typically less vulnerable to disruptions, whether from radio wave interference, physical barriers or bandwidth hogs. It can also offer a greater degree of network security and control than wireless technology, as devices must connect using physical cabling, making it difficult for outsiders to access network data or hijack bandwidth for unsanctioned devices.

How Ethernet Works

The Institute of Electrical and Electronics Engineers Inc. (IEEE) specifies in the family of standards called IEEE 802.3 that the Ethernet protocol touches both Layer 1 - the physical layer - and Layer 2 - the data link layer - on the OSI network protocol model. Ethernet defines two units of transmission: packet and frame. The frame includes not just the payload of data being transmitted, but also:

- The physical media access control (MAC) addresses of both the sender and receiver;

- VLAN tagging and quality of service information;

- Error correction information to detect transmission problems.

Each frame is wrapped in a packet that contains several bytes of information to establish the connection and mark where the frame starts.

Engineers at Xerox first developed Ethernet in the 1970s. Ethernet initially ran over coaxial cables, while a typical Ethernet LAN today uses special grades of twisted pair cables or fiber optic cabling. Early Ethernet connected multiple devices into network segments through hubs - Layer 1 devices responsible for transporting network data - using either a daisy chain or star topology.

If two devices that share a hub try to transmit data at the same time, however, the packets can collide and create connectivity problems. To alleviate these digital traffic jams, the IEEE developed the Carrier Sense Multiple Access with Collision Detection (CSMA/CD) protocol, which allows devices to check whether a given line is in use before initiating new transmissions.

Later, Ethernet hubs largely gave way to network switches, their more sophisticated and modern counterparts. Because a hub cannot discriminate between points on a network segment, it can't send data directly from point A to point B. Instead, whenever a network device sends a transmission via an input port, the hub copies the data and distributes it to all the available output ports.

In contrast, a switch intelligently sends any given port only the traffic intended for its devices rather than copies of any and all the transmissions on the network segment, improving security and efficiency.

Types of Ethernet Cables

The IEEE 802.3 working group approved the first Ethernet standard in 1983. Since then, the technology has continued to evolve and embrace new media, higher transmission speeds and changes in frame content, e.g., 802.3ac to accommodate VLAN and priority tagging - and functional requirements, e.g., 802.3af to define Power over Ethernet (POE), which is crucial to most Wi-Fi and IP telephony deployments. Wi-Fi standards, IEEE 802.11a, b, g, n, ac and ax, define the equivalent of Ethernet for Wireless LANs.

Ethernet standard IEEE 802.3u ushered in 100BASE-T - also known as Fast Ethernet with data transmission speeds of up to 100 megabits per second (Mbps). The term BASE-T indicates the use of twisted-pair cabling.

Gigabit Ethernet boasts speeds of 1,000 Mbps - 1 gigabit or 1 billion bits per second - 10-Gigabit Ethernet (GbE), up to 10 Gbps, and so on. Network engineers use 100BASE-T largely to connect end-user computers, printers and other devices; to manage servers and storage; and to achieve higher speeds for network backbone segments. Over time, the typical speed of each connection tends to increase.

Ethernet cables connect network devices to the appropriate routers or modems, with different cables working with different standards and speeds. The Category 5 (CAT5) cable supports traditional and 100BASE-T Ethernet, for example, while Category 5e (CAT5e) can handle Gigabit Ethernet and Category 6 (CAT6) works with 10 GbE.

Evolution

Ethernet has evolved to include higher bandwidth, improved medium access control methods, and different physical media. The coaxial cable was replaced with point-to-point links connected by Ethernet repeaters or switches.

Ethernet stations communicate by sending each other data packets: blocks of data individually sent and delivered. As with other IEEE 802 LANs, each Ethernet station is given a 48-bit MAC address. The MAC addresses are used to specify both the destination and the source of each data packet. Ethernet establishes link-level connections, which can be defined using both the destination and source addresses. On reception of a transmission, the receiver uses the destination address to determine whether the transmission is relevant to the station or should be ignored. A network interface normally does not accept packets addressed to other Ethernet stations. Adapters come programmed with a globally unique address

An EtherType field in each frame is used by the operating system on the receiving station to select the appropriate protocol module (e.g., an Internet Protocol version such as IPv4). Ethernet frames are said to be self-identifying, because of the EtherType field. Self-identifying frames make it possible to intermix multiple protocols on the same physical network and allow a single computer to use multiple protocols together. Despite the evolution of Ethernet technology, all generations of Ethernet (excluding early experimental versions) use the same frame formats. Mixed-speed networks can be built using Ethernet switches and repeaters supporting the desired Ethernet variants.

Due to the ubiquity of Ethernet, the ever-decreasing cost of the hardware needed to support it, and the reduced panel space needed by twisted pair Ethernet, most manufacturers now build Ethernet interfaces directly into PC motherboards, eliminating the need for installation of a separate network card.

Shared Media

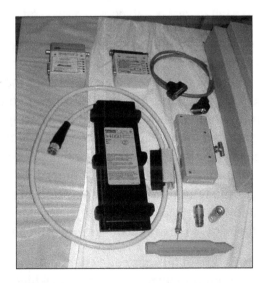

The above image shows, older Ethernet equipment: Clockwise from top-left: An Ethernet transceiver with an in-line 10BASE2 adapter, a similar model transceiver with a 10BASE5 adapter, an AUI cable, a different style of transceiver with 10BASE2 BNC T-connector, two 10BASE5 end

fittings (N connectors), an orange "vampire tap" installation tool (which includes a specialized drill bit at one end and a socket wrench at the other), and an early model 10BASE5 transceiver (h4000) manufactured by DEC. The short length of yellow 10BASE5 cable has one end fitted with a N connector and the other end prepared to have a N connector shell installed; the half-black, half-grey rectangular object through which the cable passes is an installed vampire tap.

Ethernet was originally based on the idea of computers communicating over a shared coaxial cable acting as a broadcast transmission medium. The method used was similar to those used in radio systems, with the common cable providing the communication channel likened to the Luminiferous aether in 19th century physics, and it was from this reference that the name "Ethernet" was derived.

Original Ethernet's shared coaxial cable (the shared medium) traversed a building or campus to every attached machine. A scheme known as carrier sense multiple access with collision detection (CSMA/CD) governed the way the computers shared the channel. This scheme was simpler than competing Token Ring or Token Bus technologies. Computers are connected to an Attachment Unit Interface (AUI) transceiver, which is in turn connected to the cable (with thin Ethernet the transceiver is integrated into the network adapter). While a simple passive wire is highly reliable for small networks, it is not reliable for large extended networks, where damage to the wire in a single place, or a single bad connector, can make the whole Ethernet segment unusable.

Through the first half of the 1980s, Ethernet's 10BASE5 implementation used a coaxial cable 0.375 inches (9.5 mm) in diameter, later called "thick Ethernet" or "thicknet". Its successor, 10BASE2, called "thin Ethernet" or "thinnet", used the RG-58 coaxial cable. The emphasis was on making installation of the cable easier and less costly.

Since all communication happens on the same wire, any information sent by one computer is received by all, even if that information is intended for just one destination. The network interface card interrupts the CPU only when applicable packets are received: the card ignores information not addressed to it. Use of a single cable also means that the data bandwidth is shared, such that, for example, available data bandwidth to each device is halved when two stations are simultaneously active.

A collision happens when two stations attempt to transmit at the same time. They corrupt transmitted data and require stations to re-transmit. The lost data and re-transmission reduces throughput. In the worst case, where multiple active hosts connected with maximum allowed cable length attempt to transmit many short frames, excessive collisions can reduce throughput dramatically. However, a Xerox report in 1980 studied performance of an existing Ethernet installation under both normal and artificially generated heavy load. The report claimed that 98% throughput on the LAN was observed. This is in contrast with token passing LANs (Token Ring, Token Bus), all of which suffer throughput degradation as each new node comes into the LAN, due to token waits. This report was controversial, as modeling showed that collision-based networks theoretically became unstable under loads as low as 37% of nominal capacity. Many early researchers failed to understand these results. Performance on real networks is significantly better.

In a modern Ethernet, the stations do not all share one channel through a shared cable or a simple repeater hub; instead, each station communicates with a switch, which in turn forwards that traffic to the destination station. In this topology, collisions are only possible if station and switch attempt to communicate with each other at the same time, and collisions are limited to this link. Furthermore, the 10BASE-T standard introduced a full duplex mode of operation which became common with Fast Ethernet and the de facto standard with Gigabit Ethernet. In full duplex, switch and station can send and receive simultaneously, and therefore modern Ethernets are completely collision-free.

Comparison between Original Ethernet and Modern Ethernet

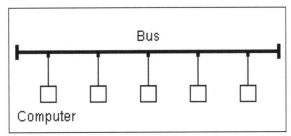

The original Ethernet implementation: shared medium, collision-prone. All computers trying to communicate share the same cable, and so compete with each other.

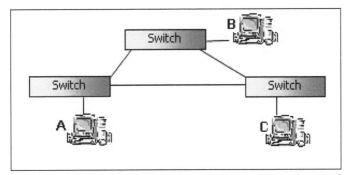

Modern Ethernet implementation: switched connection, collision-free. Each computer communicates only with its own switch, without competition for the cable with others.

Repeaters and Hubs

A 1990s ISA network interface card supporting both coaxial-cable-based 10BASE2 (BNC connector, left) and twisted pair-based 10BASE-T (8P8C connector, right).

For signal degradation and timing reasons, coaxial Ethernet segments have a restricted size. Somewhat larger networks can be built by using an Ethernet repeater. Early repeaters had only two ports, allowing, at most, a doubling of network size. Once repeaters with more than two ports became available, it was possible to wire the network in a star topology. Early experiments with star topologies (called "Fibernet") using optical fiber were published by 1978.

Shared cable Ethernet is always hard to install in offices because its bus topology is in conflict with the star topology cable plans designed into buildings for telephony. Modifying Ethernet to conform to twisted pair telephone wiring already installed in commercial buildings provided another opportunity to lower costs, expand the installed base, and leverage building design, and, thus, twisted-pair Ethernet was the next logical development in the mid-1980s.

Ethernet on unshielded twisted-pair cables (UTP) began with StarLAN at 1 Mbit/s in the mid-1980s. In 1987 SynOptics introduced the first twisted-pair Ethernet at 10 Mbit/s in a star-wired cabling topology with a central hub, later called LattisNet. These evolved into 10BASE-T, which was designed for point-to-point links only, and all termination was built into the device. This changed repeaters from a specialist device used at the center of large networks to a device that every twisted pair-based network with more than two machines had to use. The tree structure that resulted from this made Ethernet networks easier to maintain by preventing most faults with one peer or its associated cable from affecting other devices on the network.

Despite the physical star topology and the presence of separate transmit and receive channels in the twisted pair and fiber media, repeater-based Ethernet networks still use half-duplex and CSMA/CD, with only minimal activity by the repeater, primarily generation of the jam signal in dealing with packet collisions. Every packet is sent to every other port on the repeater, so bandwidth and security problems are not addressed. The total throughput of the repeater is limited to that of a single link, and all links must operate at the same speed.

Bridging and Switching

Patch cables with patch fields of two Ethernet switches.

While repeaters can isolate some aspects of Ethernet segments, such as cable breakages, they still forward all traffic to all Ethernet devices. The entire network is one collision domain, and all hosts have to be able to detect collisions anywhere on the network. This limits the number of repeaters between the farthest nodes and creates practical limits on how many machines can communicate on an Ethernet network. Segments joined by repeaters have to all operate at the same speed, making phased-in upgrades impossible.

To alleviate these problems, bridging was created to communicate at the data link layer while isolating the physical layer. With bridging, only well-formed Ethernet packets are forwarded from one Ethernet segment to another; collisions and packet errors are isolated. At initial startup, Ethernet bridges work somewhat like Ethernet repeaters, passing all traffic between segments. By observing the source addresses of incoming frames, the bridge then builds an address table associating addresses to segments. Once an address is learned, the bridge forwards network traffic destined for that address only to the associated segment, improving overall performance. Broadcast traffic is still forwarded to all network segments. Bridges also overcome the limits on total segments between two hosts and allow the mixing of speeds, both of which are critical to incremental deployment of faster Ethernet variants.

In 1989, the networking company Kalpana introduced their EtherSwitch, the first Ethernet switch. Early switches such as this used cut-through switching where only the header of the incoming packet is examined before it is either dropped or forwarded to another segment. This reduces the forwarding latency. One drawback of this method is that it does not readily allow a mixture of different link speeds. Another is that packets that have been corrupted are still propagated through the network. The eventual remedy for this was a return to the original store and forward approach of bridging, where the packet is read into a buffer on the switch in its entirety, its frame check sequence verified and only then packet is forwarded. This process is typically done using application-specific integrated circuits allowing packets to be forwarded at wire speed.

When a twisted pair or fiber link segment is used and neither end is connected to a repeater, full-duplex Ethernet becomes possible over that segment. In full-duplex mode, both devices can transmit and receive to and from each other at the same time, and there is no collision domain. This doubles the aggregate bandwidth of the link and is sometimes advertised as double the link speed (for example, 200 Mbit/s for Fast Ethernet). The elimination of the collision domain for these connections also means that all the link's bandwidth can be used by the two devices on that segment and that segment length is not limited by the need for correct collision detection.

Since packets are typically delivered only to the port they are intended for, traffic on a switched Ethernet is less public than on shared-medium Ethernet. Despite this, switched Ethernet should still be regarded as an insecure network technology, because it is easy to subvert switched Ethernet systems by means such as ARP spoofing and MAC flooding.

The bandwidth advantages, the improved isolation of devices from each other, the ability to easily mix different speeds of devices and the elimination of the chaining limits inherent in non-switched Ethernet have made switched Ethernet the dominant network technology.

Advanced Networking

A core Ethernet switch.

Simple switched Ethernet networks, while a great improvement over repeater-based Ethernet, suffer from single points of failure, attacks that trick switches or hosts into sending data to a machine even if it is not intended for it, scalability and security issues with regard to switching loops, broadcast radiation and multicast traffic, and bandwidth choke points where a lot of traffic is forced down a single link.

Advanced networking features in switches use shortest path bridging (SPB) or the spanning-tree protocol (STP) to maintain a loop-free, meshed network, allowing physical loops for redundancy (STP) or load-balancing (SPB). Advanced networking features also ensure port security, provide protection features such as MAC lockdown and broadcast radiation filtering, use virtual LANs to keep different classes of users separate while using the same physical infrastructure, employ multilayer switching to route between different classes, and use link aggregation to add bandwidth to overloaded links and to provide some redundancy.

Shortest path bridging includes the use of the link-state routing protocol IS-IS to allow larger networks with shortest path routes between devices. In 2012, it was stated by David Allan and Nigel Bragg, in 802.1aq Shortest Path Bridging Design and Evolution: The Architect's Perspective that shortest path bridging is one of the most significant enhancements in Ethernet's history. Ethernet has replaced InfiniBand as the most popular system interconnect of TOP500 supercomputers.

World Wide Web

The World Wide Web (WWW) is a network of online content that is formatted in HTML and accessed via HTTP. The term refers to all the interlinked HTML pages that can be accessed over the Internet. The World Wide Web was originally designed in 1991 by Tim Berners-Lee while he was a contractor at CERN. The World Wide Web is most often referred to simply as "the Web."

The World Wide Web is what most people think of as the Internet. It is all the Web pages, pictures, videos and other online content that can be accessed via a Web browser. The Internet, in contrast, is the underlying network connection that allows us to send email and access the World Wide Web. The early Web was a collection of text-based sites hosted by organizations that were technically gifted enough to set up a Web server and learn HTML.

HTTP

HTTP means HyperText Transfer Protocol. HTTP is the underlying protocol used by the World Wide Web and this protocol defines how messages are formatted and transmitted, and what actions Web servers and browsers should take in response to various commands.

For example, when you enter a URL in your browser, this actually sends an HTTP command to the Web server directing it to fetch and transmit the requested Web page. The other main standard that controls how the World Wide Web works is HTML, which covers how Web pages are formatted and displayed.

HTTP is a Stateless Protocol

HTTP is called a stateless protocol because each command is executed independently, without any knowledge of the commands that came before it. This is the main reason that it is difficult to implement Web sites that react intelligently to user input. This shortcoming of HTTP is being addressed in a number of new technologies, including ActiveX, Java, JavaScript and cookies.

HTTP Status Codes are Error Messages

Errors on the Internet can be quite frustrating — especially if you do not know the difference between a 404 error and a 502 error. These error messages, also called HTTP status codes are response codes given by Web servers and help identify the cause of the problem.

For example, "404 File Not Found" is a common HTTP status code. It means the Web server cannot find the file you requested. This means the webpage or other document you tried to load in your Web browser has either been moved or deleted, or you entered the wrong URL or document name.

Knowing the meaning of the HTTP status code can help you figure out what went wrong. On a 404 error, for example, you could look at the URL to see if a word looks misspelled, then correct it and try it again. If that doesn't work, backtrack by deleting information between each backslash, until you come to a page on that site that isn't a 404. From there you may be able to find the page you're looking for.

Custom 404 Error Pages

Many websites create custom 404 error pages that will help users locate a valid page or document within the website. For example, if you land on a 404 File Not Found page via Webopedia.com, a custom error page will load providing quick links to on-site navigation and site search features to help you find what you were looking for.

HTTPS

A similar abbreviation, HTTPS means Hyper Text Transfer Protocol Secure. Basically, it is the secure version of HTTP. Communications between the browser and website are encrypted by Transport Layer Security (TLS), or its predecessor, Secure Sockets Layer (SSL).

Basic Features

There are three basic features that make HTTP a simple but powerful protocol:

- HTTP is connectionless: The HTTP client, i.e., a browser initiates an HTTP request and after a request is made, the client waits for the response. The server processes the request and sends a response back after which client disconnect the connection. So client and server knows about each other during current request and response only. Further requests are made on new connection like client and server are new to each other.

- HTTP is media independent: It means, any type of data can be sent by HTTP as long as both the client and the server know how to handle the data content. It is required for the client as well as the server to specify the content type using appropriate MIME-type.

- HTTP is stateless: HTTP is connectionless and it is a direct result of HTTP being a stateless protocol. The server and client are aware of each other only during a current request. Afterwards, both of them forget about each other. Due to this nature of the protocol, neither the client nor the browser can retain information between different requests across the web pages.

Basic Architecture

The following figure shows a very basic architecture of a web application and depicts where HTTP sits:

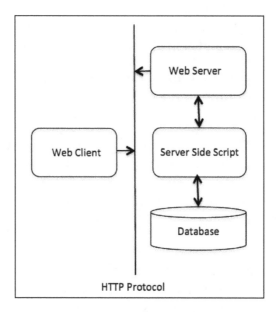

The HTTP protocol is a request/response protocol based on the client/server based architecture where web browsers, robots and search engines, etc. act like HTTP clients, and the Web server acts as a server.

Client

The HTTP client sends a request to the server in the form of a request method, URI, and protocol version, followed by a MIME-like message containing request modifiers, client information, and possible body content over a TCP/IP connection.

Server

The HTTP server responds with a status line, including the message's protocol version and a success or error code, followed by a MIME-like message containing server information, entity meta information, and possible entity-body content.

Web Caching

Web caching is a core design feature of the HTTP protocol meant to minimize network traffic while improving the perceived responsiveness of the system as a whole. Caches are found at every level of a content's journey from the original server to the browser.

Web caching works by caching the HTTP responses for requests according to certain rules. Subsequent requests for cached content can then be fulfilled from a cache closer to the user instead of sending the request all the way back to the web server.

Benefits

Effective caching aids both content consumers and content providers. Some of the benefits that caching brings to content delivery are:

- Decreased network costs: Content can be cached at various points in the network path between the content consumer and content origin. When the content is cached closer to the consumer, requests will not cause much additional network activity beyond the cache.

- Improved responsiveness: Caching enables content to be retrieved faster because an entire network round trip is not necessary. Caches maintained close to the user, like the browser cache, can make this retrieval nearly instantaneous.

- Increased performance on the same hardware: For the server where the content originated, more performance can be squeezed from the same hardware by allowing aggressive caching. The content owner can leverage the powerful servers along the delivery path to take the brunt of certain content loads.

- Availability of content during network interruptions: With certain policies, caching can be used to serve content to end users even when it may be unavailable for short periods of time from the origin servers.

Terminology

When dealing with caching, there are a few terms that you are likely to come across that might be unfamiliar. Some of the more common ones are below:

- Origin server: The origin server is the original location of the content. If you are acting as the web server administrator, this is the machine that you control. It is responsible for serving any content that could not be retrieved from a cache along the request route and for setting the caching policy for all content.

- Cache hit ratio: A cache's effectiveness is measured in terms of its cache hit ratio or hit rate. This is a ratio of the requests able to be retrieved from a cache to the total requests made. A high cache hit ratio means that a high percentage of the content was able to be retrieved from the cache. This is usually the desired outcome for most administrators.

- Freshness: Freshness is a term used to describe whether an item within a cache is still considered a candidate to serve to a client. Content in a cache will only be used to respond if it is within the freshness time frame specified by the caching policy.

- Stale content: Items in the cache expire according to the cache freshness settings in the caching policy. Expired content is "stale". In general, expired content cannot be used to respond to client requests. The origin server must be re-contacted to retrieve the new content or at least verify that the cached content is still accurate.

- Validation: Stale items in the cache can be validated in order to refresh their expiration time. Validation involves checking in with the origin server to see if the cached content still represents the most recent version of item.

- Invalidation: Invalidation is the process of removing content from the cache before its specified expiration date. This is necessary if the item has been changed on the origin server and having an outdated item in cache would cause significant issues for the client.

What can be Cached

Certain content lends itself more readily to caching than others. Some very cache-friendly content for most sites are:

- Logos and brand images.

- Non-rotating images in general (navigation icons, for example).

- Style sheets.

- General Javascript files.

- Downloadable Content.

- Media Files.

These tend to change infrequently, so they can benefit from being cached for longer periods of time.

Some items that you have to be careful in caching are:

- HTML pages,

- Rotating images,

- Frequently modified Javascript and CSS,

- Content requested with authentication cookies.

Some items that should almost never be cached are:

- Assets related to sensitive data (banking info, etc.).

- Content that is user-specific and frequently changed.

In addition to the above general rules, it's possible to specify policies that allow you to cache different types of content appropriately. For instance, if authenticated users all see the same view of your site, it may be possible to cache that view anywhere. If authenticated users see a user-sensitive view of the site that will be valid for some time, you may tell the user's browser to cache, but tell any intermediary caches not to store the view.

Locations where Web Content is Cached

Content can be cached at many different points throughout the delivery chain:

- Browser cache: Web browsers themselves maintain a small cache. Typically, the browser sets a policy that dictates the most important items to cache. This may be user-specific content or content deemed expensive to download and likely to be requested again.

- Intermediary caching proxies: Any server in between the client and your infrastructure can cache certain content as desired. These caches may be maintained by ISPs or other independent parties.

- Reverse Cache: Your server infrastructure can implement its own cache for backend services. This way, content can be served from the point-of-contact instead of hitting backend servers on each request.

Each of these locations can and often do cache items according to their own caching policies and the policies set at the content origin.

Caching Headers

Caching policy is dependent upon two different factors. The caching entity itself gets to decide whether or not to cache acceptable content. It can decide to cache less than it is allowed to cache, but never more.

The majority of caching behavior is determined by the caching policy, which is set by the content owner. These policies are mainly articulated through the use of specific HTTP headers.

Through various iterations of the HTTP protocol, a few different cache-focused headers have arisen with varying levels of sophistication. The ones you probably still need to pay attention to are below:

- Expires: The Expires header is very straight-forward, although fairly limited in scope. Basically, it sets a time in the future when the content will expire. At this point, any requests for the same content will have to go back to the origin server. This header is probably best used only as a fall back.

- Cache-Control: This is the more modern replacement for the Expires header. It is well supported and implements a much more flexible design. In almost all cases, this is preferable to Expires, but it may not hurt to set both values.

- Etag: The Etag header is used with cache validation. The origin can provide a unique Etag-for an item when it initially serves the content. When a cache needs to validate the content it has on-hand upon expiration, it can send back the Etagit has for the content. The origin will either tell the cache that the content is the same, or send the updated content (with the new Etag).

- Last-Modified: This header specifies the last time that the item was modified. This may be used as part of the validation strategy to ensure fresh content.

- Content-Length: While not specifically involved in caching, the Content-Length header is important to set when defining caching policies. Certain software will refuse to cache content if it does not know in advanced the size of the content it will need to reserve space for.

- Vary: A cache typically uses the requested host and the path to the resource as the key with which to store the cache item. The Vary header can be used to tell caches to pay attention to an additional header when deciding whether a request is for the same item. This is most commonly used to tell caches to key by the Accept-Encoding header as well, so that the cache will know to differentiate between compressed and uncompressed content.

Systems

Web caches can be used in various systems (as viewed from direction of delivery of Web content):

Forward Position System: Recipient or Client Side

A forward cache is a cache outside the Web server's network, e.g. on the client computer, in an ISP or within a corporate network. A network-aware forward cache is just like a forward cache but only caches heavily accessed items. A client, such as a Web browser, can also store Web content for re-use. For example, if the back button is pressed, the local cached version of a page may be displayed instead of a new request being sent to the Web server. A Web proxy sitting between the client and the server can evaluate HTTP headers and choose whether to store Web content.

Reverse Position System: Content Provider or Web-server Side

A reverse cache sits in front of one or more Web servers and Web applications, accelerating requests from the Internet, reducing peak Web server load. A content delivery network (CDN) can retain copies of Web content at various points throughout a network. A search engine may also cache a website; it provides a way of retrieving information from websites that have recently gone down or a way of retrieving data more quickly than by clicking the direct link. Google, for instance, does so.

Cache control

HTTP defines three basic mechanisms for controlling caches: freshness, validation, and invalidation.

Freshness

It allows a response to be used without re-checking it on the origin server, and can be controlled by both the server and the client. For example, the Expires response header gives a date when the document becomes stale, and the Cache-Control: max-age directive tells the cache how many seconds the response is fresh for.

Validation

It can be used to check whether a cached response is still good after it becomes stale. For example, if the response has a Last-Modified header, a cache can make a conditional request using the If-Modified-Since header to see if it has changed. The ETag (entity tag) mechanism also allows for both strong and weak validation.

Invalidation

It is usually a side effect of another request that passes through the cache. For example, if a URL associated with a cached response subsequently gets a POST, PUT or DELETE request, the cached response will be invalidated.

Intranet

An intranet is a private network accessible only to an organization's staff. Often, a wide range of information and services are available on an organization's internal intranet that are unavailable to the public, unlike the Internet. A company-wide intranet can constitute an important focal point of internal communication and collaboration, and provide a single starting point to access internal and external resources. In its simplest form, an intranet is established with the technologies for local area networks (LANs) and wide area networks (WANs). Many modern intranets have search engines, user profiles, blogs, mobile apps with notifications, and events planning within their infrastructure.

Intranets began to appear in a range of larger organizations from 1994. Increasingly, intranets are being used to deliver tools, e.g. collaboration (to facilitate working in groups and teleconferencing) or sophisticated corporate directories, sales and customer relationship management tools, project management etc.

Intranets are also being used as corporate culture-change platforms. For example, large numbers of employees discussing key issues in an intranet forum application could lead to new ideas in management, productivity, quality, and other corporate issues.

In large intranets, website traffic is often similar to public website traffic and can be better understood by using web metrics software to track overall activity. User surveys also improve intranet website effectiveness.

Larger businesses allow users within their intranet to access public internet through firewall servers. They have the ability to screen messages coming and going, keeping security intact. When part of an intranet is made accessible to customers and others outside the business, it becomes part of an extranet. Businesses can send private messages through the public network, using special encryption/decryption and other security safeguards to connect one part of their intranet to another.

Intranet user-experience, editorial, and technology teams work together to produce in-house sites. Most commonly, intranets are managed by the communications, HR or CIO departments of large organizations, or some combination of these.

Because of the scope and variety of content and the number of system interfaces, intranets of many organizations are much more complex than their respective public websites. Intranets and their use are growing rapidly. According to the Intranet design annual 2007 from Nielsen Norman Group, the number of pages on participants' intranets averaged 200,000 over the years 2001 to 2003 and has grown to an average of 6 million pages over 2005–2007.

- Workforce productivity: Intranets can help users to locate and view information faster and use applications relevant to their roles and responsibilities. With the help of a web browser interface, users can access data held in any database the organization wants to make available, anytime and— subject to security provisions— from anywhere within the company workstations, increasing the employees ability to perform their jobs faster, more accurately, and with confidence that they have the right information. It also helps to improve the services provided to the users.

- Time: Intranets allow organizations to distribute information to employees on an as-needed basis; Employees may link to relevant information at their convenience, rather than being distracted indiscriminately by email.

- Communication: Intranets can serve as powerful tools for communication within an organization, vertically strategic initiatives that have a global reach throughout the organization. The type of information that can easily be conveyed is the purpose of the initiative and what the initiative is aiming to achieve, who is driving the initiative, results achieved to date, and who to speak to for more information. By providing this information on the intranet, staff have the opportunity to keep up-to-date with the strategic focus of the organization. Some examples of communication would be chat, email, and blogs. A great real-world example of where an intranet helped a company communicate is when Nestle had a number of food processing plants in Scandinavia. Their central support system had to deal with a number of queries every day. When Nestle decided to invest in an intranet, they quickly realized the savings. McGovern says the savings from the reduction in query calls was substantially greater than the investment in the intranet.

- Web publishing allows cumbersome corporate knowledge to be maintained and easily accessed throughout the company using hypermedia and Web technologies. Examples include: employee manuals, benefits documents, company policies, business standards, news feeds, and even training, can be accessed using common Internet standards (Acrobat files, Flash files, CGI applications). Because each business unit can update the online copy of a document, the most recent version is usually available to employees using the intranet.

- Business operations and management: Intranets are also being used as a platform for developing and deploying applications to support business operations and decisions across the internetworked enterprise.

- Workflow: A collective term that reduces delay, such as automating meeting scheduling and vacation planning.

- Cost-effective: Users can view information and data via web-browser rather than maintaining physical documents such as procedure manuals, internal phone list and requisition forms. This can potentially save the business money on printing, duplicating documents, and the environment as well as document maintenance overhead. For example, the HRM company PeopleSoft "derived significant cost savings by shifting HR processes to the intranet". McGovern goes on to say the manual cost of enrolling in benefits was found to be USD109.48 per enrollment. "Shifting this process to the intranet reduced the cost per enrollment to $21.79; a saving of 80 percent". Another company that saved money on expense reports was Cisco. "In 1996, Cisco processed 54,000 reports and the amount of dollars processed was USD19 million".

- Enhance collaboration: Information is easily accessible by all authorised users, which enables teamwork. Being able to communicate in real-time through integrated third party tools, such as an instant messenger, promotes the sharing of ideas and removes blockages to communication to help boost a business' productivity.

- Cross-platform capability: Standards-compliant web browsers are available for Windows, Mac, and UNIX.

- Built for one audience: Many companies dictate computer specifications which, in turn, may allow Intranet developers to write applications that only have to work on one browser (no cross-browser compatibility issues). Being able to specifically address your "viewer" is a great advantage. Since Intranets are user-specific (requiring database/network authentication prior to access), you know exactly who you are interfacing with and can personalize your Intranet based on role (job title, department) or individual.

- Promote common corporate culture: Every user has the ability to view the same information within the Intranet.

- Immediate updates: When dealing with the public in any capacity, laws, specifications, and parameters can change. Intranets make it possible to provide your audience with "live" changes so they are kept up-to-date, which can limit a company's liability.

- Supports a distributed computing architecture: The intranet can also be linked to a company's management information system, for example a time keeping system.

- Employee Engagement: Since "involvement in decision making" is one of the main drivers of employee engagement, offering tools (like forums or surveys) that foster peer-to-peer collaboration and employee participation can make employees feel more valued and involved.

Most organizations devote considerable resources into the planning and implementation of their intranet as it is of strategic importance to the organization's success. Some of the planning would include topics such as determining the purpose and goals of the intranet, identifying persons or departments responsible for implementation and management and devising functional plans, page layouts and designs.

The appropriate staff would also ensure that implementation schedules and phase-out of existing systems were organized, while defining and implementing security of the intranet and ensuring it lies within legal boundaries and other constraints. In order to produce a high-value end product, systems planners should determine the level of interactivity desired.

Planners may also consider whether the input of new data and updating of existing data is to be centrally controlled or devolve. These decisions sit alongside to the hardware and software considerations (like content management systems), participation issues (like good taste, harassment, confidentiality), and features to be supported.

Intranets are often static sites; they are a shared drive, serving up centrally stored documents alongside internal articles or communications (often one-way communication). By leveraging firms which specialise in 'social' intranets, organisations are beginning to think of how their intranets can become a 'communication hub' for their entire team. The actual implementation would include steps such as securing senior management support and funding., conducting a business requirement analysis and identifying users' information needs.

From the technical perspective, there would need to be a co-ordinated installation of the web server and user access network, the required user/client applications and the creation of document framework (or template) for the content to be hosted.

The end-user should be involved in testing and promoting use of the company intranet, possibly through a parallel adoption methodology or pilot programme. In the long term, the company should carry out ongoing measurement and evaluation, including through benchmarking against other company services.

Password Management - Rather than have a Password manager manage two or more dozen passwords, Single Sign-on (SSO) allows a single password to cover multiple applications. This is a relatively new development.

Some aspects are non-static. An intranet structure needs key personnel committed to maintaining the Intranet and keeping content current. For feedback on the intranet, social networking can be done through a forum for users to indicate what they want and what they do not like.

A short item in "Top Five Intranet Trends for 2019" was titled Data Privacy concerns come to the intranet. Part of the force behind this is the European Union's General Data Protection Regulation which went into effect May 2018.

An enterprise private network is a computer network built by a business to interconnect its various company sites (such as production sites, offices and shops) in order to share computer resources.

Beginning with the digitalisation of telecommunication networks, started in the 1970s in the USA by AT&T, and propelled by the growth in computer systems availability and demands, enterprise networks have been built for decades without the need to append the term private to them. The networks were operated over telecommunication networks and, as for voice communications, a certain amount of security and secrecy was expected and delivered.

But with the Internet in the 1990s came a new type of network, virtual private networks, built over this public infrastructure, using encryption to protect the data traffic from eaves-dropping. So the enterprise networks are now commonly referred to enterprise private networks in order to clarify that these are private networks, in contrast to public networks.

Extranet

An extranet is a controlled private network that allows access to partners, vendors and suppliers or an authorized set of customers – normally to a subset of the information accessible from an organization's intranet. An extranet is similar to a DMZ in that it provides access to needed services for authorized parties, without granting access to an organization's entire network.

Historically the term was occasionally also used in the sense of two organizations sharing their internal networks over a virtual private network (VPN).

Enterprise Applications

During the late 1990s and early 2000s, several industries started to use the term 'extranet' to describe centralized repositories of shared data (and supporting applications) made accessible via the web only to authorized members of particular work groups - for example, geographically dispersed, multi-company project teams. Some applications are offered on a software as a service (SaaS) basis.

For example, in the construction industry, project teams may access a project extranet to share drawings, photographs and documents, and use online applications to mark-up and make comments and to manage and report on project-related communications. In 2003 in the United Kingdom, several of the leading vendors formed the Network for Construction Collaboration Technology Providers (NCCTP) to promote the technologies and to establish data exchange standards between the different data systems. The same type of construction-focused technologies have also been developed in the United States, Australia and mainland Europe.

Advantages

- Exchange large volumes of data using Electronic Data Interchange (EDI).

- Share product catalogs exclusively with trade partners.

- Collaborate with other companies on joint development efforts.

- Jointly develop and use training programs with other companies.

- Provide or access services provided by one company to a group of other companies, such as an online banking application managed by one company on behalf of affiliated banks.

- Improved efficiency: since the customers are satisfied with the information provided it can be an advantage for the organisation where they will get more customers which increases the efficiency.

Disadvantages

- Extranets can be expensive to implement and maintain within an organization (e.g., hardware, software, employee training costs), if hosted internally rather than by an application service provider.

- Security of extranets can be a concern when hosting valuable or proprietary information.

Internet

By the 1980s other U.S. governmental bodies were heavily involved with networking, including the National Science Foundation (NSF), the Department of Energy, and the National Aeronautics and Space Administration (NASA). While DARPA had played a seminal role in creating a small-scale version of the Internet among its researchers, NSF worked with DARPA to expand access to the entire scientific and academic community and to make TCP/IP the standard in all federally supported research networks. In 1985–86 NSF funded the first five supercomputing centres—at Princeton University, the University of Pittsburgh, the University of California, San Diego, the University of Illinois, and Cornell University. In the 1980s NSF also funded the development and operation of the

NSFNET, a national "backbone" network to connect these centres. By the late 1980s the network was operating at millions of bits per second. NSF also funded various nonprofit local and regional networks to connect other users to the NSFNET. A few commercial networks also began in the late 1980s; these were soon joined by others, and the Commercial Internet Exchange (CIX) was formed to allow transit traffic between commercial networks that otherwise would not have been allowed on the NSFNET backbone. In 1995, after extensive review of the situation, NSF decided that support of the NSFNET infrastructure was no longer required, since many commercial providers were now willing and able to meet the needs of the research community, and its support was withdrawn. Meanwhile, NSF had fostered a competitive collection of commercial Internet backbones connected to one another through so-called network access points (NAPs).

From the Internet's origin in the early 1970s, control of it steadily devolved from government stewardship to private-sector participation and finally to private custody with government oversight and forbearance. Today a loosely structured group of several thousand interested individuals known as the Internet Engineering Task Force participates in a grassroots development process for Internet standards. Internet standards are maintained by the nonprofit Internet Society, an international body with headquarters in Reston, Virginia. The Internet Corporation for Assigned Names and Numbers (ICANN), another nonprofit, private organization, oversees various aspects of policy regarding Internet domain names and numbers.

The Internet (portmanteau of interconnected network) is the global system of interconnected computer networks that use the Internet protocol suite (TCP/IP) to link devices worldwide. It is a network of networks that consists of private, public, academic, business, and government networks of local to global scope, linked by a broad array of electronic, wireless, and optical networking technologies. The Internet carries a vast range of information resources and services, such as the inter-linked hypertext documents and applications of the World Wide Web (WWW), electronic mail, telephony, and file sharing.

The origins of the Internet date back to research commissioned by the federal government of the United States in the 1960s to build robust, fault-tolerant communication with computer networks. The primary precursor network, the ARPANET, initially served as a backbone for interconnection of regional academic and military networks in the 1980s. The funding of the National Science Foundation Network as a new backbone in the 1980s, as well as private funding for other commercial extensions, led to worldwide participation in the development of new networking technologies, and the merger of many networks. The linking of commercial networks and enterprises by the early 1990s marked the beginning of the transition to the modern Internet, and generated a sustained exponential growth as generations of institutional, personal, and mobile computers were connected to the network. Although the Internet was widely used by academia since the 1980s, commercialization incorporated its services and technologies into virtually every aspect of modern life.

Most traditional communication media, including telephony, radio, television, paper mail and newspapers are reshaped, redefined, or even bypassed by the Internet, giving birth to new services such as email, Internet telephony, Internet television, online music, digital newspapers, and video streaming websites. Newspaper, book, and other print publishing are adapting to website technology, or are reshaped into blogging, web feeds and online news aggregators. The Internet has enabled and accelerated new forms of personal interactions through instant messaging, Internet forums, and social networking. Online shopping has grown exponentially both for major retailers and small businesses and entrepreneurs, as it enables firms to extend their "brick and mortar" presence to serve a larger market or even sell goods and services entirely online. Business-to-business and financial services on the Internet affect supply chains across entire industries.

The Internet has no single centralized governance in either technological implementation or policies for access and usage; each constituent network sets its own policies. The overreaching definitions of the two principal name spaces in the Internet, the Internet Protocol address (IP address) space and the Domain Name System (DNS), are directed by a maintainer organization, the Internet Corporation for Assigned Names and Numbers (ICANN). The technical underpinning and standardization of the core protocols is an activity of the Internet Engineering Task Force (IETF), a non-profit organization of loosely affiliated international participants that anyone may associate with by contributing technical expertise. In November 2006, the Internet was included on USA Today's list of New Seven Wonders.

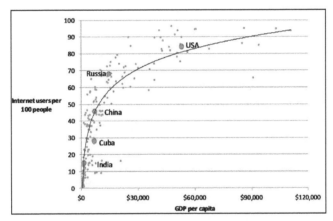

Internet users per 100 population members and GDP per capita for selected countries.

Terminology

The Internet Messenger by Buky Schwartz.

When the term Internet is used to refer to the specific global system of interconnected Internet Protocol (IP) networks, the word is a proper noun that should be written with an initial capital letter. In common use and the media, it is often not capitalized, viz. the internet. Some guides specify that the word should be capitalized when used as a noun, but not capitalized when used as an adjective. The Internet is also often referred to as the Net, as a short form of network. Historically, as early as 1849, the word internetted was used uncapitalized as an adjective, meaning interconnected or interwoven. The designers of early computer networks used internet both as a noun and as a verb in shorthand form of internetwork or internetworking, meaning interconnecting computer networks.

The terms Internet and World Wide Web are often used interchangeably in everyday speech; it is common to speak of "going on the Internet" when using a web browser to view web pages. However, the World Wide Web or the Web is only one of a large number of Internet services. The Web is a collection of interconnected documents (web pages) and other web resources, linked by hyperlinks and URLs. As another point of comparison, Hypertext Transfer Protocol, or HTTP, is the language used on the Web for information transfer, yet it is just one of many languages or protocols that can be used for communication on the Internet. The term Interweb is a portmanteau of Internet and World Wide Web typically used sarcastically to parody a technically unsavvy user.

Governance

ICANN headquarters in the Playa Vista.

The Internet is a global network that comprises many voluntarily interconnected autonomous networks. It operates without a central governing body. The technical underpinning and standardization of the core protocols (IPv4 and IPv6) is an activity of the Internet Engineering Task Force (IETF), a non-profit organization of loosely affiliated international participants that anyone may associate with by contributing technical expertise. To maintain interoperability, the principal name spaces of the Internet are administered by the Internet Corporation for Assigned Names and Numbers (ICANN). ICANN is governed by an international board of directors drawn from across the Internet technical, business, academic, and other non-commercial communities. ICANN coordinates the assignment of unique identifiers for use on the Internet, including domain names, Internet Protocol (IP) addresses, application port numbers in the transport protocols, and many other parameters. Globally unified name spaces are essential for maintaining the global reach of the Internet. This role of ICANN distinguishes it as perhaps the only central coordinating body for the global Internet.

Regional Internet Registries (RIRs) allocate IP addresses:

- African Network Information Center (AfriNIC) for Africa.

- American Registry for Internet Numbers (ARIN) for North America.

- Asia-Pacific Network Information Centre (APNIC) for Asia and the Pacific region.

- Latin American and Caribbean Internet Addresses Registry (LACNIC) for Latin America and the Caribbean region.

- Réseaux IP Européens – Network Coordination Centre (RIPE NCC) for Europe, the Middle East, and Central Asia.

The National Telecommunications and Information Administration, an agency of the United States Department of Commerce, had final approval over changes to the DNS root zone until the IANA stewardship transition on 1 October 2016. The Internet Society (ISOC) was founded in 1992 with a mission to "assure the open development, evolution and use of the Internet for the benefit of all people throughout the world". Its members include individuals (anyone may join) as well as corporations, organizations, governments, and universities. Among other activities ISOC provides an administrative home for a number of less formally organized groups that are involved in developing and managing the Internet, including: the Internet Engineering Task Force (IETF), Internet Architecture Board (IAB), Internet Engineering Steering Group (IESG), Internet Research Task Force (IRTF), and Internet Research Steering Group (IRSG). On 16 November 2005, the United Nations-sponsored World Summit on the Information Society in Tunis established the Internet Governance Forum (IGF) to discuss Internet-related issues.

Infrastructure

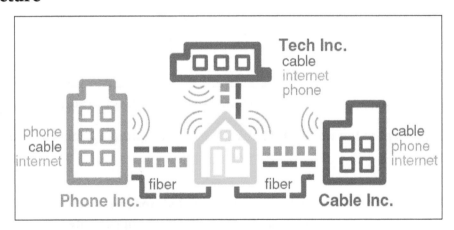

The communications infrastructure of the Internet consists of its hardware components and a system of software layers that control various aspects of the architecture.

Routing and Service Tiers

Internet service providers (ISPs) establish the worldwide connectivity between individual networks at various levels of scope. End-users who only access the Internet when needed to perform a function or obtain information, represent the bottom of the routing hierarchy. At the top of the routing hierarchy are the tier 1 networks, large telecommunication companies that exchange traffic directly with each other via very high speed fibre optic cables and governed by peering agreements. Tier 2 and lower level networks buy Internet transit from other providers to reach at least some parties on the global Internet, though they may also engage in peering. An ISP may use a single upstream provider for connectivity, or implement multihoming to achieve redundancy and load balancing. Internet exchange points are major traffic exchanges with physical connections to multiple ISPs. Large organizations, such as academic institutions, large enterprises, and governments, may perform the same function as ISPs, engaging in peering and purchasing transit on behalf of their internal networks. Research networks tend to interconnect with large subnetworks such as GEANT, GLORIAD, Internet2, and the UK's national research and education network, JANET. Both the Internet IP routing structure and hypertext links of the World Wide Web are examples of scale-free networks. Computers and routers use routing tables in their operating system to direct IP packets to the next-hop router or destination. Routing tables are maintained by manual configuration or automatically by routing protocols. End-nodes typically use a default route that points toward an ISP providing transit, while ISP routers use the Border Gateway Protocol to establish the most efficient routing across the complex connections of the global Internet.

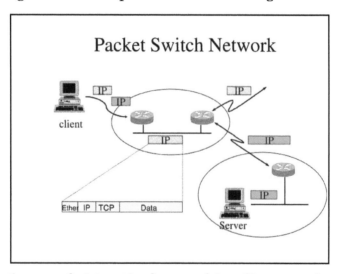

Packet routing across the Internet involves several tiers of Internet service providers.

An estimated 70 percent of the world's Internet traffic passes through Ashburn, Virginia.

Access

Common methods of Internet access by users include dial-up with a computer modem via telephone circuits, broadband over coaxial cable, fiber optics or copper wires, Wi-Fi, satellite, and cellular telephone technology (e.g. 3G, 4G). The Internet may often be accessed from computers in libraries and Internet cafes. Internet access points exist in many public places such as airport halls and coffee shops. Various terms are used, such as public Internet kiosk, public access terminal, and Web payphone. Many hotels also have public terminals that are usually fee-based. These terminals are widely accessed for various usages, such as ticket booking, bank deposit, or online payment. Wi-Fi provides wireless access to the Internet via local computer networks. Hotspots providing such access include Wi-Fi cafes, where users need to bring their own wireless devices such as a laptop or PDA. These services may be free to all, free to customers only, or fee-based.

Grassroots efforts have led to wireless community networks. Commercial Wi-Fi services covering large city areas are in many cities, such as New York, London, Vienna, Toronto, San Francisco,

Philadelphia, Chicago and Pittsburgh. The Internet can then be accessed from places, such as a park bench. Apart from Wi-Fi, there have been experiments with proprietary mobile wireless networks like Ricochet, various high-speed data services over cellular phone networks, and fixed wireless services. High-end mobile phones such as smartphones in general come with Internet access through the phone network. Web browsers such as Opera are available on these advanced handsets, which can also run a wide variety of other Internet software. Internet usage by mobile and tablet devices exceeded desktop worldwide for the first time in October 2016. An Internet access provider and protocol matrix differentiates the methods used to get online.

Mobile Communication

in billions

3.89
in 2012

4.83
in 2016

5.69
in 2020

Number of mobile cellular subscriptions 2012–2016.

The International Telecommunication Union (ITU) estimated that, by the end of 2017, 48% of individual users regularly connect to the Internet, up from 34% in 2012. Mobile Internet connectivity has played an important role in expanding access in recent years especially in Asia and the Pacific and in Africa. The number of unique mobile cellular subscriptions increased from 3.89 billion in 2012 to 4.83 billion in 2016, two-thirds of the world's population, with more than half of subscriptions located in Asia and the Pacific. The number of subscriptions is predicted to rise to 5.69 billion users in 2020. As of 2016, almost 60% of the world's population had access to a 4G broadband cellular network, up from almost 50% in 2015 and 11% in 2012. The limits that users face on accessing information via mobile applications coincide with a broader process of fragmentation of the Internet. Fragmentation restricts access to media content and tends to affect poorest users the most.

Zero-rating, the practice of Internet service providers allowing users free connectivity to access specific content or applications without cost, has offered opportunities to surmount economic hurdles, but has also been accused by its critics as creating a two-tiered Internet. To address the issues with zero-rating, an alternative model has emerged in the concept of 'equal rating' and is being tested in experiments by Mozilla and Orange in Africa. Equal rating prevents prioritization of one type of content and zero-rates all content up to a specified data cap. A study published by Chatham House, 15 out of 19 countries researched in Latin America had some kind of hybrid or zero-rated product offered. Some countries in the region had a handful of plans to choose from (across all mobile network operators) while others, such as Colombia, offered as many as 30 pre-paid and 34 post-paid plans.

A study of eight countries in the Global South found that zero-rated data plans exist in every country, although there is a great range in the frequency with which they are offered and actually used in each. The study looked at the top three to five carriers by market share in Bangladesh, Colombia, Ghana, India, Kenya, Nigeria, Peru and Philippines. Across the 181 plans examined, 13 per cent were offering zero-rated services. Another study, covering Ghana, Kenya, Nigeria and South Africa.

Protocols

While the hardware components in the Internet infrastructure can often be used to support other software systems, it is the design and the standardization process of the software that characterizes the Internet and provides the foundation for its scalability and success. The responsibility for the architectural design of the Internet software systems has been assumed by the Internet Engineering Task Force (IETF). The IETF conducts standard-setting work groups, open to any individual, about the various aspects of Internet architecture. Resulting contributions and standards are published as Request for Comments (RFC) documents on the IETF web site. The principal methods of networking that enable the Internet are contained in specially designated RFCs that constitute the Internet Standards. Other less rigorous documents are simply informative, experimental, or historical, or document the best current practices (BCP) when implementing Internet technologies.

The Internet standards describe a framework known as the Internet protocol suite, or in short as TCP/IP, based on the first two components. This is a model architecture that divides methods into a layered system of protocols, originally documented in RFC 1122 and RFC 1123. The layers correspond to the environment or scope in which their services operate. At the top is the application layer, space for the application-specific networking methods used in software applications. For example, a web browser program uses the client-server application model and a specific protocol of interaction between servers and clients, while many file-sharing systems use a peer-to-peer paradigm. Below this top layer, the transport layer connects applications on different hosts with a logical channel through the network with appropriate data exchange methods.

Underlying these layers are the networking technologies that interconnect networks at their borders and exchange traffic across them. The Internet layer enables computers to identify and locate each other by Internet Protocol (IP) addresses, and routes their traffic via intermediate (transit) networks. At the bottom of the architecture is the link layer, which provides logical connectivity between hosts on the same network link, such as a local area network (LAN) or a dial-up connection. The model is designed to be independent of the underlying hardware used for the physical connections, which the model does not concern itself with in any detail. Other models have been developed, such as the OSI model, that attempt to be comprehensive in every aspect of communications. While many similarities exist between the models, they are not compatible in the details of description or implementation. Yet, TCP/IP protocols are usually included in the discussion of OSI networking.

The most prominent component of the Internet model is the Internet Protocol (IP), which provides addressing systems, including IP addresses, for computers on the network. IP enables internetworking and, in essence, establishes the Internet itself. Internet Protocol Version 4 (IPv4) is the initial version used on the first generation of the Internet and is still in dominant use. It was designed to address up to $\approx$4.3 billion (109) hosts. However, the explosive growth of the Internet has led to IPv4 address exhaustion, which entered its final stage in 2011, when the global address allocation pool was exhausted. A new protocol version, IPv6, was developed in the mid-1990s, which provides vastly larger addressing capabilities and more efficient routing of Internet traffic. IPv6 is currently in growing deployment around the world, since Internet address registries (RIRs) began to urge all resource managers to plan rapid adoption and conversion.

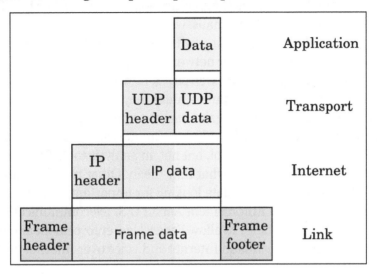

As user data is processed through the protocol stack, each abstraction layer adds encapsulation information at the sending host. Data is transmitted over the wire at the link level between hosts and routers. Encapsulation is removed by the receiving host. Intermediate relays update link encapsulation at each hop, and inspect the IP layer for routing purposes.

IPv6 is not directly interoperable by design with IPv4. In essence, it establishes a parallel version of the Internet not directly accessible with IPv4 software. Thus, translation facilities must exist for internetworking or nodes must have duplicate networking software for both networks. Essentially all modern computer operating systems support both versions of the Internet Protocol. Network infrastructure, however, has been lagging in this development. Aside from the complex array of physical connections that make up its infrastructure, the Internet is facilitated by bi- or multi-lateral commercial contracts, e.g., peering agreements, and by technical specifications or protocols that describe the exchange of data over the network. Indeed, the Internet is defined by its interconnections and routing policies.

Security

Internet resources, hardware, and software components are the target of criminal or malicious attempts to gain unauthorized control to cause interruptions, commit fraud, engage in blackmail or access private information.

Malware

Malware is malicious software used and distributed via the Internet. It includes computer viruses which are copied with the help of humans, computer worms which copy themselves automatically, software for denial of service attacks, ransomware, botnets, and spyware that reports on the activity and typing of users. Usually, these activities constitute cybercrime. Defense theorists have also speculated about the possibilities of cyber warfare using similar methods on a large scale.

Surveillance

The vast majority of computer surveillance involves the monitoring of data and traffic on the Internet. In the United States for example, under the Communications Assistance For Law Enforcement Act, all phone calls and broadband Internet traffic (emails, web traffic, instant messaging, etc.) are required to be available for unimpeded real-time monitoring by Federal law enforcement agencies. Packet capture is the monitoring of data traffic on a computer network. Computers communicate over the Internet by breaking up messages (emails, images, videos, web pages, files, etc.) into small chunks called "packets", which are routed through a network of computers, until they reach their destination, where they are assembled back into a complete "message" again. Packet Capture Appliance intercepts these packets as they are traveling through the network, in order to examine their contents using other programs. A packet capture is an information gathering tool, but not an analysis tool. That is it gathers "messages" but it does not analyze them and figure out what they mean. Other programs are needed to perform traffic analysis and sift through intercepted data looking for important/useful information. Under the Communications Assistance For Law Enforcement Act all U.S. telecommunications providers are required to install packet sniffing technology to allow Federal law enforcement and intelligence agencies to intercept all of their customers' broadband Internet and voice over Internet protocol (VoIP) traffic.

The large amount of data gathered from packet capturing requires surveillance software that filters and reports relevant information, such as the use of certain words or phrases, the access of certain types of web sites, or communicating via email or chat with certain parties. Agencies, such as the Information Awareness Office, NSA, GCHQ and the FBI, spend billions of dollars per year to develop, purchase, implement, and operate systems for interception and analysis of data. Similar systems are operated by Iranian secret police to identify and suppress dissidents. The required hardware and software was allegedly installed by German Siemens AG and Finnish Nokia.

Censorship

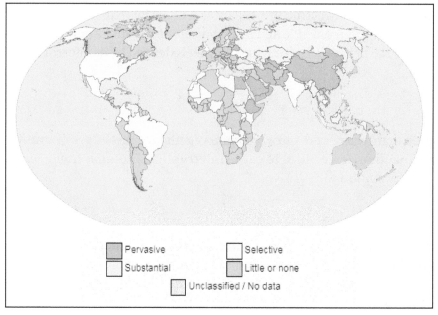

Internet Surveillance and censorship by country.

Some governments, such as those of Burma, Iran, North Korea, the Mainland China, Saudi Arabia and the United Arab Emirates restrict access to content on the Internet within their territories, especially to political and religious content, with domain name and keyword filters.

In Norway, Denmark, Finland, and Sweden, major Internet service providers have voluntarily agreed to restrict access to sites listed by authorities. While this list of forbidden resources is supposed to contain only known child pornography sites, the content of the list is secret. Many countries, including the United States, have enacted laws against the possession or distribution of certain material, such as child pornography, via the Internet, but do not mandate filter software. Many free or commercially available software programs, called content-control software are available to users to block offensive websites on individual computers or networks, in order to limit access by children to pornographic material or depiction of violence.

ISP

An Internet service provider (ISP) is an organization that provides services for accessing, using, or participating in the Internet. Internet service providers may be organized in various forms, such as commercial, community-owned, non-profit, or otherwise privately owned.

Internet services typically provided by ISPs include Internet access, Internet transit, domain name registration, web hosting, Usenet service, and colocation.

Local ISP in installing fiber for provisioning Internet access.

Classifications

Access Providers

Access provider ISPs provide Internet access, employing a range of technologies to connect users to their network. Available technologies have ranged from computer modems with acoustic couplers to telephone lines, to television cable (CATV), Wi-Fi, and fiber optics.

For users and small businesses, traditional options include copper wires to provide dial-up, DSL, typically asymmetric digital subscriber line (ADSL), cable modem or Integrated Services Digital Network (ISDN) (typically basic rate interface). Using fiber-optics to end users is called Fiber To The Home or similar names.

For customers with more demanding requirements (such as medium-to-large businesses, or other ISPs) can use higher-speed DSL (such as single-pair high-speed digital subscriber line), Ethernet, metropolitan Ethernet, gigabit Ethernet, Frame Relay, ISDN Primary Rate Interface, ATM (Asynchronous Transfer Mode) and synchronous optical networking (SONET).

Wireless access is another option, including cellular and satellite Internet access.

Mailbox Providers

A mailbox provider is an organization that provides services for hosting electronic mail domains with access to storage for mail boxes. It provides email servers to send, receive, accept, and store email for end users or other organizations.

Many mailbox providers are also access providers, while others are not (e.g., Gmail, Yahoo Mail, Outlook.com, AOL Mail, Po box). The task is typically accomplished by implementing Simple Mail Transfer Protocol (SMTP) and possibly providing access to messages through Internet Message Access Protocol (IMAP), the Post Office Protocol, Webmail, or a proprietary protocol.

Hosting Isps

Internet hosting services provide email, web-hosting, or online storage services. Other services include virtual server, cloud services, or physical server operation.

Transit Isps

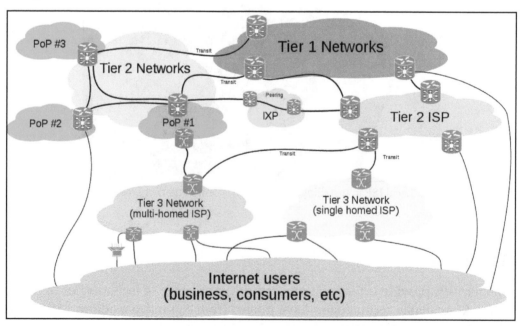

Tiers 1 and 2 ISP interconnections

Just as their customers pay them for Internet access, ISPs themselves pay upstream ISPs for Internet access. An upstream ISP usually has a larger network than the contracting ISP or is able to provide the contracting ISP with access to parts of the Internet the contracting ISP by itself has no access to.

In the simplest case, a single connection is established to an upstream ISP and is used to transmit data to or from areas of the Internet beyond the home network; this mode of interconnection is often cascaded multiple times until reaching a tier 1 carrier. In reality, the situation is often more complex. ISPs with more than one point of presence (PoP) may have separate connections to an upstream ISP at multiple PoPs, or they may be customers of multiple upstream ISPs and may have connections to each one of them at one or more point of presence. Transit ISPs provide large amounts of bandwidth for connecting hosting ISPs and access ISPs.

Virtual Isps

A virtual ISP (VISP) is an operation that purchases services from another ISP, sometimes called a wholesale ISP in this context, which allow the VISP's customers to access the Internet using services and infrastructure owned and operated by the wholesale ISP. VISPs resemble mobile virtual network operators and competitive local exchange carriers for voice communications.

Free Isps

Free ISPs are Internet service providers that provide service free of charge. Many free ISPs display advertisements while the user is connected; like commercial television, in a sense they are selling the user's attention to the advertiser. Other free ISPs, sometimes called freenets, are run on a non-profit basis, usually with volunteer staff.

Wireless Isp

A wireless Internet service provider (WISP) is an Internet service provider with a network based on wireless networking. Technology may include commonplace Wi-Fi wireless mesh networking, or proprietary equipment designed to operate over open 900 MHz, 2.4 GHz, 4.9, 5.2, 5.4, 5.7, and 5.8 GHz bands or licensed frequencies such as 2.5 GHz (EBS/BRS), 3.65 GHz (NN) and in the UHF band (including the MMDS frequency band) and LMDS.

Peering

ISPs may engage in peering, where multiple ISPs interconnect at peering points or Internet exchange points (IXs), allowing routing of data between each network, without charging one another for the data transmitted—data that would otherwise have passed through a third upstream ISP, incurring charges from the upstream ISP.

ISPs requiring no upstream and having only customers (end customers or peer ISPs) are called Tier 1 ISPs.

Network hardware, software and specifications, as well as the expertise of network management personnel are important in ensuring that data follows the most efficient route, and upstream connections work reliably. A tradeoff between cost and efficiency is possible.

URL

A Uniform Resource Locator (URL), colloquially termed a web address, is a reference to a web resource that specifies its location on a computer network and a mechanism for retrieving it. A URL is a specific type of Uniform Resource Identifier (URI), although many people use the two terms interchangeably.URLs occur most commonly to reference web pages (http), but are also used for file transfer (ftp), email (mailto), database access (JDBC), and many other applications.

Most web browsers display the URL of a web page above the page in an address bar. A typical URL could have the form http://www.example.com/index.html, which indicates a protocol (http), a hostname (www.example.com), and a file name (index.html).

Syntax

Every HTTP URL conforms to the syntax of a generic URL. The URL generic syntax consists of a hierarchical sequence of five components:

URL = scheme:[//authority]path[?query][#fragment]

where the authority component divides into three subcomponents:

authority = [userinfo@]host[:port]

This is represented in a syntax as:

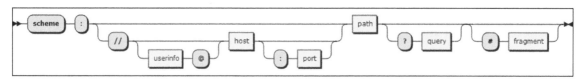

The URL comprises:

- A non-empty scheme component followed by a colon (:), consisting of a sequence of characters beginning with a letter and followed by any combination of letters, digits, plus (+), period (.), or hyphen (-). Although schemes are case-insensitive, the canonical form is lowercase and documents that specify schemes must do so with lowercase letters. Examples of popular schemes include http, https, ftp, mailto, file, data, and irc. URL schemes should be registered with the Internet Assigned Numbers Authority (IANA), although non-registered schemes are used in practice.

- An optional authority component preceded by two slashes (//), comprising:

  ○ An optional userinfo subcomponent that may consist of a user name and an optional password preceded by a colon (:), followed by an at symbol (@). Use of the format username:-password in the userinfo subcomponent is deprecated for security reasons. Applications should not render as clear text any data after the first colon (:) found within a userinfo subcomponent unless the data after the colon is the empty string (indicating no password).

  ○ An optional host subcomponent, consisting of either a registered name (including but not limited to a hostname), or an IP address. IPv4 addresses must be in dot-decimal notation, and IPv6 addresses must be enclosed in brackets ([]).

 ○ An optional port subcomponent preceded by a colon (:).

- A path component, consisting of a sequence of path segments separated by a slash (/). A path is always defined for a URL, though the defined path may be empty (zero length). A segment may also be empty, resulting in two consecutive slashes (//) in the path component. A path component may resemble or map exactly to a file system path, but does not always imply a relation to one. If an authority component is present, then the path component must either be empty or begin with a slash (/). If an authority component is absent, then the path cannot begin with an empty segment, that is with two slashes (//), as the following characters would be interpreted as an authority component. The final segment of the path may be referred to as a 'slug'.

- An optional query component preceded by a question mark (?), containing a query string of non-hierarchical data. Its syntax is not well defined, but by convention is most often a sequence of attribute–value pairs separated by a delimiter.

- An optional fragment component preceded by a hash (#). The fragment contains a fragment identifier providing direction to a secondary resource. When the primary resource is an HTML document, the fragment is often an id attribute of a specific element, and web browsers will scroll this element into view.

Query delimiter	Example
Ampersand (&)	key1=value1&key2=value2
Semicolon (;)	key1=value1;key2=value2

Internationalized URL

Internet users are distributed throughout the world using a wide variety of languages and alphabets and expect to be able to create URLs in their own local alphabets. An Internationalized Resource Identifier (IRI) is a form of URL that includes Unicode characters. All modern browsers support IRIs. The parts of the URL requiring special treatment for different alphabets are the domain name and path.

The domain name in the IRI is known as an Internationalized Domain Name (IDN). Web and Internet software automatically convert the domain name into punycode usable by the Domain Name System.

The URL path name can also be specified by the user in the local writing system. If not already encoded, it is converted to UTF-8, and any characters not part of the basic URL character set are escaped as hexadecimal using percent-encoding.

Protocol-relative URLs

Protocol-relative links (PRL), also known as protocol-relative URLs (PRURL), are URLs that have no protocol specified. For example, //example.com will use the protocol of the current page, either HTTP or HTTPS.

Cookies

Cookies are messages that web servers pass to your web browser when you visit Internet sites. Your browser stores each message in a small file, called cookie.txt. When you request another page from the server, your browser sends the cookie back to the server. These files typically contain information about your visit to the web page, as well as any information you've volunteered, such as your name and interests.

The term "cookie" is an allusion to a Unix program called Fortune Cookie that produces a different message, or fortune, each time it runs.

Examples of Cookies

Cookies are most commonly used to track website activity. When you visit some sites, the server gives you a cookie that acts as your identification card. Upon each return visit to that site, your browser passes that cookie back to the server. In this way, a web server can gather information about which web pages are used the most, and which pages are gathering the most repeat hits.

Cookies are also used for online shopping. Online stores often use cookies that record any personal information you enter, as well as any items in your electronic shopping cart, so that you don't need to re-enter this information each time you visit the site.

Servers can use cookies to provide personalized web pages. When you select preferences at a site that uses this option, the server places the information in a cookie. When you return, the server uses the information in the cookie to create a customized page for you.

Security Concerns

Only the website that creates a cookie can read it, so other servers do not have access to your information. Additionally, web servers can use only information that you provide or choices that you make while visiting the website as content in cookies.

Webmasters have always been able to track access to their sites, but cookies make it easier to do so. In some cases, cookies come not from the site you're visiting, but from advertising companies that manage the banner ads for a set of sites. These advertising companies can develop detailed profiles of the people who select ads across their customers' sites.

Accepting a cookie does not give a server access to your computer or any of your personal information (except for any information that you may have purposely given, as with online shopping). Also, it is not possible to execute code from a cookie, and not possible to use a cookie to deliver a virus.

Services

Communication

Email is an important communications service available on the Internet. The concept of sending electronic text messages between parties in a way analogous to mailing letters or memos predates the creation of the Internet. Pictures, documents, and other files are sent as email attachments. Emails can be cc-ed to multiple email addresses.

Internet telephony is another common communications service made possible by the creation of the Internet. VoIP stands for Voice-over-Internet Protocol, referring to the protocol that underlies all Internet communication. The idea began in the early 1990s with walkie-talkie-like voice applications for personal computers. In recent years many VoIP systems have become as easy to use and as convenient as a normal telephone. The benefit is that, as the Internet carries the voice traffic, VoIP can be free or cost much less than a traditional telephone call, especially over long distances and especially for those with always-on Internet connections such as cable or ADSL and mobile data. VoIP is maturing into a competitive alternative to traditional telephone service. Interoperability between different providers has improved and the ability to call or receive a call from a traditional telephone is available. Simple, inexpensive VoIP network adapters are available that eliminate the need for a personal computer.

Voice quality can still vary from call to call, but is often equal to and can even exceed that of traditional calls. Remaining problems for VoIP include emergency telephone number dialing and reliability. Currently, a few VoIP providers provide an emergency service, but it is not universally available. Older traditional phones with no "extra features" may be line-powered only and operate during a power failure; VoIP can never do so without a backup power source for the phone equipment and the Internet access devices. VoIP has also become increasingly popular for gaming applications, as a form of communication between players. Popular VoIP clients for gaming include Ventrilo and Teamspeak. Modern video game consoles also offer VoIP chat features.

Data Transfer

File sharing is an example of transferring large amounts of data across the Internet. A computer file can be emailed to customers, colleagues and friends as an attachment. It can be uploaded to a website or File Transfer Protocol (FTP) server for easy download by others. It can be put into a "shared location" or onto a file server for instant use by colleagues. The load of bulk downloads to many users can be eased by the use of "mirror" servers or peer-to-peer networks. In any of these cases, access to the file may be controlled by user authentication, the transit of the file over the Internet may be obscured by encryption, and money may change hands for access to the file. The price can be paid by the remote charging of funds from, for example, a credit card whose details are also passed – usually fully encrypted – across the Internet. The origin and authenticity of the file received may be checked by digital signatures or by MD5 or other message digests. These simple features of the Internet, over a worldwide basis, are changing the production, sale, and distribution of anything that can be reduced to a computer file for transmission. This includes all manner of print publications, software products, news, music, film, video, photography, graphics and the other arts. This in turn has caused seismic shifts in each of the existing industries that previously controlled the production and distribution of these products.

Streaming media is the real-time delivery of digital media for the immediate consumption or enjoyment by end users. Many radio and television broadcasters provide Internet feeds of their live audio and video productions. They may also allow time-shift viewing or listening such as Preview, Classic Clips and Listen Again features. These providers have been joined by a range of pure Internet "broadcasters" who never had on-air licenses. This means that an Internet-connected device, such as a computer or something more specific, can be used to access on-line media in much the same way as was previously possible only with a television or radio receiver. The range of available types of content is much wider, from specialized technical webcasts to on-demand popular multimedia services. Podcasting is a variation on this theme, where – usually audio – material is downloaded and played back on a computer or shifted to a portable media player to be listened to on the move. These techniques using simple equipment allow anybody, with little censorship or licensing control, to broadcast audio-visual material worldwide.

Digital media streaming increases the demand for network bandwidth. For example, standard image quality needs 1 Mbit/s link speed for SD 480p, HD 720p quality requires 2.5 Mbit/s, and the top-of-the-line HDX quality needs 4.5 Mbit/s for 1080p.

Webcams are a low-cost extension of this phenomenon. While some webcams can give full-frame-rate video, the picture either is usually small or updates slowly. Internet users can watch animals around an African waterhole, ships in the Panama Canal, traffic at a local roundabout or monitor their own premises, live and in real time. Video chat rooms and video conferencing are also popular with many uses being found for personal webcams, with and without two-way sound. YouTube was founded on 15 February 2005 and is now the leading website for free streaming video with a vast number of users. It uses a HTML5 based web player by default to stream and show video files. Registered users may upload an unlimited amount of video and build their own personal profile. YouTube claims that its users watch hundreds of millions, and upload hundreds of thousands of videos daily.

Social Impact

The Internet has enabled new forms of social interaction, activities, and social associations. This phenomenon has given rise to the scholarly study of the sociology of the Internet.

Users

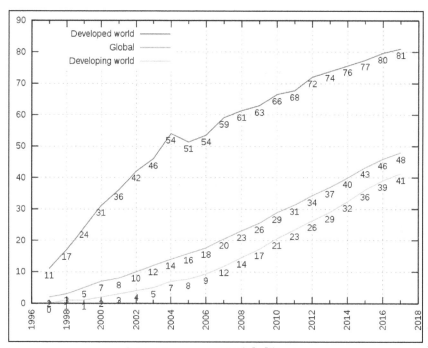

Internet users per 100 inhabitants.

Internet usage has grown tremendously. From 2000 to 2009, the number of Internet users globally rose from 394 million to 1.858 billion. By 2010, 22 percent of the world's population had access to computers with 1 billion Google searches every day, 300 million Internet users reading blogs, and 2 billion videos viewed daily on YouTube. In 2014 the world's Internet users surpassed 3 billion or 43.6 percent of world population, but two-thirds of the users came from richest countries, with 78.0 percent of Europe countries population using the Internet, followed by 57.4 percent of the Americas. However, by 2018, this trend had shifted so tremendously that Asia alone accounted for 51% of all Internet users, with 2.2 billion out of the 4.3 billion Internet users in the world coming from that region. The number of China's Internet users surpassed a major miletsone in 2018, when the country's Internet regulatory authority, China Internet Network Information Centre, announced that there were 802 million Internet users in China. By 2019, China was the world's leading country in terms of Internet users, with more than 800 million users, followed closely by India, with some 700 million users, with USA a distant third with 275 million users. However, in terms of penetration, China has a 38.4% penetration rate compared to India's 40% and USA's 80%.

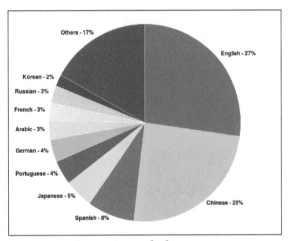

Internet users by language.

The prevalent language for communication via the Internet has been English. This may be a result of the origin of the Internet, as well as the language's role as a lingua franca. Early computer systems were limited to the characters in the American Standard Code for Information Interchange (ASCII), a subset of the alphabet.

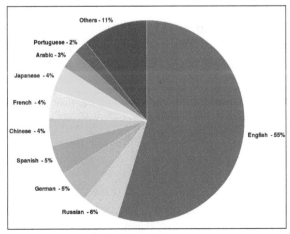

Website content languages.

After English (27%), the most requested languages on the World Wide Web are Chinese (25%), Spanish (8%), Japanese (5%), Portuguese and German (4% each), Arabic, French and Russian (3% each), and Korean (2%). By region, 42% of the world's Internet users are based in Asia, 24% in Europe, 14% in North America, 10% in Latin America and the Caribbean taken together, 6% in Africa, 3% in the Middle East and 1% in Australia/Oceania. The Internet's technologies have developed enough in recent years, especially in the use of Unicode, that good facilities are available for development and communication in the world's widely used languages. However, some glitches such as mojibake (incorrect display of some languages' characters) still remain.

In an American study in 2005, the percentage of men using the Internet was very slightly ahead of the percentage of women, although this difference reversed in those under 30. Men logged on more often, spent more time online, and were more likely to be broadband users, whereas women tended to make more use of opportunities to communicate (such as email). Men were more likely to use the Internet to pay bills, participate in auctions, and for recreation such as downloading music and videos. Men and women were equally likely to use the Internet for shopping and banking. More recent studies indicate that in 2008, women significantly outnumbered men on most social networking sites, such as Facebook and Myspace, although the ratios varied with age. In addition, women watched more streaming content, whereas men downloaded more. In terms of blogs, men were more likely to blog in the first place; among those who blog, men were more likely to have a professional blog, whereas women were more likely to have a personal blog.

Forecasts predict that 44% of the world's population will be users of the Internet by 2020. Splitting by country, in 2012 Iceland, Norway, Sweden, the Netherlands, and Denmark had the highest Internet penetration by the number of users, with 93% or more of the population with access.

Several neologisms exist that refer to Internet users: Netizen (as in "citizen of the net") refers to those actively involved in improving online communities, the Internet in general or surrounding political affairs and rights such as free speech, Internaut refers to operators or technically highly capable users of the Internet, digital citizen refers to a person using the Internet in order to engage in society, politics, and government participation.

Usage

The Internet allows greater flexibility in working hours and location, especially with the spread of unmetered high-speed connections. The Internet can be accessed almost anywhere by numerous means, including through mobile Internet devices. Mobile phones, datacards, handheld game consoles and cellular routers allow users to connect to the Internet wirelessly. Within the limitations imposed by small screens and other limited facilities of such pocket-sized devices, the services of the Internet, including email and the web, may be available. Service providers may restrict the services offered and mobile data charges may be significantly higher than other access methods.

Educational material at all levels from pre-school to post-doctoral is available from websites. Examples range from CBeebies, through school and high-school revision guides and virtual universities, to access to top-end scholarly literature through the likes of Google Scholar. For distance education, help with homework and other assignments, self-guided learning, whiling away spare time, or just looking up more detail on an interesting fact, it has never been easier for people to access educational information at any level from anywhere. The Internet in general and the World Wide Web in particular are important enablers of both formal and informal education. Further, the Internet allows universities, in particular, researchers from the social and behavioral sciences, to conduct research remotely via virtual laboratories, with profound changes in reach and generalizability of findings as well as in communication between scientists and in the publication of results.

The low cost and nearly instantaneous sharing of ideas, knowledge, and skills have made collaborative work dramatically easier, with the help of collaborative software. Not only can a group cheaply communicate and share ideas but the wide reach of the Internet allows such groups more easily to form. An example of this is the free software movement, which has produced, among other things, Linux, Mozilla Firefox, and OpenOffice.org (later forked into LibreOffice). Internet chat, whether using an IRC chat room, an instant messaging system, or a social networking website, allows colleagues to stay in touch in a very convenient way while working at their computers during the day. Messages can be exchanged even more quickly and conveniently than via email. These systems may allow files to be exchanged, drawings and images to be shared, or voice and video contact between team members.

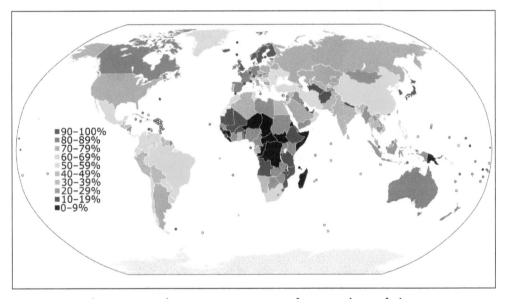

Internet users in 2015 as a percentage of a country's population.

Content management systems allow collaborating teams to work on shared sets of documents simultaneously without accidentally destroying each other's work. Business and project teams can share calendars as well as documents and other information. Such collaboration occurs in a wide variety of areas including scientific research, software development, conference planning, political activism and creative writing. Social and political collaboration is also becoming more widespread as both Internet access and computer literacy spread.

The Internet allows computer users to remotely access other computers and information stores easily from any access point. Access may be with computer security, i.e. authentication and encryption technologies, depending on the requirements. This is encouraging new ways of working from home, collaboration and information sharing in many industries. An accountant sitting at home can audit the books of a company based in another country, on a server situated in a third country that is remotely maintained by IT specialists in a fourth. These accounts could have been created by home-working bookkeepers, in other remote locations, based on information emailed to them from offices all over the world. Some of these things were possible before the widespread use of the Internet, but the cost of private leased lines would have made many of them infeasible in practice. An office worker away from their desk, perhaps on the other side of the world on a business trip or a holiday, can access their emails, access their data using cloud computing, or open a remote desktop session into their office PC using a secure virtual private network (VPN) connection on the Internet. This can give the worker complete access to all of their normal files and data, including email and other applications, while away from the office. It has been referred to among system administrators as the Virtual Private Nightmare, because it extends the secure perimeter of a corporate network into remote locations and its employees' homes.

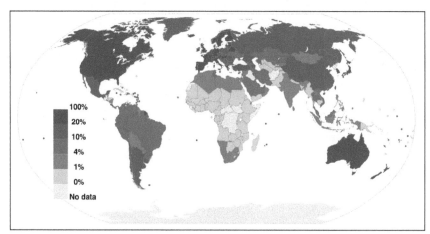

Fixed broadband Internet subscriptions in 2012 as a percentage of a country's population.

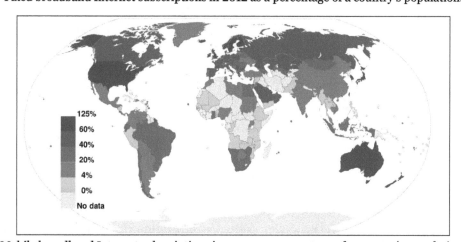

Mobile broadband Internet subscriptions in 2012 as a percentage of a country's population.

Social Networking and Entertainment

Many people use the World Wide Web to access news, weather and sports reports, to plan and book vacations and to pursue their personal interests. People use chat, messaging and email to make and stay in touch with friends worldwide, sometimes in the same way as some previously had pen pals. Social networking websites such as Facebook, Twitter, and Myspace have created new ways to socialize and interact. Users of these sites are able to add a wide variety of information to pages, to pursue common interests, and to connect with others. It is also possible to find existing acquaintances, to allow communication among existing groups of people. Sites like LinkedIn foster commercial and business connections. YouTube and Flickr specialize in users' videos and photographs. While social networking sites were initially for individuals only, today they are widely used by businesses and other organizations to promote their brands, to market to their customers and to encourage posts to "go viral". "Black hat" social media techniques are also employed by some organizations, such as spam accounts and astroturfing.

A risk for both individuals and organizations writing posts (especially public posts) on social networking websites, is that especially foolish or controversial posts occasionally lead to an unexpected and possibly large-scale backlash on social media from other Internet users. This is also a risk in relation to controversial offline behavior, if it is widely made known. The nature of this backlash can range widely from counter-arguments and public mockery, through insults and hate speech, to, in extreme cases, rape and death threats. The online disinhibition effect describes the tendency of many individuals to behave more stridently or offensively online than they would in person. A significant number of feminist women have been the target of various forms of harassment in response to posts they have made on social media, and Twitter in particular has been criticised in the past for not doing enough to aid victims of online abuse.

For organizations, such a backlash can cause overall brand damage, especially if reported by the media. However, this is not always the case, as any brand damage in the eyes of people with an opposing opinion to that presented by the organization could sometimes be outweighed by strengthening the brand in the eyes of others. Furthermore, if an organization or individual gives in to demands that others perceive as wrong-headed, that can then provoke a counter-backlash.

Some websites, such as Reddit, have rules forbidding the posting of personal information of individuals (also known as doxxing), due to concerns about such postings leading to mobs of large numbers of Internet users directing harassment at the specific individuals thereby identified. In particular, the Reddit rule forbidding the posting of personal information is widely understood to imply that all identifying photos and names must be censored in Facebook screenshots posted to Reddit. However, the interpretation of this rule in relation to public Twitter posts is less clear, and in any case, like-minded people online have many other ways they can use to direct each other's attention to public social media posts they disagree with.

Children also face dangers online such as cyberbullying and approaches by sexual predators, who sometimes pose as children themselves. Children may also encounter material which they may find upsetting, or material which their parents consider to be not age-appropriate. Due to naivety, they may also post personal information about themselves online, which could put them or their families at risk unless warned not to do so. Many parents choose to enable Internet filtering, and supervise their children's online activities, in an attempt to protect their children from inappropriate material on the Internet. The most popular social networking websites, such as Facebook and Twitter, commonly forbid users under the age of 13. However, these policies are typically trivial to circumvent by registering an account with a false birth date, and a significant number of children aged under 13 join such sites anyway. Social networking sites for younger children, which claim to provide better levels of protection for children, also exist.

The Internet has been a major outlet for leisure activity since its inception, with entertaining social experiments such as MUDs and MOOs being conducted on university servers, and humor-related Usenet groups receiving much traffic. Many Internet forums have sections devoted to games and funny videos. The Internet pornography and online gambling industries have taken advantage of the World Wide Web, and often provide a significant source of advertising revenue for other websites. Although many governments have attempted to restrict both industries' use of the Internet, in general, this has failed to stop their widespread popularity.

Another area of leisure activity on the Internet is multiplayer gaming. This form of recreation creates communities, where people of all ages and origins enjoy the fast-paced world of multiplayer games. These range from MMORPG to first-person shooters, from role-playing video games to online gambling. While online gaming has been around since the 1970s, modern modes of online gaming began with subscription services such as GameSpy and MPlayer. Non-subscribers were limited to certain types of game play or certain games. Many people use the Internet to access and download music, movies and other works for their enjoyment and relaxation. Free and fee-based services exist for all of these activities, using centralized servers and distributed peer-to-peer technologies. Some of these sources exercise more care with respect to the original artists' copyrights than others.

Cybersectarianism is a new organizational form which involves: "highly dispersed small groups of practitioners that may remain largely anonymous within the larger social context and operate in relative secrecy, while still linked remotely to a larger network of believers who share a set of practices and texts, and often a common devotion to a particular leader. Overseas supporters provide funding and support; domestic practitioners distribute tracts, participate in acts of resistance, and share information on the internal situation with outsiders. Collectively, members and practitioners of such sects construct viable virtual communities of faith, exchanging personal testimonies and engaging in the collective study via email, on-line chat rooms, and web-based message boards." In particular, the British government has raised concerns about the prospect of young British Muslims being indoctrinated into Islamic extremism by material on the Internet, being persuaded to join terrorist groups such as the so-called "Islamic State", and then potentially committing acts of terrorism on returning to Britain after fighting in Syria or Iraq.

Cyberslacking can become a drain on corporate resources; the average UK employee spent 57 minutes a day surfing the Web while at work, according to a 2003 study by Peninsula Business Services. Internet addiction disorder is excessive computer use that interferes with daily life. Nicholas G. Carr believes that Internet use has other effects on individuals, for instance improving skills of scan-reading and interfering with the deep thinking that leads to true creativity.

Electronic Business

Electronic business (e-business) encompasses business processes spanning the entire value chain: purchasing, supply chain management, marketing, sales, customer service, and business relationship. E-commerce seeks to add revenue streams using the Internet to build and enhance relationships with clients and partners. According to International Data Corporation, the size of worldwide e-commerce, when global business-to-business and -consumer transactions are combined, equate to $16 trillion for 2013. A report by Oxford Economics adds those two together to estimate the total size of the digital economy at $20.4 trillion, equivalent to roughly 13.8% of global sales.

While much has been written of the economic advantages of Internet-enabled commerce, there is also evidence that some aspects of the Internet such as maps and location-aware services may serve to reinforce economic inequality and the digital divide. Electronic commerce may be responsible for consolidation and the decline of mom-and-pop, brick and mortar businesses resulting in increases in income inequality.

Author Andrew Keen, a long-time critic of the social transformations caused by the Internet, has recently focused on the economic effects of consolidation from Internet businesses. Keen cites a 2013 Institute for Local Self-Reliance report saying brick-and-mortar retailers employ 47 people for every $10 million in sales while Amazon employs only 14. Similarly, the 700-employee room rental start-up Airbnb was valued at $10 billion in 2014, about half as much as Hilton Worldwide, which employs 152,000 people. At that time, transportation network company Uber employed 1,000 full-time employees and was valued at $18.2 billion, about the same valuation as Avis Rent a Car and The Hertz Corporation combined, which together employed almost 60,000 people.

Telecommuting

Telecommuting is the performance within a traditional worker and employer relationship when it is facilitated by tools such as groupware, virtual private networks, conference calling, videoconferencing, and voice over IP (VOIP) so that work may be performed from any location, most conveniently the worker's home. It can be efficient and useful for companies as it allows workers to communicate over long distances, saving significant amounts of travel time and cost. As broadband Internet connections become commonplace, more workers have adequate bandwidth at home to use these tools to link their home to their corporate intranet and internal communication networks.

Collaborative Publishing

Wikis have also been used in the academic community for sharing and dissemination of information across institutional and international boundaries. In those settings, they have been found useful for collaboration on grant writing, strategic planning, departmental documentation, and committee work. The United States Patent and Trademark Office uses a wiki to allow the public to collaborate on finding prior art relevant to examination of pending patent applications. Queens, New York has used a wiki to allow citizens to collaborate on the design and planning of a local park. The English Wikipedia has the largest user base among wikis on the World Wide Web and ranks in the top 10 among all Web sites in terms of traffic.

Politics and Political Revolutions

The Internet has achieved new relevance as a political tool. The presidential campaign of Howard Dean in 2004 in the United States was notable for its success in soliciting donation via the Internet.

Many political groups use the Internet to achieve a new method of organizing for carrying out their mission, having given rise to Internet activism, most notably practiced by rebels in the Arab Spring. The New York Times suggested that social media websites, such as Facebook and Twitter, helped people organize the political revolutions in Egypt, by helping activists organize protests, communicate grievances, and disseminate information.

Banner in Bangkok during the 2014 Thai coup d'état, informing the Thai public that 'like' or 'share' activities on social media could result in imprisonment.

Many have understood the Internet as an extension of the Habermasian notion of the public sphere, observing how network communication technologies provide something like a global civic forum. However, incidents of politically motivated Internet censorship have now been recorded in many countries, including western democracies.

Philanthropy

The spread of low-cost Internet access in developing countries has opened up new possibilities for peer-to-peer charities, which allow individuals to contribute small amounts to charitable projects for other individuals. Websites, such as DonorsChoose and GlobalGiving, allow small-scale donors to direct funds to individual projects of their choice. A popular twist on Internet-based philanthropy is the use of peer-to-peer lending for charitable purposes. Kiva pioneered this concept in 2005, offering the first web-based service to publish individual loan profiles for funding. Kiva raises funds for local intermediary microfinance organizations which post stories and updates on behalf of the borrowers. Lenders can contribute as little as $25 to loans of their choice, and receive their money back as borrowers repay. Kiva falls short of being a pure peer-to-peer charity, in that loans are disbursed before being funded by lenders and borrowers do not communicate with lenders themselves.

However, the recent spread of low-cost Internet access in developing countries has made genuine international person-to-person philanthropy increasingly feasible. In 2009, the US-based nonprofit Zidisha tapped into this trend to offer the first person-to-person microfinance platform to link lenders and borrowers across international borders without intermediaries. Members can fund loans for as little as a dollar, which the borrowers then use to develop business activities that improve their families' incomes while repaying loans to the members with interest. Borrowers access the Internet via public cybercafes, donated laptops in village schools, and even smart phones, then create their own profile pages through which they share photos and information about themselves and their businesses. As they repay their loans, borrowers continue to share updates and dialogue with lenders via their profile pages. This direct web-based connection allows members themselves to take on many of the communication and recording tasks traditionally performed by local organizations, bypassing geographic barriers and dramatically reducing the cost of microfinance services to the entrepreneurs.

Deep Web

The deep web, invisible web, or hidden web are parts of the World Wide Web whose contents are not indexed by standard web search engines. The opposite term to the deep web is the surface web, which is accessible to anyone using the Internet. Computer scientist Michael K. Bergman is credited with coining the term deep web in 2001 as a search indexing term.

The content of the deep web is hidden behind HTTP forms and includes many very common uses such as web mail, online banking, private or otherwise restricted access social media pages and profiles, some web forums that require registration for viewing content, and services that users must pay for, and which are protected by paywalls, such as video on demand and some online magazines and newspapers.

The content of the deep web can be located and accessed by a direct URL or IP address, and may require a password or other security access past the public website page.

Indexing Methods

Methods that prevent web pages from being indexed by traditional search engines may be categorized as one or more of the following:

1. Contextual web: Pages with content varying for different access contexts (e.g., ranges of client IP addresses or previous navigation sequence).

2. Dynamic content: Dynamic pages, which are returned in response to a submitted query or accessed only through a form, especially if open-domain input elements (such as text fields) are used; such fields are hard to navigate without domain knowledge.

3. Limited access content: Sites that limit access to their pages in a technical way (e.g., using the Robots Exclusion Standard or CAPTCHAs, or no-store directive, which prohibit search engines from browsing them and creating cached copies).

4. Non-HTML/text content: Textual content encoded in multimedia (image or video) files or specific file formats not handled by search engines.

5. Private web: sites that require registration and login (password-protected resources).

6. Scripted content: Pages that are only accessible through links produced by JavaScript as well as content dynamically downloaded from Web servers via Flash or Ajax solutions.

7. Software: Certain content is intentionally hidden from the regular Internet, accessible only with special software, such as Tor, I2P, or other darknet software. For example, Tor allows users to access websites using the .onion server address anonymously, hiding their IP address.

8. Unlinked content: Pages which are not linked to by other pages, which may prevent web crawling programs from accessing the content. This content is referred to as pages without backlinks (also known as inlinks). Also, search engines do not always detect all backlinks from searched web pages.

9. Web archives: Web archival services such as the Wayback Machine enable users to see archived versions of web pages across time, including websites which have become inaccessible, and are not indexed by search engines such as Google.

Content Types

While it is not always possible to directly discover a specific web server's content so that it may be indexed, a site potentially can be accessed indirectly (due to computer vulnerabilities).

To discover content on the web, search engines use web crawlers that follow hyperlinks through known protocol virtual port numbers. This technique is ideal for discovering content on the surface web but is often ineffective at finding deep web content. For example, these crawlers do not attempt to find dynamic pages that are the result of database queries due to the indeterminate number of queries that are possible. It has been noted that this can be (partially) overcome by providing links to query results, but this could unintentionally inflate the popularity for a member of the deep web.

DeepPeep, Intute, Deep Web Technologies, Scirus, and Ahmia.fi are a few search engines that have accessed the deep web. Intute ran out of funding and is now a temporary static archive as of July 2011. Scirus retired near the end of January 2013.

Researchers have been exploring how the deep web can be crawled in an automatic fashion, including content that can be accessed only by special software such as Tor. In 2001, Sriram Raghavan and Hector Garcia-Molina (Stanford Computer Science Department, Stanford University) presented an architectural model for a hidden-Web crawler that used key terms provided by users or collected from the query interfaces to query a Web form and crawl the Deep Web content. Alexandros Ntoulas, Petros Zerfos, and Junghoo Cho of UCLA created a hidden-Web crawler that automatically generated meaningful queries to issue against search forms. Several form query languages (e.g., DEQUEL) have been proposed that, besides issuing a query, also allow extraction of structured data from result pages. Another effort is DeepPeep, a project of the University of Utah sponsored by the National Science Foundation, which gathered hidden-web sources (web forms) in different domains based on novel focused crawler techniques.

Commercial search engines have begun exploring alternative methods to crawl the deep web. The Sitemap Protocol (first developed, and introduced by Google in 2005) and OAI-PMH are mechanisms that allow search engines and other interested parties to discover deep web resources on particular web servers. Both mechanisms allow web servers to advertise the URLs that are accessible on them, thereby allowing automatic discovery of resources that are not directly linked to the surface web. Google's deep web surfacing system computes submissions for each HTML form and adds the resulting HTML pages into the Google search engine index. The surfaced results account for a thousand queries per second to deep web content. In this system, the pre-computation of submissions is done using three algorithms:

- Selecting input values for text search inputs that accept keywords,

- Identifying inputs which accept only values of a specific type (e.g., date),

- Selecting a small number of input combinations that generate URLs suitable for inclusion into the Web search index.

In 2008, to facilitate users of Tor hidden services in their access and search of a hidden .onion suffix, Aaron Swartz designed Tor2web—a proxy application able to provide access by means of common web browsers. Using this application, deep web links appear as a random string of letters followed by the .onion TLD.

Dark Net

Dark Net (or Darknet) is an umbrella term describing the portions of the Internet purposefully not open to public view or hidden networks whose architecture is superimposed on that of the Internet. "Darknet" is often associated with the encrypted part of the Internet called Tor network where illicit trading takes place such as the infamous online drug bazaar called Silk Road. It is also considered part of the Deep Web. Anonymous communication between whistle-blowers, journalists and news organisations is facilitated by the "Darknet" Tor network through use of applications including SecureDrop.

Uses

Darknets in general may be used for various reasons, such as:

- Computer crime (cracking, file corruption, etc.).

- Protecting dissidents from political reprisal.

- File sharing (warez, personal files, pornography, confidential files, illegal or counterfeit software, etc.).

- To better protect the privacy rights of citizens from targeted and mass surveillance.

- Sale of restricted goods on darknet markets.

- Whistleblowing and news leaks.

- Purchase or sale of illicit or illegal goods or services.

- Circumventing network censorship and content-filtering systems, or bypassing restrictive firewall policies.

Software

All darknets require specific software installed or network configurations made to access them, such as Tor, which can be accessed via a customised browser from Vidalia (aka the Tor browser bundle), or alternatively via a proxy configured to perform the same function.

Active

- anoNet is a decentralized friend-to-friend network built using VPNs and software BGP routers.

- Decentralized network 42 (not for anonymity but research purposes).

- Freenet is a popular darknet (friend-to-friend) by default; since version 0.7 it can run as a "opennet" (peer nodes are discovered automatically).

- GNUnet can be utilised as a darknet if the "F2F (network) topology" option is enabled.

- I2P (Invisible Internet Project) is another overlay network that features a darknet whose sites are called "Eepsites".

- OneSwarm can be run as a darknet for friend-to-friend file-sharing.

- RetroShare can be run as a darknet (friend-to-friend) by default to perform anonymous file transfers if DHT and Discovery features are disabled.

- Riffle is a client-server darknet system that simultaneously provides secure anonymity (as long as at least one server remains uncompromised), efficient computation, and minimal bandwidth burden.

- Syndie is software used to publish distributed forums over the anonymous networks of I2P, Tor and Freenet.

- Tor (The onion router) is an anonymity network that also features a darknet – its "hidden services". It is the most popular instance of a darknet.

- Tribler can be run as a darknet for file-sharing.

- Zeronet is open source software aimed to build an internet-like computer network of peer-to-peer users of Tor.

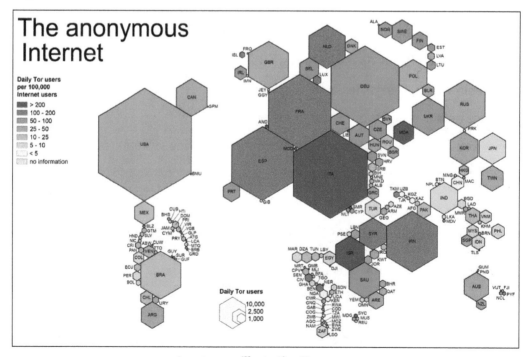

A cartogram illustrating Tor usage.

Cloud Computing

Cloud computing is a general term for anything that involves delivering hosted services over the Internet. These services are broadly divided into three categories: Infrastructure-as-a-Service (IaaS), Platform-as-a-Service (PaaS) and Software-as-a-Service (SaaS). The name cloud computing was inspired by the cloud symbol that's often used to represent the Internet in flowcharts and diagrams.

A cloud service has three distinct characteristics that differentiate it from traditional web hosting. It is sold on demand, typically by the minute or the hour; it is elastic - a user can have as much or as little of a service as they want at any given time; and the service is fully managed by the provider (the consumer needs nothing but a personal computer and Internet access). Significant innovations in virtualization and distributed computing, as well as improved access to high-speed Internet, have accelerated interest in cloud computing.

A cloud can be private or public. A public cloud sells services to anyone on the Internet. A private cloud is a proprietary network or a data center that supplies hosted services to a limited number of people. Private or public, the goal of cloud computing is to provide easy, scalable access to computing resources and IT services.

Cloud Computing Deployment Models

Private cloud services are delivered from a business's data center to internal users. This model offers the versatility and convenience of the cloud, while preserving the management, control and security common to local data centers. Internal users may or may not be billed for services through IT chargeback. Common private cloud technologies and vendors include VMware and OpenStack.

In the public cloud model, a third-party cloud service provider delivers the cloud service over the internet. Public cloud services are sold on demand, typically by the minute or hour, though long-term commitments are available for many services. Customers only pay for the CPU cycles, storage or bandwidth they consume. Leading public cloud service providers include Amazon Web Services (AWS), Microsoft Azure, IBM and Google Cloud Platform.

A hybrid cloud is a combination of public cloud services and an on-premises private cloud, with orchestration and automation between the two. Companies can run mission-critical workloads or sensitive applications on the private cloud and use the public cloud to handle workload bursts or spikes in demand.The goal of a hybrid cloud is to create a unified, automated, scalable environment that takes advantage of all that a public cloud infrastructure can provide, while still maintaining control over mission-critical data.

In addition, organizations are increasingly embracing a multicloud model, or the use of multiple infrastructure-as-a-service providers. This enables applications to migrate between different cloud providers or to even operate concurrently across two or more cloud providers. Organizations adopt multicloud for various reasons. For example, they could do so to minimize the risk of a cloud service outage or to take advantage of more competitive pricing from a particular provider. Multicloud implementation and application development can be a challenge because of the differences between cloud providers' services and application program interfaces (APIs). Multicloud deployments should become easier, however, as providers' services and APIs converge and become more homogeneous through industry initiatives such as the Open Cloud Computing Interface

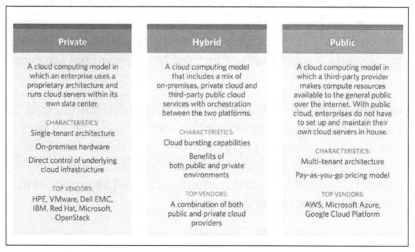

Main cloud deployment models.

Cloud Computing Characteristics and Benefits

Cloud computing boasts several attractive benefits for businesses and end users. Five of the main benefits of cloud computing are:

- Self-service provisioning: End users can spin up compute resources for almost any type of workloadon demand. This eliminates the traditional need for IT administrators to provision and manage compute resources.

- Elasticity: Companies can scale up as computing needs increase and scale down again as demands decrease. This eliminates the need for massive investments in local infrastructure, which may or may not remain active.

- Pay per use: Computer resources are measured at a granular level, enabling users to pay only for the resources and workloads they use.

- Workload resilience: Cloud service providers often implement redundant resources to ensure resilient storage and to keep users' important workloads running - often across multiple global regions.

- Migration flexibility: Organizations can move certain workloads to or from the cloud - or to different cloud platforms - as desired or automatically for better cost savings or to use new services as they emerge.

Types of Cloud Computing Services

Although cloud computing has changed over time, it has been divided into three broad service categories: infrastructure as a service (IaaS), platform as a service (PaaS) and software as a service (SaaS).

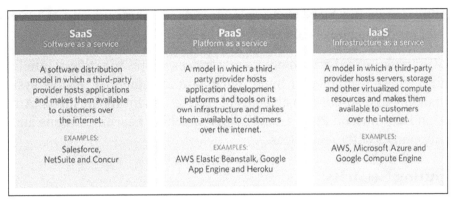

Cloud service categories.

IaaS providers, such as AWS, supply a virtual server instance and storage, as well as APIs that enable users to migrate workloads to a VM. Users have an allocated storage capacity and can start, stop, access and configure the VM and storage as desired. IaaS providers offer small, medium, large, extra-large and memory- or compute-optimized instances, in addition to customized instances, for various workload needs.

In the PaaS model, cloud providers host development tools on their infrastructures. Users access these tools over the internet using APIs, web portals or gateway software. PaaS is used for general software development, and many PaaS providers host the software after it's developed. Common PaaS providers include Salesforce's Force.com, AWS Elastic Beanstalk and Google App Engine.

SaaS is a distribution model that delivers software applications over the internet; these applications are often called web services. Users can access SaaS applications and services from any location using a computer or mobile device that has internet access. One common example of a SaaS application is Microsoft Office 365 for productivity and email services.

Emerging Cloud Technologies and Services

Cloud providers are competitive, and they constantly expand their services to differentiate themselves. This has led public IaaS providers to offer far more than common compute and storage instances.

For example, serverless, or event-driven computing is a cloud service that executes specific functions, such as image processing and database updates. Traditional cloud deployments require users to establish a compute instance and load code into that instance. Then, the user decides how long to run - and pay for - that instance.

With serverless computing, developers simply create code, and the cloud provider loads and executes that code in response to real-world events, so users don't have to worry about the server or instance aspect of the cloud deployment. Users only pay for the number of transactions that the function executes. AWS Lambda, Google Cloud Functions and Azure Functions are examples of serverless computing services.

Public cloud computing also lends itself well to big data processing, which demands enormous compute resources for relatively short durations. Cloud providers have responded with big data services, including Google BigQuery for large-scale data warehousing and Microsoft Azure Data Lake Analytics for processing huge data sets.

Another crop of emerging cloud technologies and services relates to artificial intelligence (AI) and machine learning. These technologies build machine understanding, enable systems to mimic human understanding and respond to changes in data to benefit the business. Amazon Machine Learning, Amazon Lex, Amazon Polly, Google Cloud Machine Learning Engine and Google Cloud Speech API are examples of these services.

Cloud Computing Security

Security remains a primary concern for businesses contemplating cloud adoption - especially public cloud adoption. Public cloud service providers share their underlying hardware infrastructure between numerous customers, as public cloud is a multi-tenant environment. This environment demands copious isolation between logical compute resources. At the same time, access to public cloud storage and compute resources is guarded by account login credentials.

Many organizations bound by complex regulatory obligations and governance standards are still hesitant to place data or workloads in the public cloud for fear of outages, loss or theft. However, this resistance is fading, as logical isolation has proven reliable, and the addition of data encryption and various identity and access management tools has improved security within the public cloud.

References

- Ethernet, definition: techtarget.com, Retrieved 19 April, 2019

- Charles M. Kozierok (September 20, 2005). "Data Link Layer (Layer 2)". Tcpipguide.com. Retrieved January 9, 2016

- World-wide-web-www, 5217, definition: techopedia.com, Retrieved 25 February, 2019

- "Ethernet Prototype Circuit Board". Smithsonian National Museum of American History. 1973. Retrieved September 2, 2007

- Overview: tutorialspoint.com, Retrieved 8 January, 2019

- Gerald W. Brock (September 25, 2003). The Second Information Revolution. Harvard University Press. P. 151. ISBN 0-674-01178-3

- HTTP, TERM: webopedia.com, Retrieved 26 July, 2019

- "What Is Employee Engagement? The Ultimate Definition!". Myhub Intranet Solutions. 2016-05-03. Retrieved 2018-09-12

- Web-caching-basics-terminology-http-headers-and-caching-strategies, tutorials, community: digitalocean.com, Retrieved 13 May, 2019

- Wilkinson, Paul (2005). Construction Collaboration Technologies: The Extranet Evolution. Taylor & Francis. ISBN 0-415-35859-0

- Foundation-of-the-Internet, Internet, technology: britannica.com, Retrieved 14 July, 2019

- Wyatt, Edward (23 April 2014). "F.C.C., in 'Net Neutrality' Turnaround, Plans to Allow Fast Lane". The New York Times. Retrieved 23 April 2014

- Gayard, Laurent (2018). Darknet: Geopolitics and Uses. Hoboken, NJ: John Wiley & Sons. P. 158. ISBN 9781786302021

Permissions

All chapters in this book are published with permission under the Creative Commons Attribution Share Alike License or equivalent. Every chapter published in this book has been scrutinized by our experts. Their significance has been extensively debated. The topics covered herein carry significant information for a comprehensive understanding. They may even be implemented as practical applications or may be referred to as a beginning point for further studies.

We would like to thank the editorial team for lending their expertise to make the book truly unique. They have played a crucial role in the development of this book. Without their invaluable contributions this book wouldn't have been possible. They have made vital efforts to compile up to date information on the varied aspects of this subject to make this book a valuable addition to the collection of many professionals and students.

This book was conceptualized with the vision of imparting up-to-date and integrated information in this field. To ensure the same, a matchless editorial board was set up. Every individual on the board went through rigorous rounds of assessment to prove their worth. After which they invested a large part of their time researching and compiling the most relevant data for our readers.

The editorial board has been involved in producing this book since its inception. They have spent rigorous hours researching and exploring the diverse topics which have resulted in the successful publishing of this book. They have passed on their knowledge of decades through this book. To expedite this challenging task, the publisher supported the team at every step. A small team of assistant editors was also appointed to further simplify the editing procedure and attain best results for the readers.

Apart from the editorial board, the designing team has also invested a significant amount of their time in understanding the subject and creating the most relevant covers. They scrutinized every image to scout for the most suitable representation of the subject and create an appropriate cover for the book.

The publishing team has been an ardent support to the editorial, designing and production team. Their endless efforts to recruit the best for this project, has resulted in the accomplishment of this book. They are a veteran in the field of academics and their pool of knowledge is as vast as their experience in printing. Their expertise and guidance has proved useful at every step. Their uncompromising quality standards have made this book an exceptional effort. Their encouragement from time to time has been an inspiration for everyone.

The publisher and the editorial board hope that this book will prove to be a valuable piece of knowledge for students, practitioners and scholars across the globe.

Index

Printed in the USA
CPSIA information can be obtained
at www.ICGtesting.com
JSHW051420221024
72173JS00006B/1381